A Martial Artist's Guide to Korean Terms, Translation, and Han-gŭl

By   **Richard L. Mitchell**
Heather Stanton Breiting
Tammy Kay Hayward

February 1998

Published in the United States of America
    by Lilley Gulch TKD.

Copyright © 1998 by   Richard L. Mitchell
                          Heather Stanton Breiting
                          Tammy Kay Hayward

Library of Congress Catalog Card Number 97-78390
ISBN 1-884583-00-8

Artwork by Heather Stanton Breiting

Dedication

The authors would like to dedicate this book to our spouses; Malinda Mitchell, Brian Breiting, and John Hayward, who have persevered through our numerous lengthy editorial meetings, and without whose steadfast patience and support, this book would not have been completed.

Acknowledgment

We would like to express our appreciation to those senior ranked instructors who have inspired us to pursue a greater understanding of the background of our martial art. We would also like to thank Sean Cavins, Barry Staver, and Simon Tsuo for their advice and guidance.

Table of Contents   mok-ch'a (목 차)

Introduction

For the serious student, learning a martial art is a lifelong process. Each art has a style that reflects the customs and heritage of its founders. In most traditional Taekwon-Do schools, and most other Korean martial arts, aspects of Korean culture are woven throughout the art and its instruction. For example, the uniforms, customs such as meditation before and after class, and the language used in class commands and/or technique descriptions are all influenced by this founding culture. In order to have a thorough knowledge of any martial art, it is helpful to have an understanding of the customs, language, and culture from which the art stems. In the case of many Korean-based martial arts, a basic knowledge of the Korean language as it applies to martial art techniques and class instruction is very useful. This understanding can improve pronunciation of commands, enhance technical understanding, and avoid misunderstandings in translation from Korean to English.

This book is designed for the English speaking student who practices a Korean martial art such as Taekwon-Do. It is a reference guide for the Korean language as it applies to Korean martial art techniques and offers some basic knowledge of Han-gŭl (Korean alphabet), and a few simple conversational phrases. It is hoped that this book will help martial artists use some simple Korean greetings; read Han-gŭl on certificates and flags; understand and pronounce many of the Korean terms used in his/her martial arts class, and increase understanding of technical terms. Many Korean martial arts terms have lost some of their full meaning in the process of translation. This book has been laid out as a reference guide that can be leafed through and used in the to-jang (often written as do-jang) to find words on an as needed basis. It can also be used as a study guide for the serious student who wishes to obtain an in-depth knowledge of Han-gŭl and Korean terms as they apply to martial art techniques.

Many of the terms presented in this book come from general terminology used by Korean martial artists as well as the standardized technical terms of the two largest organizations Taekwon-Do, the International Taekwon-Do Federation (ITF), and the Taekwon-Do Federation (WTF). This book can provide the martial artist with a unique insight into the differences and similarities between the terms used by the ITF and WTF. Terms specifically used in either of these two organizations have been identified as such in order for the martial artist to obtain a better understanding. Unmarked terms should be assumed to be general Korean language terms used by both organizations.

The authors are traditional martial artists who have devoted time into research on Han-gŭl translation and Korean martial arts terminology. However, they do not claim to have a complete understanding of the Korean language nor are they fluent in Korean. This book is not structured to provide the reader with an understanding of the complexities of the Korean language, address Korean grammar, correct the formulation of Korean sentences, instruct in the usage of formal and informal terms, nor to provide the martial artist with a sufficient vocabulary to do anything other than understand Korean terminology as used in martial arts classes. All terms in this book have been referenced using official ITF and WTF sources written in Han-gŭl. These terms have been cross-referenced using web pages and several of the standard Korean dictionaries, and the books College Korean and Functional Korean listed in the bibliography, as well as reviewed by a Korean editorial service. As this is the first edition, it is also recognized that there may be an occasional error, and corrections for future editions are invited. Except for personal names and "traditional" nomenclature, all terms have been Romanized using a single system which is defined in Appendices A through D.

Many of the references in the Bibliography (such as books College Korean and Functional Korean) can also be used by the martial arts student to learn more about the Korean language and culture.

How to use each section of this book

The information in this book is divided into four Chapters and four Appendices. Chapter 1 describes the history of Han-gŭl and the subsequent development of a translation system. For thousands of years, Korean was an oral language. In the 1400's, Han-gŭl was invented by King Se-jong to improve the life of the Korean people by giving them an alphabet that was easy to learn, and that fit the language well.

The Korean language has several sounds which are not found in English. Therefore, the Han-gŭl letters associated with these sounds have no English equivalent and no Roman letters to directly represent them. In order to Romanize Han-gŭl characters from Korean to English, a system had to be developed to convert the Korean phonetic sounds into English. Several Romanization systems have been used over the years, however, the most widely used is the McCune-Reischauer Romanization system.

Chapter 2 is basically an English to Korean dictionary tailored for the martial artist. If the martial artist wishes to find a specific Korean word, he/she will not only find the Korean word under its English equivalent, but also the Korean word written in Han-gŭl. The martial artist may find Chapter 2 useful in making banners and pattern diagrams.

Chapter 3 is a Korean to English dictionary designed to help the student recognize techniques that are related and connected to each other. For instance, an English term that has two possible translations, one used by the ITF, and the other used by the WTF. This chapter also contains definitions for specific Korean terms including many root verbs, as well as some Chinese characters from which the terms have been derived.

The terms in Chapter 4 are sorted into 21 sections. Each section was designed to help the martial artist find groups of related terms such as commands, kicks, blocks, or phrases. For example, students interested in compiling a list of the Tenets of Taekwon-Do will find the section addressing moral culture more useful than looking each tenet up one by one in Chapters 2 and 3.

The four appendices are designed to enhance the student's understanding of Han-gŭl. Appendix A describes the formation of Han-gŭl and Korean syllables, along with a discussion of the difficulties that often occur in the Romanization of Han-gŭl. Appendix B provides a description of Han-gŭl vowels. Appendix C provides a similar description for Han-gŭl consonants along with several rules used in Romanization. Appendix D contains a set of McCune-Reischauer Romanization tables to be used in identifying the formation and pronunciation of Han-gŭl consonant-vowel combinations. These tables can be used by the martial artist as a quick reference for the conversion of Han-gŭl to Romanized Korean words. It is hoped that the information presented in these four appendices will help the martial artist to better read, write, and pronounce the Han-gŭl terms included in this book.

The authors have designed these four chapters and four appendices to allow the martial artist to quickly find what he or she needs, as well as to provide background and references to support their further research into the subject. As a reference guide for Korean martial artists, it is not necessary to read the book from cover to cover. The sections were designed for information to be accessed as needed; yet provide the resources for the reader to access additional related information in other sections. Chapter 1 lists the history of Han-gŭl, and the appendices can provide a deeper understanding of Han-gŭl and rules for pronunciation. While Chapter 2 provides Korean words for a given martial arts term in English, the student can often get a further definition for that term in Chapter 3. Chapter 4 arranges the terms from previous chapters and organizes those terms into groups that can be beneficial when seen as a whole. The book therefore, can be used either as a quick guide, or as a research text with enough information included not only to enhance your understanding of techniques, but to enhance your knowledge of the Korean language and Korean martial arts terminology. It is hoped that you will find this book to be a useful tool and an educational experience that enriches your art.

Chapter 1
(제 1 장)

Korea's King Se-jong and the Development of Han-gŭl
(the Korean alphabet)

The Korean alphabet used extensively in this book, was invented by King Se-jong, the 4th monarch of the Choson Dynasty (1393-1910), along with help from seven of his best scholars. This unique phonetic alphabet was invented, not evolved, as are almost all other forms of writing in the world.

The Korean language, like the Korean culture, is an ancient one. The legend of Dan-Gun describes the birth of Korea, dating back as far as 2333 B.C., and illustrates the age of this culture. The spoken language of Korea, having developed since that time, is understandably complex and unique. Like other ancient cultures, it was many centuries before the Koreans had a written language. Chinese writing systems came to the Korean peninsula near the 4th century B.C., and were in widespread use around the 2nd or 3rd century A.D. In order to read and write Chinese, an extensive knowledge of many thousands of Chinese characters was required. Because this took a significant amount of free time to learn, only the elite Korean

7

aristocracy were educated and literate. King Se-jong reigned from 1418-1450 with an emphasis on improving the quality of life for his people. In support of the arts, he founded the Royal Academy named the Jade Hall (chip-hyon-jon) and staffed it with a group of the 20 best scholars in the country. Their sole purpose was to study and to invent tools to improve life for the Korean people.

Among other social improvements developed with the help of the staff of the Jade Hall, King Se-jong was convinced that a simple phonetic alphabet could help his people significantly. He felt that by creating a phonetic writing system, a peasant could memorize a few simple letters, and in a short time be able to start reading and writing. This is something they could not do using Chinese. To help him, he assigned seven of the best linguists from the Jade Hall to work on an alphabet. These scholars provided approximately 100 man-years of effort for the completion and debugging of this new alphabet. When completed in 1443, King Se-jong had the seven scholars write an instruction book for the new Korean alphabet. It was called the hun-min-chong-um, meaning *the correct pronunciation of letters for the instruction of the people*. In 28th year of his reign, on October 9, 1446, after approximately three more years of perfecting the system, the King presented this book to his people. In the preface of his proclamation he stated:

> "Being of foreign origin, Chinese characters are incapable of capturing uniquely Korean meanings. Therefore, many common people have no way to express their thoughts and feelings. Out of my sympathy for their difficulties, I have created a set of twenty-eight letters. The letters are very easy to learn, and it is my fervent hope that they improve the quality of life of all people."

The original hun-min-chong-um consisting of these twenty-eight letters was made up of seventeen consonants and eleven vowels. These have been reduced over time to only twenty-four letters made up of fourteen basic consonants and ten basic vowels. The student should take note that the letters in Han-gŭl have only one form and cannot be capitalized. Therefore, it is only proper that the Romanized form should also only contain lower case letters. In this text, only proper names for individuals, names of arts, official organizations, patterns, and the beginning of phrases and sentences are capitalized.

The teaching of this hun-min-chong-um system of writing was very popular among the people and received a wide public distribution. However, it received a lot of resistance from the aristocracy, who called it the ŏn-mun "vulgar script" and feared it would weaken their position as the only educated people in the country. When Japan invaded Korea, the Korean language was banned. Despite its creation in 1443, it has been most widely used and accepted since Korea was liberated from Japan at the end of World War II. The contemporary name for this system, Han-gŭl (meaning "Great Letters" or "Korean writing"), was coined by Chou Si Kyong (1876-1914). It also often referred to by the names ka-na-da (after the first three consonants in the alphabet) and kung-mun (National Script).

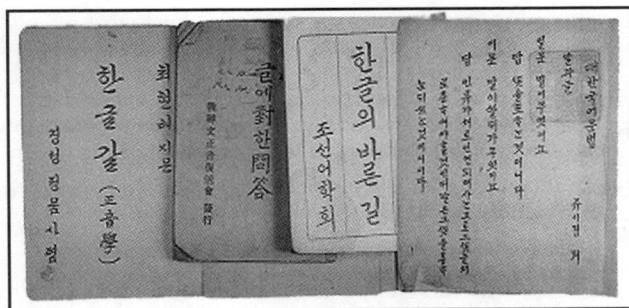

There were previously at least two other forms of written language used during the Choson Dynasty; one using a system of adding particles to the traditional Chinese symbols in use at the time, and therefore borrowing pronunciation from these ideograms. The second written form was created by Sol Ch'ong, the son of the great monk Won Hyo. As stated earlier, both of these required an extensive education in Chinese to use.

King Se-jong was also very interested in music and wanted a written language that would be read like musical notes. The vowels were created out of the three basic tones of nature. First, the [|], is a high pitch representing man. The second, the [—], is a low pitch representing land. The last symbol was the [•], which represented the empty heavens. These three symbols when combined in different ways formed all of the vowels used in Han-gŭl. Over the years, the [•] has evolved into small horizontal or vertical dashes [–]. (See Appendix B for more information on Han-gŭl vowels.)

The consonants in Han-gŭl are directly related to the formation of the mouth as it creates the sounds they represent. For example, the letter shi-ot (ㅅ) is the shape of the tongue touching the teeth and has the sound that is made by moving air past the teeth. The letter ch'i-ŭt (ㅈ) is in the same family. The letter mi-ŭm (ㅁ) is the symbol for closed lips or a mouth, the same formation needed to make the sound of an **m**, with the letter pi-ŭp (ㅂ) being in this same family. The consonant i–ŭng (ㅇ) is the symbol that is in the shape of an open throat and in its initial position it is silent. (See Appendix C for more information on Han-gŭl consonants.)

Using Han-gŭl, Korean can be written horizontally (left to right, top to bottom as in English) or vertically (top to bottom, right to left as in Chinese). Because both Han-gŭl and English are used together in this book, we have chosen the standard English approach common to both for this book. This format also allows for the inclusion of traditional Chinese characters (han-ja) within the text.

Because Han-gŭl was developed to be a written representation of an existing oral language, it is not surprising that it is complex in nature. Unfortunately, many of the advantages inherent in the elegant phonetics of Han-gŭl are disadvantages for those trying to transliterate Korean words into Roman letters. Many sounds in the Korean language do not have an "exact" counterpart in English. In most Romanization of Korean words, things are written exactly as they sound. Because Han-gŭl was invented as a phonetic alphabet, there is no representation for sounds that are not in the Korean language.

Some Korean martial arts texts have been transliterated into Roman letters by writing terms as they sound. Often an attempt is made to form "Korean" sounds with only the Roman alphabet. This unfortunately, allows too much latitude, and the result is that we have a multitude of

10

spellings for the same Korean word, depending on the accent of the translator. As an example, the Korean word mak-kki (딱기, meaning block) can be spelled in Romanized form as mak-ki, mak-gi, ma-ki, ma-gi, etc. Because of these different pronunciations and Romanizations, Korean words seldom sound exactly like they are written. The Korean letter piŭp (ㅂ) is often written in Romanized form as either a **b** or a **p**. Neither is exactly correct. Piŭp is actually a lighter version of how we say a **p** but harder than we say a **b**. Similarly, the Korean letter ki-yŏk (ㄱ) is a lighter version of how we say would say a **k** but harder than we say a **g**. The Korean letter shi-ot (ㅅ) is a heavier version of how we say an **s** but a lighter version of how we would say **ch**. (See Appendix C for further information.)

The martial artist will note that Romanized Korean appears in many forms depending on the source and the Romanization system employed. On the other hand, Han-gŭl terms almost always appear in the same form, since this is simply the most accurate way to depict Korean terms.

Attempts have been made to provide transliteration systems that allow the reader to better pronounce Korean words written in Romanized form. Often two or more letters are used to try to force a sequence of Roman-letter sounds to coincide with a Korean sound. The most notable Romanization systems in Korea were the Korean Ministry of Education version, and the most widely accepted McCune-Reischauer system. The later was created, in 1939 by G.M. McCune and Edwin O. Reischauer [Transactions of the Korea Branch of the Royal Asiatic Society 29 (1939): 1-55]. But, even these are not universally accepted, as many Korean books and dictionaries state that they use a "modified" version of one of these systems. Since these modifications are individualized, we still wind up with a variety of ways to Romanize a given Korean word.

In choosing a Romanization system to use, one must decide on one of two approaches: 1) if pronunciation is not an issue then simple single Roman letters are used; or 2) if pronunciation is the most important issue then a complex set of Roman letters and symbols must be used. To this end, there are a multitude of systems in use. These are usually referred to as a "modified McCune-Reischauer system" or something similar. This book is no different, as it will use a version of the McCune-Reischauer System.

Unfortunately, many words used in Taekwon-Do are specialized and are not found in a standard Korean Dictionary. Given these problems, it seems the best approach is to transliterate all appropriate words compiled from several sources into Han-gŭl, and then translate their meanings back into English using a single transliteration format – the McCune-Reischauer Romanization system.

To keep the translation as close to the McCune-Reischauer System as possible, it was necessary to incorporate the use of several new letters. These include the letter ŏ which sounds like the **ah** in the word caught, and the letter ŭ which sounds like the **uh** in the word cut. We have also used an apostrophe (') to add an intensity to specific Korean letters (e.g., k'i-yŏk and p'i-ŭp). Finally, there are five "twin-letters" in Korean. The best way to describe them, is that they are pronounced in a tense manner with the tongue and mouth tensed up. An example is the "twin-s" (ㅆ - ssang shi-ot) which would sound more like the **sc** in the word **sc**ientific than like its single relative shi-ot (ㅅ), which sounds more like the **s** in **s**upper. These twin-letters when translated into English are written as multiple letters **kk**, **dd**, **pp**, **ss**, and **tch**. However, they should not be thought of, or pronounced as two letters, but as a single letter that is pronounced as a very tense version of their single relatives. The reader is referred to the appendices for a more detailed discussion of the rules of pronunciation of Han-gŭl letters, as well as a list of Romanization rules regarding consonants changing sound within syllable groups.

King Se-jong and his seven scholars have created an elegant alphabet based on the shape of the vocal system and the three basic sounds of nature as viewed by Korean culture. The Han-gŭl alphabet is easy to learn and, by far, the best way to depict Korean terms. A better understanding of Han-gŭl will offer the martial artist greater insight in conducting classes, and reading and writing Korean martial arts terms.

Chapter 2
(제 2 장)

English-Korean Dictionary
yŏng-han sajŏn
(영 한 사 전)

This chapter is designed to introduce the Romanization of Korean martial arts terms from English to Han-gŭl. It can also be used to learn more about specific Korean terms for a given English word. Each term is presented in alphabetical order, followed by Romanized Korean with the Han-gŭl letters presented below it. This allows a term to be viewed in both languages at the same time, as well as to illustrate how it is written in Han-gŭl. There are many ways to describe a given technique in both English and Korean. Several terms have been listed in word groupings, such as flying side pushing kick, or hand blade trunk pushing block. Each of these terms may be found in the book separately, but when more than one word is combined to express a complex technique, the written structure or word format may be changed according to complicated rules of Korean grammar. We have provided several examples of these word groupings in Chapter 4 in order to provide a better understanding of possible phrase structure for a given term. Once the Korean translation of a specific English term is identified, further definitions of a Korean term can be found in Chapter 3. It is hoped that this format will be beneficial in obtaining a better understanding of Korean terminology as it relates to giving commands in a martial arts class, or understanding Korean nomenclature. (Please note that certain terms such as "ax kick" will not be covered in this book since they are either terms derived from Japanese Karate or American slang and not supported by Han-gŭl terms for specific techniques.)

A

Abdomen	pok-bu 복부
About Face (ITF&WTF)	twi-ro to-ra 뒤로 돌아
Absolute, the Great	t'ae-gŭk 태극
Achilles Heel	twi-ch'uk yak-jŏm 뒤축 약점
Achilles Tendon	twi-ch'uk him-jul 뒤축 힘줄

Actions	tong-jak 동작
Adam's Apple	kyŏl-hu 결후
Again	ta-shi 다시
Air Shield (ITF)	kong-gi pang-p'ae 공기 방패
Angle Fingertip (ITF)	ho-mi son-kkŭt 호미 손끝
Angle of the Mandible [upper jaw]	wit t'ŏk 윗 턱
Angle Punch (ITF)	ki-yŏk-ja tchi-rŭ-gi 기역자 찌르기
Ankle	pal-mok 발 목
Ankle Joint	pal-mok kwan-jŏl 발목 관절
Arc Fist (WTF)	a-gwi-son 아귀 손
Arc Hand (ITF)	pan-dal-son 반달 손
Arc-hand Rising Block (ITF)	pan-dal-son ch'u-k'yŏ mak-ki 반달손 추켜 막기
Arc Kick (WTF)	pan tol-lyŏ ch'a-gi 반 돌려 차기
Arm	p'al 팔
Armpit	kyŏ-dŭ-rang-i 겨드랑이
Art	-Do [Sino-Korean] 도

Artery	tong-maek 동맥
Assistant Instructor (ITF)	pu-sa-bŏm 부사범
Assistant Instructor Sir (ITF)	pu-sa-bŏm-nim 부사범 님
Assisting Block (WTF)	kŏ-dŭ-rŏ mak-ki 거들어 막기
Assisting Face Block (WTF)	kŏ-dŭ-rŏ ŏl-gul mak-ki 거들어 얼굴 막기
Assisting Face Outer Hit (WTF)	kŏ-dŭ-rŏ ŏl-gul pa-kkat ch'i-gi 거들어 얼굴 바깥 치기
Assisting Face Side Block (WTF)	kŏ-dŭ-rŏ ŏl-gul yŏp mak-ki 거들어 얼굴 옆 막기
Assisting Hand-blade Block (WTF)	kŏ-dŭ-rŏ son-nal mak-ki 거들어 손날 막기
Assisting Stance (WTF)	kyŏt-da-ri sŏ-gi 곁 다리 서기
Assisting Trunk Block (WTF)	kŏ-dŭ-rŏ mom-t'ong mak-ki 거들어 몸통 막기
Assisting Underneath Block (WTF)	kŏ-dŭ-rŏ a-rae mak-ki 거들어 아래 막기
At Ease (ITF&WTF)	swi-ŏt 쉬엇
At Ease Stance (WTF)	p'yŏn-hi sŏ-gi 편히 서기
Attack	kong-gyŏk 공격
Attack Techniques or	kong-gyŏk-ki (ITF) 공격기 kong-gyŏk ki-sul (WTF) 공격 기술

Attacking Tools (ITF)   kong-gyŏk pu-wi
                                    공격 부위

Attention (ITF&WTF)   ch'a-ryŏt
                                    차렷

Attention Stance (ITF&WTF)   ch'a-ryŏt sŏ-gi
                                    차렷 서기

Attention Stance (WTF)   twi-ch'uk mo-a sŏ-gi
                                    뒤축 모아 서기

B

Back   twi , twit or tŭng
                                    뒤 , 뒷 or 등

Back Elbow   twit p'al-gup
                                    뒷 팔굽

Back Elbow Strike (ITF)   twit p'al-gup ttae-ri-gi
                                    뒷 팔굽 때리기

Back Elbow Thrust (ITF)   twit p'al-gup ttul-ki
                                    뒷 팔굽 뚫기

Backfist (ITF&WTF)   tŭng chu-mŏk
                                    등 주먹

Backfist Assisting   tŭng chu-mŏk kŏ-dŭ-rŏ
    Front Hit (WTF)   ap ch'i-gi
                                    등 주먹 거들 앞 치기

Backfist Strike (ITF)   tŭng chu-mŏk ttae-ri-gi
                                    등 주먹 때리기

Backfist Face Front Hit (WTF)   tŭng chu-mŏk ŏl-gul ap ch'i-gi
                                        pa-kkat ch'i-gi
                                    등 주먹 얼굴 앞 치기

Backfist Face Outer Hit (WTF)   tŭng ŏl-gul pa-kkat ch'i-gi
                                    등 주먹 얼굴 바깥 치기

Back Forearm   tŭng p'al-mok
    [at the wrist]   등 팔목

Backhand

son-dŭng

손등

Back Heel

twi-ch'uk or pal twi-ch'uk

뒤축 or 발 뒤축

Back Hit (WTF)

twi ch'i-gi

뒤 치기

Back Inflection Stance (WTF)

twit ku-bi

뒷 굽이

Back Kick (ITF&WTF)

twit ch'a-gi

뒷 차기

Back Leg

twit-da-ri

뒷 다리

Back Piercing Kick (ITF)

twit ch'a-tchi-rŭ-gi

뒷 차 찌르기

Back Punch (WTF)

twi chi-rŭ-gi

뒤 지르기

Back Pushing Kick (ITF)

twit ch'a-mil-gi

뒷 차 밀기

Back Snap Kick (ITF)
  [smashing]

twit ch'a-pu-su-gi

뒷 차 부수기

Back Sole
  [of the foot]

twi-ch'uk

뒤 축

Back Sole (ITF)
  [heel area]

twi-kkum-ch'i

뒤 꿈치

Back Strike (ITF)

twi ttae-ri-gi

뒤 때리기

Back Tibia
  [Achilles tendon area]

twit kyŏng-gol

뒷 경골

Backward Cross Stance (WTF)

twit kko-a sŏ-gi

뒷 꼬아 서기

Back Wrist Artery

tŭng son-mok tong-maek

등 손목 동맥

Backward Double Step-turning (ITF)
twi-ro i-bo om-gyŏ ti-di-myŏ tol-gi
뒤 로 이보 옮겨 디디며 돌기

Backward Lifting Kick (WTF)
twi ol-lyŏ ch'a-gi
뒤 올려 차기

Backward Sliding Punch (ITF)
mi-kkŭ-rŭm-bal-lo tchi-rŭ-myŏ tŭ-rŏ-o-gi
미끄름발로 찌르며 들어오기

Backward Stepping (ITF)
tŭ-rŏ o-gi
들어오기

Backward Step-turning (ITF)
twi-ro om-gyŏ ti-di-myŏ tol-gi
뒤 로 옮겨 디디며 돌기

Balance
chung-shim
중심

Ball of the Foot
ap-kkum-ch'i
앞 꿈치

Base of Knifehand (ITF)
son-k'al pa-t'ang
손칼 바 탕

Basic
ki-bon
기 본

Basic Ready Stance (WTF)
ki-bon chun-bi sŏ-gi
기본 준비 서기

Bayonet
ch'ong-gŏm
총검

Bear Hand (ITF&WTF)
kom-son
곰 손

Begin
shi-jak
시작

Beginning Black Belt (ITF&WTF)
ch'ŏt-dan
첫 단

Beginning Junior Black Belt (WTF)
ch'ŏt-pum
첫 붐

Belt	tti
	띠
Belt Color	tti saek
	띠 색
Bending Ready Stance (ITF)	ku-bu-ryŏ chun-bi sŏ-gi
	구부려 준비 서기
Bending Stance (ITF)	ku-bu-ryŏ sŏ-gi
	구부려 서기
Black Color	kŏ-mŭn saek
	검은 색
Black Belt (ITF&WTF)	kŏ-mŭn tti
	검은 띠
Block - Backward Stepping (ITF)	ma-gŭ-myŏ tŭ-rŏ o-gi
	막으며 들어오기
Block - Forward Stepping (ITF)	ma-gŭ-myŏ na-ga-gi
	막으며 나가기
Block or Blocking (ITF&WTF)	mak-ki
	막기
Blocking Apparatus (ITF)	mak-ki tae
	막기 대
Blocking Tools (ITF)	mak-ki pu-wi
	막기 부위
Blue Color	p'u-rŭn saek
	푸른 색
Blue Belt (ITF&WTF)	p'u-rŭn tti
	푸른 띠
Blue Belt with a Red Stripe (ITF&WTF)	p'u-rŭn tti-e ppal-gan sŏn
	푸른 띠에 빨간 선
Blue Contestant (WTF)	ch'ŏng sŏn-su
	청 선수
Blue Contestant Mark (WTF)	ch'ŏng k'on-a
	청 코나

Body   mom
몸

Body Dropping (ITF)   mom nat-ch'u-gi
몸 낮추기

Body - Middle Section (WTF)   mom-t'ong pu-wi
몸통 부위

Body Turning Kick (WTF)   mom tol-lyŏ ch'a-gi
몸 돌려 차기

Bone   kol or ppyŏ
골 or 뼈

Bout   shi-hap or kyŏ-ru-gi
시합 or 겨루기

Bow   kyŏng-nye
경례

Bow Wrist (WTF)   ku-p'in son-mok
굽힌 손 목

Bow Wrist (ITF)   son-mok dŭng
손목 등

Bow Wrist Block (ITF)   son-mok dŭng mak-ki
손목 등 막기

Bow Wrist Trunk Block (WTF)   ku-p'in son-mok mom-t'ong
    mak-ki
굽힌 손목   몸통 막기

Bow Wrist Face Block (WTF)   ku-p'in son-mok
    ŏl-gul mak-ki
굽힌 손목 얼굴 막기

Bowing Posture (ITF)   kyŏng-nye cha-se
경례 자세

Brachial Plexus   sang-wan shin-gyŏng
상완 신경

Break (WTF)   kal-lyŏ
  [separate fighters]   갈려

Breaking	kyŏk-p'a-gi 격파기
Breath Control (ITF)	ho-hŭp cho-jŏl 호흡 조절
Breathing	ho-hŭp 호흡
Bridge of the Nose	mi-gan 미간
Bull Block (WTF)	hwang-so mak-ki 황 소 막기

C

Calisthenics (ITF)	to-su dal-lyŏn 도수 단련
Center of Gravity	chung-nyŏk chung-shim 중력 중심
Certain Victory	p'il-sŭng 필승
Certificate	cha-gyŏk-jŭng 자격 증
Cervical Bundle	kyŏng-bu 경부
Cervical Vertebrae (WTF)	kyŏng-gol 경골
Change Direction (WTF)	pang-hyang pa-kku-gi 방향 바꾸기
Checking (ITF)	mŏm-ch'u-gi 멈추기
Checking Block (ITF)	mŏm-ch'wo mak-ki 멈 춰 막기
Checking Kick (ITF)	ch'a-mŏm-ch'u-gi 차 멈추기

Cheek Bone	kwang-dae ppyŏ 광대 뼈
Chest	ka-sŭm 가슴
Chestnut Fist (WTF)	pam chu-mŏk 밤 주먹
Chin	t'ŏk 틱
Chin-up	t'ŏk-gŏ-ri 틱걸이
Choi Hong Hi, General	Choi Hong Hi, Chang-gun 최 홍 희 장군
Choson Dynasty	Cho-sŏn shi-dae 조선 시대
Circular Block (ITF)	tol-li-myŏ mak-ki 돌리며 막기
Classification of Instructor (ITF)	sa-bŏm pu-ryu 사범 부류
Classification of Umpire (ITF)	shim-p'an pu-ryu 심판 부류
Clavicle	swae-gol 쇄골
Clockwise (turn) (ITF)	o-rŭn-tchok-ŭ-ro to-nŭn 오른 쪽으로 도는
Close Attention stance (WTF)	mo chu-ch'um sŏ-gi 모 주춤 서기
Close Ready Stance (ITF)	mo-a chun-bi sŏ-gi 모아 준비 서기
Close Stance (ITF&WTF)	mo-a sŏ-gi 모아 서기
Club	kon-bong 곤봉

Coccyx	mi-gol 미골
Cold Showers and Baths	naeng-su ma-ch'al 냉수 마찰
Combination (ITF)	hon-hap 혼합
Combination Attack (ITF)	hon-hap kong-gyŏk 혼합 공격
Combination Kick (ITF)	hon-hap ch'a-gi 혼합 차기
Combined All-fingertip (WTF)	mo-dŭm son-kkŭt 모 듬 손끝
Combined All-fingertip Hit (WTF)	mo-dŭm son-kkŭt ch'i-gi 모 듬 손끝 치기
Combined Three-fingertip Hit (WTF)	mo-ŭn se son-kkŭt ch'i-gi 모은 세 손끝 치기
Combined Three-fingertip Thrust (WTF)	mo-ŭn se son-kkŭt tchi-rŭ-gi 모은 세 손끝 찌르기
Combined Three Flat-fingertip (WTF)	mo-ŭn se p'yŏn son-kkŭt 모은 세 편 손끝
Combined Two-fingertip Hit (WTF)	mo-ŭn tu son-kkŭt ch'i-gi 모은 두 손끝 치기
Combined Two-fingertip Thrust (WTF)	mo-ŭn tu son-kkŭt tchi-rŭ-gi 모은 두 손끝 찌르기
Combined Two Flat-fingertip (WTF)	mo-ŭn tu p'yŏn son-kkŭt 모은 두 편 손끝
Commence (ITF)	shi-jak 시작
Competition (ITF)	kyŏng-gi 경기
Composition (ITF)	ku-sŏng 구성

Concentration (WTF)	chip-jung 집중
Concentration (ITF&WTF)	ki-hap 기합
Connecting Motion (ITF)	i-ŏ-jin tong-jak 이어진 동작
Consecutive Attack (ITF)	yŏn-sok kong-gyŏk 연속 공격
Consecutive Kick (ITF)	yŏn-sok ch'a-gi 연속 차기
Contestant (WTF)	sŏn-su 선수
Continue	gye-sok 계 속
Continuous (ITF)	yŏn-sok 연속
Continuous Motion (ITF)	yŏn-sok tong-jak 연속 동작
Correct	o-rŭm 옳음
Counter Attack (ITF)	pan-gyŏk 반격
Counter Clockwise (ITF) [turn]	oen-tchok-ŭ-ro to-nŭn 왼쪽으로 도는
Counter Kick (ITF)	pa-da ch'a-gi 받아 차기
Courtesy	ye-ŭi 예의
Covered-fist Ready Stance (WTF)	po chu-mŏk chun-bi sŏ-gi 보 주먹 준비 서기
Covering (ITF)	ka-ri-u-gi 가리우기

Covering Fist (WTF)	po chu-mŏk 보 주먹
Crane Diamond Block (WTF)	hak-da-ri kŭm-gang mak-ki 학다리 금강 막기
Crane Stance (WTF)	hak-da-ri sŏ-gi 학다리 서기
Crane Stance Hinge (WTF)	hak-da-ri tol-tchŏ-gwi 학다리 돌쩌귀
Crane Thrust (WTF)	hak-da-ri tchi-rŭ-gi 학다리 찌르기
Crescent Kick (ITF)	pan-dal ch'a-gi 반달 차기
Crescent Punch (ITF)	pan-dal tchi-rŭ-gi 반달 찌르기
Crescent Strike (ITF)	pan-dal ttae-ri-gi 반달 때리기
Cross Block (WTF)	ŏt-gal-lyŏ mak-ki 엇갈려 막기
Cross-cut (ITF)	kŭt-gi 굿기
Crossing	kko-gi 꼬기
Cross Stance (WTF)	kko-a sŏ-gi 꼬아 서기
Cross Underneath Block (WTF)	ŏt-gal-lyŏ a-rae mak-ki 엇갈려 아래 막기
Crouched Stance (ITF)	o-gŭ-ryŏ sŏ-gi 오그려 서기

D

Dagger	tan-do
	단도
Deduction (WTF) [minus-1]	kam-jŏm [ha-na]
	감점 [하나]
Defense (ITF)	pang-ŏ
	방어
Defense Against a Bayonet (ITF)	tae ch'ong-gŏm
	대 총검
Defense Against a Club (ITF)	tae kon-bong
	대 곤봉
Defense Against a Dagger (ITF)	tae tan-do
	대 단도
Defense Against a Pistol (ITF)	tae kwŏn-ch'ong
	대 권총
Defense Against a Pole (ITF)	tae mong-dung-i
	대 몽둥이
Defense Against a Sudden Attack (ITF)	tae pu-ri kong-gyŏk
	대 불의 공격
Defense Against an Armed Opponent (ITF)	tae mu-gi
	대 무기
Defensive Techniques (ITF)	pang-ŏ-gi
	방어기
Degree - Black Belt Ranking (ITF&WTF)	-dan
	단
Degree Certificate (ITF)	tan-jŭng
	단 증
Demonstration (ITF)	shi-bŏm
	시범
Diagonal Stance (ITF)	sa-sŏn sŏ-gi
	사선 서기

Diamond Block (WTF)	kŭm-gang mak-ki 금강 막기
Diamond Forward Punch (WTF)	kŭm-gang ap tchi-rŭ-gi 금강 앞 찌르기
Diamond Side Punch (WTF)	kŭm-gang yŏp tchi-rŭ-gi 금강 옆 찌르기
Diamond Trunk Block (WTF)	kŭm-gang mom-t'ong mak-ki 금강 몸통 막기
Dichotomy Kick (WTF)	pan-dal ch'a-gi 반달 차기
Dismissed	hae-san 해산
Disqualification	shil-kyŏk 실격
Dodging (ITF&WTF)	p'i-ha-gi 피하기
Dodging Attack (ITF)	p'i-ha-myŏ kong-gyŏk 피하며 공격
Dodging Kick (ITF)	p'i-ha-myŏ ch'a-gi 피하며 차기
Dodging Punch (ITF)	p'i-ha-myŏ tchi-rŭ-gi 피하며 찌르기
Dodging Strike (ITF)	p'i-ha-myŏ ttae-ri-gi 피하며 때리기
Dodging Technique (ITF&WTF)	p'i-ha-myŏ ki-sul 피하며 기술
Dodging Thrust (ITF)	p'i-ha-myŏ ttul-ki 피하며 뚫기
Double Arc-hand Block (ITF)	tu-ban-dal-son mak-ki 두 반달 손 막기
Double Attack (ITF)	i-jung kong-gyŏk 이 중 공격

Double Backhand (ITF)	tu-son-dŭng 두 손등
Double Finger (ITF)	tu-son-ga-rak 두 손가락

Double Finger Spear (ITF)	ka-wi son-kkŭt or
	  tu-son-ga-rak ttul-ki
	가위 손끝 or
	  두 손가락 뚫기

Double Fist Punch (ITF)	tu-ju-mŏk tchi-rŭ-gi 두 주먹 찌르기
Double Forearm (ITF)	tu-p'al-mok 두 팔목
Double Forearm Block (ITF)	tu-p'al-mok mak-ki 두 팔목 막기
Double Front Snap Kick (ITF) [smashing]	i-jung ap ch'a-pu-su-gi 이 중 앞 차 부수기
Double Kick (ITF)	i-jung ch'a-gi 이 중 차기
Double Side Elbow (ITF)	tu yŏp p'al-gup 두 옆 팔굽
Double Side Elbow Thrust (ITF)	tu yŏp p'al-gup ttul-ki 두 옆 팔굽 뚫기
Double Stepping (ITF)	i-bo om-gyŏ ti-di-gi 이보 옮겨 디디기
Double Stepping Turn (ITF)	i-bo om-gyŏ ti-di-myŏ tol-gi 이보 옮겨 디디며 돌기
Double Strike (ITF)	i-jung ttae-ri-gi 이 중 때리기
Downward	nae-ryŏ 내려
Downward Block (ITF)	nae-ryŏ mak-ki 내려 막기

Downward Kick (ITF&WTF)	nae-ryŏ ch'a-gi 내려 차기
Downward Punch (ITF)	nae-ryŏ tchi-rŭ-gi 내려 찌르기
Downward Strike (ITF)	nae-ryŏ ttae-ri-gi 내려 때리기
Downward Strike (WTF)	nae-ryŏ ch'i-gi 내려 치기
Downward Thrust (ITF)	nae-ryŏ ttul-ki 내려 뚫기
Downward X-Block (ITF)	nae-ryŏ kyo-ch'a mak-ki 내려 교차 막기
Downward X-Fist Block (ITF)	nae-ryŏ kyo-ch'a chu-mŏk mak-ki 내려 교차 주먹 막기
Downward X-Knifehand Block (ITF)	nae-ryŏ kyo-ch'a son-k'al mak-ki 내려 교차 손칼 막기
Drawing the Feet together (ITF)	mo-dŭm-bal 모듬발
Drawing up (WTF)	kkŭ-rŏ ol-li-gi 끌어 올리기
Ducking (ITF)	nat-ch'u-gi 낮추기
Dynamic Stability (ITF)	tong-jŏk an-jŏng 동적 안정
Dynasty	shi-dae 시대

31

E

Ear	kwi 귀
Edge of the Foot (ITF) [see Footsword or Foot-blade]	pal-lal 발날
Edge of the Hand (WTF) [see Hand-blade or Knifehand]	son-nal 손날
Eight [in Native Korean]	yŏ-dŏl 여덟
Eight [in Sino-Korean]	p'al 팔
Eight-Diagrams	p'al-gwae 팔괘
Eighth [in Native Korean]	yŏ-dŏl-tchae 여덟 째
Eighth [in Sino-Korean]	che-p'al 제 팔
Eighth Degree Black Belt (ITF&WTF)	p'al-dan 팔 단
Eighth Grade (ITF&WTF) [Low Yellow Belt]	p'al-gŭp 팔 급
Elbow [bottom]	p'al-gup 팔 굽
Elbow [general area]	p'al-kkum-ch'i 팔꿈치
Elbow Back Strike (WTF)	p'al-gup twi ch'i-gi 팔굽 뒤 치기
Elbow Downward Strike (ITF)	p'al-gup nae-ryŏ ttae-ri-gi 팔굽 내려 때리기
Elbow Downward Strike (WTF)	p'al-gup nae-ryŏ ch'i-gi 팔굽 내려 치기

Elbow Downward Thrust (ITF)	p'al-gup nae-ryŏ ttul-ki
	팔굽 내려 뚫기
Elbow Front Strike (WTF)	p'al-gup ap ch'i-gi
	팔굽 앞 치기
Elbow Joint	p'al-gup kwan-jŏl
	팔굽 관절
Elbow Rise-up Strike (WTF)	p'al-gup ol-lyŏ ch'i-gi
	팔굽 올려 치기
Elbow Side Strike (WTF)	p'al-gup yŏp ch'i-gi
	팔굽 옆 치기
Elbow Strike (WTF)	p'al-gup ch'i-gi
	팔굽 치기
Elbow Strike (ITF)	p'al-gup ttae-ri-gi
	팔굽 때리기
Elbow Target Strike (WTF)	p'al-gup p'yo-jŏk ch'i-gi
	팔굽 표적 치기
Elbow Turning Strike (WTF)	p'al-gup tol-lyŏ ch'i-gi
	팔굽 돌려 치기
End	kkŭt
	끝
Equilibrium	kyun-hyŏng
	균형
Erected-fist Punch (WTF)	se-wŏ chi-rŭ-gi
	세워 지르기
Eternity	t'ae-gŭk
	태극
Etiquette	ye-jŏl
	예 절
Exercise (ITF)	un-dong
	운동
Exercises (ITF)	yŏn-sŭp
	연습

Extremities	p'al-gwa-da-ri 팔과다리
Excuse me	shil-lye ham-ni-da 실례 합니다
Eye	nun 눈
Eye [region]	an-bu 안부
Eyeball	an-gu 안구

F

Face (WTF)	ŏl-gul 얼굴
Face Area [Sino-Korean]	an-myŏn 안면
Face Block (WTF)	ŏl-gul mak-ki 얼굴 막기
Face Cross Block (WTF)	ŏl-gul ŏt-gal-lyŏ mak-ki 얼굴 엇갈려 막기
Face Inner Block (WTF)	ŏl-gul an mak-ki 얼굴 안 막기
Face Foot-blade Rising Block (WTF)	ŏl-gul yŏp ch'a-ol-lyŏ mak-ki 얼굴 옆 차 올려 막기
Face Front Hit (WTF)	ŏl-gul ap ch'i-gi 얼굴 앞 치기
Face Front-sole Rising Block (WTF)	ŏl-gul ap ch'a-ol-lyŏ mak-ki 얼굴 앞 차 올려 막기
Face Outer Block (WTF)	ŏl-gul pa-kkat mak-ki 얼굴 바깥 막기
Face Parts (WTF)	ŏl-gul pu-wi 얼굴 부위

Face Punch (WTF)	ŏl-gul chi-rŭ-gi
	얼굴 지르기
Face Pushing Block (WTF)	ŏl-gul he-ch'yŏ mak-ki
	얼굴 헤쳐 막기
Face Side Block (WTF)	ŏl-gul yŏp mak-ki
	얼굴 옆 막기
Face the [National] Flag	kuk-ki-e tae-ha-yŏ
	국기에 대하여
Face the Instructor	sa-bŏm-nim kke
	사범 님 께
Face Twist Block (WTF)	ŏl-gul pi-t'ŭ-rŏ mak-ki
	얼굴 비틀어 막기
Fake or Faking (ITF)	so-gim
	속임
Fall or Falling (ITF)	ttŏ-rŏ-ji-gi
	떨어지기
Fast Motion (ITF)	ppa-rŭn tong-jak
	빠른 동작
Federation	yŏn-maeng
	연맹
Femur	tae-t'wi-gol
	대퇴골
Fibula	pi-gol
	비골
Fifth [in Native Korean]	ta-sŏt-tchae
	다섯 째
Fifth [in Sino-Korean]	che-o
	제 오
Fifth Degree Black Belt (ITF&WTF)	o-dan
	오 단
Fifth Grade (ITF&WTF) [High Green Belt]	o-gŭp
	오 급

35

Fighting Stance (WTF)
kyŏ-rum-se sŏ-gi
겨룸세 서기

Finger Belly (ITF)
[bottom]
son-ga-rak pa-dak
손가락 바닥

Finger Joint
son-ga-rak kwan-jŏl
손가락 관절

Finger Pincers (ITF)
chip-ge-son
집게 손

Fingertip
son-kkŭt
손끝

First [in Native Korean]
ch'ŏt-tchae
첫 째

First [in Sino-Korean]
che-il
제 일

First Degree Black Belt
(ITF&WTF)
il-dan
일 단

First Grade (ITF&WTF)
[High Red Belt]
il-gŭp
일 급

First Degree Junior Black Belt
(WTF)
il-pum
일 붐

Fist (ITF&WTF)
chu-mŏk
주먹

Fist
kwŏn [Sino-Korean]
권

Fists on the Waist Ready
Stance (WTF)
tu-ju-mŏk hŏ-ri chun-bi sŏ-gi
두 주먹 허리 준비 서기

Five [in Native Korean]
ta-sŏt
다섯

Five [in Sino-Korean]
o
오

Fixed Stance (ITF)
ko-jŏng sŏ-gi
고정 서기

Flag [National]   kuk-ki
                                           국기

Flank or Side   yŏp-gu-ri
                                           옆 구리

Flat Fingertip (WTF)   p'yŏn son-kkŭt
                                           편 손끝

Flat Fingertip (ITF)   ŏ-pŭn son-kkŭt
                                           엎은 손끝

Flat Fingertip Erect Thrust (WTF)   p'yŏn son-kkŭt se-wŏ tchi-rŭ-gi
                                           편 손끝 세워 찌르기

Flat-fingertip Flat Thrust (WTF)   p'yŏn son-kkŭt ŏ-p'ŭn tchi-rŭ-gi
                                           편 손끝 엎은 찌르기

Flat-fingertip Front Thrust (WTF)   p'yŏn son-kkŭt ap tchi-rŭ-gi
                                           편 손끝 앞 찌르기

Flat-fingertip Palm Upward Punch   p'yŏn son-kkŭt
   (WTF)   che-ch'yŏ chi-rŭ-gi
                                           편 손끝 제쳐 지르기

Flat-fingertip Palm Upward   p'yŏn son-kkŭt che-ch'yŏ
   Thrust (WTF)   tchi-rŭ-gi
                                           편 손끝 제쳐 찌르기

Flat-fingertip Vertical   p'yŏn son-kkŭt se-wŏ chi-rŭ-gi
   Punch (WTF)   편 손끝 세워 지르기

Flat-fist (WTF)   p'yŏn chu-mŏk
                                           편 주먹

Flat-fist Reverse Straight   p'yŏn chu-mŏk pan-dae
   Punch (WTF)   chi-rŭ-gi
                                           편 주먹 반대 지르기

Flat-fist Reverse Straight   p'yŏn chu-mŏk pan-dae
   Vertical Punch (WTF)   se-wŏ chi-rŭ-gi
                                           편 주먹 반대 세워 지르기

Flat-fist Straight Punch (WTF)   p'yŏn chu-mŏk pa-ro chi-rŭ-gi
                                           편 주먹 바로 지르기

Flat-fist Straight Vertical
   Punch (WTF)

p'yŏn chu-mŏk pa-ro
  se-wŏ chi-rŭ-gi
편 주먹　바로
세워 지르기

Flexibility

shin-ch'uk
신 축

Floating Rib [Sino-Korean]

yu-ri nŭk-gol
유리 늑골

Flying (ITF)
  [jumping]

ttwi-gi
뛰기

Flying Combination Attack
  [jumping] (ITF)

ttwi-myŏ hon-hap kong-gyŏk
뛰며 혼합 공 격

Flying Combination Kick
  [jumping] (ITF)

ttwi-myŏ hon-hap ch'a-gi
뛰며 혼합 차기

Flying Consecutive Attack
  [jumping] (ITF)

ttwi-myŏ yŏn-sok kong-gyŏk
뛰며 연속 공 격

Flying Consecutive Kick
  [jumping] (ITF)

ttwi-myŏ yŏn-sok ch'a-gi
뛰며 연속 차 기

Flying Consecutive Kick (WTF)

kong-jung yŏn-sok ch'a-gi
공중 연속 차기

Flying Consecutive Punch
  [jumping] (ITF)

ttwi-myŏ yŏn-sok tchi-rŭ-gi
뛰며 연속 찌 르 기

Flying Consecutive Strike
  [jumping] (ITF)

ttwi-myŏ yŏn-sok ttae-ri-gi
뛰며 연속 때 리 기

Flying Consecutive Thrust
  [jumping] (ITF)

ttwi-myŏ yŏn-sok ttul-ki
뛰며 연속 뚫기

Flying Double Attack
  [jumping] (ITF)

ttwi-myŏ i-jung kong-gyŏk
뛰며 이 중 공 격

Flying Double Foot Side Pushing
  Kick [jumping] (ITF)

ttwi-myŏ tu-bal yŏp ch'a-mil-gi
뛰며 두 발 옆 차 밀기

Flying Front and Twisting Kick
  [jumping] (ITF)

ttwi-myŏ ap ch'ago
  pi-t'ŭ-rŏ ch'a-gi
뛰며 앞 차고 비틀어 차 기

Flying Kick [jumping] (ITF)	ttwi-myŏ ch'a-gi 뛰며 차기
Flying Overhead Kick [jumping] (ITF)	ttwi-myŏ nŏ-mŏ ch'a-gi 뛰며 너머 차기
Flying Overhead Punch [jumping] (ITF)	ttwi-myŏ nŏ-mŏ tchi-rŭ-gi 뛰며 너머 찌르기
Flying Punch [jumping] (ITF)	ttwi-myŏ tchi-rŭ-gi 뛰며 찌르기
Flying Scissors-shape Kick [jumping] (ITF)	ttwi-myŏ ka-wi ch'a-gi 뛰며 가위 차기
Flying Spiral Kick [jumping] (ITF)	ttwi-myŏ ra-sŏn-shik ch'a-gi 뛰며 라선식 차기
Flying Strike [jumping] (ITF)	ttwi-myŏ ttae-ri-gi 뛰며 때리기
Flying Techniques [jumping] (ITF)	ttwi-myŏ ki-sul 뛰며 기술
Flying to Evade [jumping] (ITF)	ttwi-gi 뛰 기
Flying Triple Attack [jumping] (ITF)	ttwi-myŏ sam-jung kong-gyŏk 뛰며 삼 중 공격
Flying Thrust [jumping] (ITF)	ttwi-myŏ ttul-ki 뛰며 뚫기
Flying Twin-foot Closed Kick (WTF)	kong-jung mo-dŭm-bal ch'a-gi 공중 모 듬발 차기
Flying Twisting Kick [jumping] (ITF)	ttwi-myŏ pi-t'ŭ-rŏ ch'a-gi 뛰며 비틀어 차기
Focus Point (ITF)	ch'o-jŏm 초점
Focus Shield (ITF)	ch'o-jŏm pang-p'ae 초점 방패

Foot	pal (-bal) or t'ae [Sino-Korean] 발 or 태
Foot-back [instep]	pal-dŭng 발 등
Foot Back Sole [Heel]	pal twi-kkum-ch'i 발 뒤꿈치
Foot-blade (WTF) [see edge of foot or footsword]	pal-lal 발 날
Foot-blade Back (WTF)	pal-lal dŭng 발날 등
Foot-blade Underneath Counter Block (WTF)	a-rae pa-da mak-ki 아래 받아 막기
Foot-fist-way [Korean martial art]	T'ae-kwŏn-Do 태권도
Foot Back Sole (WTF) [heel]	pal twi-kkum-ch'i or pal twi-ch'uk 발 뒤 꿈치 or 발 뒤축
Foot Lifting (ITF)	pal tŭl-gi 발 들기
Foot Parts (ITF) [lower half of body]	ha-ban-shin 하 반신
Foot-sole [foot bottom]	pal-ba-dak 발 바닥
Foot Sparring (ITF)	pal mat-sŏ-gi 발 맞서기
Foot Tackling (ITF)	pal kŏl-gi 발 걸기
Foot Techniques (ITF&WTF)	pal ki-sul 발 기술
Footsword	pal-lal (WTF) or pal-k'al (ITF) 발날 or 발 칼

Force	him 힘
Forearm Wedging Block (ITF)	p'al-mok he-ch'yŏ mak-ki 팔목 헤쳐 막기
Forearm [near the elbow]	p'al-gup 팔굽
Forearm [near the elbow]	p'al-kkum-ch'i 팔꿈치
Forearm [near the wrist]	p'al-mok 팔목
Forefinger (ITF)	han son-ga-rak 한 손가락
Forefist (ITF)	ap chu-mŏk 앞 주먹
Forehead	i-ma 이마
Fore-knuckle Fist (ITF)	in-ji chu-mŏk 인지 주먹
Forging (ITF)	tal-lyŏn 단련
Forging Bag (ITF)	tal-lyŏn ppaek 단련 빽
Forging Post (ITF)	tal-lyŏn chu 단련 주
Fork-shape Punch (WTF)	ch'et-da-ri chi-rŭ-gi 쳇다리 지르기
Forward Cross Stance (WTF)	ap kko-a sŏ-gi 앞 꼬아 서기
Forward Double Step-turning (ITF)	a-p'ŭ-ro i-bo om-gyŏ ti-dim-yŏ tol-gi 앞으로 이보 옮겨 디디며 돌기

Forward Inflection Stance (WTF)	ap ku-bi 앞 굽 이
Forward Riding Stance (WTF)	ap chu-ch'um sǒ-gi 앞 주춤 서기
Forward Sliding Punch (ITF)	mi-kkǔ-rǔm-bal-lo tchi-rǔ-myǒ na-ga-gi 미끄름발로 찌르며 나가기
Forward Stepping (ITF)	na-ga-gi 나가기
Forward Step-turning (ITF)	a-p'ǔ-ro om-gyǒ ti-di-myǒ tol-gi 앞으로 옮겨 디디며 돌기
Forward Stance (WTF)	ap sǒ-gi 앞 서기
Fossa of the knee	o-gǔm 오금
Foundation	ki-bon 기본
Four [in Native Korean]	net 넷
Four [in Sino-Korean]	sa 사
Four-direction Block (ITF)	sa-ju mak-ki 사 주 막기
Four-direction Kick (WTF)	sa-bang hyang ch'a-gi 사 방 향 차기
Four-direction Kick (ITF)	sa-bang ch'a-gi 사 방 차기
Four-direction Punch (ITF)	sa-ju tchi-rǔ-gi 사 주 찌르기
Four-direction Thrust (ITF)	sa-ju ttul-ki 사 주 뚫기

Fourth [in Native Korean]	ne-tchae 넷 째
Fourth [in Sino-Korean]	che-sa 제 사
Fourth Degree Black Belt (ITF&WTF)	sa-dan 사 단
Fourth Grade (ITF&WTF) [Low Blue Belt]	sa-gŭp 사 급
Free Sparring (ITF)	cha-yu mat-sŏ-gi 자유 맞서기
Free Sparring (WTF)	cha-yu tae-ryŏn 자유 대련
Front	ap 앞
Front Block (ITF)	ap mak-ki 앞 막기
Front Checking Kick (ITF)	ap ch'a-mŏm-ch'u-gi 앞 차 멈추기
Front Downward Strike (ITF)	ap nae-ryŏ ttae-ri-gi 앞 내려 때리기
Front Elbow (ITF)	ap p'al-gup 앞 팔굽
Front Elbow Strike (ITF)	ap p'al-gup ttae-ri-gi 앞 팔굽 때리기
Front Elbow Thrust (ITF)	ap p'al-gup ttul-ki 앞 팔굽 뚫기
Front Hit (WTF)	ap ch'i-gi 앞 치기
Front Kick (ITF&WTF)	ap ch'a-gi 앞 차기
Front Leg (ITF)	ap ta-ri 앞 다리

Front Leg Kick (ITF)	ap ta-ri ch'a-gi 앞다리 차기
Front Piercing Kick (ITF)	ap ch'a-tchi-rŭ-gi 앞 차 찌르기
Front Punch (ITF)	ap tchi-rŭ-gi 앞 찌르기
Front Punching Kick (ITF)	ap tchi-rŭ-myŏ ch'a-gi 앞 찌르며 차기
Front Pushing Kick (ITF)	ap ch'a-mil-gi 앞 차 밀기
Front Rising Kick (WTF)	pal ap ol-lyŏ ch'a-gi 발 앞 올려 차기
Front Rising Kick (ITF)	ap ch'a-ol-li-gi 앞 차 올리기
Front Snap Kick (ITF) [smashing]	ap ch'a-pu-su-gi 앞 차 부수기
Front-sole (WTF)	ap-ch'uk 앞축
Front Strike (ITF)	ap ttae-ri-gi 앞 때리기
Full Facing (ITF)	on-mom 온 몸
Fundamental Exercises	ki-bon yŏn-sŭp 기본 연습

G

Grab [Grasp]	chap-gi 잡기
Grade (WTF)	p'um-gye 품계
Grade - Colored Belt Ranking (ITF&WTF)	-gŭp 급

Grade Certificate	kŭp-jŭng 급증
Grand Master (ITF)	sa-sŏng 사성
Grand Master Sir (ITF)	sa-sŏng-nim 사성 님
Grand Master (WTF)	kwan-jang 관 장
Grand Master Sir (WTF)	kwan-jang nim 관 장 님
Grasping Block (ITF)	put-ja-ba mak-ki 붙잡아 막기
Grasp and Kick (ITF)	put-jap-go ch'a-gi 붙잡고 차기
Great Absolute	t'ae-gŭk 태극
Green Color	ch'o-rok saek 초록 색
Green Belt (ITF&WTF)	ch'o-rok tti 초록 띠
Green Belt with a Blue Stripe (ITF&WTF)	ch'o-rok tti-e p'u-rŭn sŏn 초록 띠에 푸른 선
Groin	sa-t'a-gu-ni 사타구니
Ground Dodging (ITF)	nu-wŏ p'i-ha-gi 누워 피하기
Ground Foot Technique (ITF)	nu-wŏ pal ki-sul 누워 발 기술
Ground Hand Technique (ITF)	nu-wŏ son ki-sul 누워 손 기술
Ground Knee Bending (ITF)	nu-wŏ mu-rŭp ku-bu-ri-gi 누워 무릎 구부 리기

Ground Leg Crossing (ITF)	nu-wŏ ta-ri kko-gi 누워 다리 꼬기
Ground Technique (ITF)	nu-wŏ ki-sul 누워 기술
Ground Kick (ITF)	nu-wŏ ch'a-gi 누워 차기
Ground Punch (ITF)	nu-wŏ tchi-rŭ-gi 누워 찌르기
Ground Thrust (ITF)	nu-wŏ ttul-ki 누워 뚫기
Ground Strike (ITF)	nu-wŏ ttae-ri-gi 누워 때리기
Guard or Guarding (ITF)	tae-bi 대비
Guarding Block (ITF)	tae-bi mak-ki 대비 막기

H

Half Facing (ITF)	pan-mom 반몸
Half Turning Kick [arc kick] (WTF)	pan tol-lyŏ ch'a-gi 반 돌려 차기
Hammer-fist (WTF)	me chu-mŏk 메 주먹
Hand	son 손
Hand-back (WTF)	son-dŭng 손등
Hand-blade (WTF) [see Knifehand or Edge of the Hand]	son-nal 손날
Hand-blade Back (WTF)	son-nal tŭng 손날 등

Hand-blade Back Face Block (WTF)	son-nal tŭng ŏl-gul mak-ki 손날 등 얼굴 막기
Hand-blade Back Trunk Block (WTF)	son-nal tŭng mom-t'ong mak-ki 손날 등 몸통 마기
Hand-blade Back Trunk Pushing Block (WTF)	son-nal tŭng mom-t'ong he-ch'yŏ mak-ki 손날 등 몸통 헤 쳐 막기
Hand-blade Back Underneath Block (WTF)	son-nal tŭng a-rae mak-ki 손날 등 아래 막기
Hand-blade Back Wide-open Block (WTF)	son-nal tŭng san-t'ŭl mak-ki 손날 등 산틀 막기
Hand-blade Diamond Block (WTF)	son-nal kŭm-gang mak-ki 손날 금강 막기
Hand-blade Single-hand Wide-open Block (WTF)	son-nal oe san-t'ŭl mak-ki 손날 외 산틀 막기
Hand-blade Trunk Block (WTF)	son-nal mom-t'ong mak-ki 손날 몸통 막기
Hand-blade Trunk Pushing Block (WTF)	son-nal mom-t'ong he-ch'yŏ mak-ki 손날 몸통 헤 쳐 막기
Hand-blade Trunk Side Block (WTF)	son-nal mom-t'ong yŏp mak-ki 손날 몸통 옆 막기
Hand-blade Underneath Block (WTF)	son-nal a-rae mak-ki 손날 아래 막기
Hand-blade Underneath Cross Block (WTF)	son-nal a-rae ŏt-gal-lyŏ mak-ki 손날 아래 엇갈려 막기
Hand-blade Underneath Pushing Block (WTF)	son-nal a-rae he-ch'yŏ mak-ki 손날 아래 헤 쳐 막기
Hand Parts (ITF) [upper half of body]	sang-ban-shin 상 반신
Hand Techniques (ITF)	son ki-sul 손 기술

47

Head	mŏ-ri 머리
Head-on Attack (ITF)	mat-ba-da kong-gyŏk 맞받아 공격
Headquarters of the WTF	Kuk-ki-wŏn 국기원
Heart	shim-jang 심장
Heaven Hand Stance (ITF)	ha-nŭl-son sŏ-gi 하늘 손 서기
Heel (WTF) [back of the foot]	twi-kkum-ch'i 뒤 꿈치
Heel of the Foot	pal twi-kkum-ch'i 발 뒤 꿈치
High (ITF)	no-p'ŭn-dae 높은대
High Abdomen	sang-bok-bu 상 복부
High Attack (ITF)	no-p'ŭn-dae kong-gyŏk 높은대 공격
High Block (ITF)	no-p'ŭn-dae mak-ki 높은대 막기
High Elbow Strike (ITF)	no-p'ŭn-dae p'al-gup ttae-ri-gi 높은대 팔굽 때리기
High Elbow Thrust (ITF)	no-p'ŭn-dae p'al-gup ttul-ki 높은대 팔굽 뚫기
High Kick (ITF)	no-p'i ch'a-gi 높이 차기
High Level (ITF) [Sino-Korean]	sang-dan 상 단
High Punch (ITF)	no-p'ŭn-dae tchi-rŭ-gi 높은대 찌르기

High Section (ITF)	no-p'ŭn pu-bun (ITF) or ŏl-gul (WTF)
	높은 부분 or 얼굴
High Strike (ITF)	no-p'ŭn-dae ttae-ri-gi
	높은대 때리기
High Thrust (ITF)	no-p'ŭn-dae ttul-ki
	높은대 뚫기
High Twisting Kick (ITF)	no-p'i pi-t'ŭ-rŏ ch'a-gi
	높이 비틀어 차기
Hip Joint	ŏng-dŏng-i kwan-jŏl
	엉덩이 관절
History	yŏk-sa
	역사
Hitting (WTF)	ch'i-gi
	치기
Holding (ITF)	pat-ch'i-gi
	받치기
Holding Front Kick (WTF)	chap-go ap ch'a-gi
	잡고 앞 차기
Holding Kick (WTF)	chap-go ch'a-gi
	잡고 차기
Holding Side Kick (WTF)	chap-go yŏp ch'a-gi
	잡고 옆 차기
Holding Turning Kick (WTF)	chap-go tol-lyŏ ch'a-gi
	잡고 돌려 차기
Hook Kick (ITF)	kŏ-rŏ ch'a-gi
	걸어 차기
Hook Kick (WTF)	na-ga ch'a-gi
	나가 차기
Hooking Block (ITF)	kŏl-ch'ŏ mak-ki
	걸처 막기
Hooking Kick (ITF)	kŏl-ch'ŏ ch'a-gi
	걸처 차기

Hooking Punch (ITF)	kŏrŏ tchi-rŭ-gi 걸어 찌르기
Horizontal Elbow Strike (ITF)	su-p'yŏng p'al-gup ttae-ri-gi 수평 팔굽 때리기
Horizontal Forearm (ITF)	su-p'yŏng p'al-mok 수평 팔목
Horizontal Forearm Block (ITF)	su-p'yŏng p'al-mok mak-ki 수평 팔목 막기
Horizontal Punch (ITF)	su-p'yŏng tchi-rŭ-gi 수평 찌르기
Horizontal Strike (ITF)	su-p'yŏng ttae-ri-gi 수평 때리기
Horizontal Striking Kick (ITF)	su-p'yŏng ttae-ri-myŏ ch'a-gi 수평 때리며 차기
Horizontal Thrust (ITF)	su-p'yŏng ttul-ki 수평 뚫기
Horizontal Wave (ITF)	su-p'yŏng p'a-do 수평 파도
Humanity	in-gan-mi 인간미
Humerus	sang-bak-gol 상박 골
Humility	kyŏm-son 겸손
Hwarang Code of Ethics	Hwa-rang Do 화랑 도

I

Incorrect	t'ŭl-lim 틀림
Indomitable Spirit	paek-jŏl-bul-gul 백 절 불 굴

Inflection (WTF)	ku-bi 굽 이
Injury	pu-sang 부상
Inner	an 안
Inner Ankle Joint	an pal-mok kwan-jŏl 안 발목 관절
Inner-block (WTF)	an mak-ki 안 막기
Inner Downward Kick (WTF)	an nae-ryŏ ch'a-gi 안 내려 차기
Inner Forearm (ITF&WTF) [at the wrist]	an p'al-mok 안 팔목
Inner-forearm Assisting Trunk Block (WTF)	an p'al-mok kŏ-dŭ-rŏ mom-t'ong mak-ki 안 팔목 거들어 몸통 막기
Inner-forearm Block (ITF&WTF)	an p'al-mok mak-ki 안 팔목 막기
Inner-forearm Face Outer Block (WTF)	an p'al-mok ŏl-gul pa-kkat mak-ki 안 팔목 얼굴 바깥 막기
Inner-forearm Face Twist Block (WTF)	an p'al-mok ŏl-gul pi-t'ŭ-rŏ mak-ki 안 팔목 얼굴 비틀어 막기
Inner-forearm Trunk Outer Block (WTF)	an p'al-mok mom-t'ong pa-kkat mak-ki 안 팔목 몸통 바깥 막기
Inner-forearm Trunk Pushing Block (WTF)	an p'al-mok mom-t'ong he-ch'yŏ mak-ki 안 팔목 몸통 헤쳐 막기
Inner-forearm Trunk Twist Block (WTF)	an p'al-mok mom-t'ong pi-t'ŭ-rŏ mak-ki 안 팔목 몸통 비틀어 막기

Inner Open Stance (ITF)	an p'al-ja sŏ-gi 안 팔자 서기
Inner Tibia	an kyŏng-gol 안 경 골
Inside Block (ITF)	an mak-ki 안 막기
Inside Thigh	an-tchok hŏ-bŏk-da-ri 안쪽 허벅 다리
Inside [area]	an-tchok 안쪽
Instantaneous Attack (ITF)	chŭk-shi kong-gyŏk 즉시 공 격
Instep	pal-dŭng 발등
Instructor - Teacher (ITF&WTF)	sa-bŏm 사범
Instructor Classification (ITF)	sa-bŏm pu-ryu 사범 부류
Instructor Sir - Teacher Sir (ITF&WTF)	sa-bŏm-nim 사범 님
Integrity	yŏm-ch'i 염 치
Intercostal Nerve	nŭk-gol shin-gyŏng 늑골 신경
International	kuk-je 국제
International Taekwon-Do Federation (ITF)	Kuk-je T'ae-kwŏn-Do Yŏn-maeng 국제 태권도 연맹
Inverted "T"-Shape Stance (WTF)	o-ja sŏ-gi 오자 서기

Inward	an-ŭ-ro 안으로
Inward Block (ITF)	an-ŭ-ro mak-ki 안으로 막기
Inward Cross-cut (ITF)	an-ŭ-ro kŭt-gi 안으로 긋기
Inward Hit (WTF)	an ch'i-gi 안 치기
Inward Kick (ITF)	an-ŭ-ro ch'a-gi 안으로 차기
Inward Riding Stance (WTF)	an-tchok chu-ch'um sŏ-gi 안쪽 주춤 서기
Inward Stance (WTF)	an-tchok sŏ-gi 안쪽 서기
Inward Strike (ITF)	an-ŭ-ro ttae-ri-gi 안으로 때리기
Inward Vertical Kick (ITF)	an-ŭ-ro se-wŏ ch'a-gi 안으로 세워 차기

J

Jaw or Chin	t'ŏk 턱
Joint	kwan-jŏl 관절
Joint-feet Kick (WTF)	mo-dŭm-bal ch'a-gi 모듬발 차기
Judge	pu-shim 부심
Jumping to Evade (ITF)	ttwi-gi 뛰 기
Jump Kick (WTF)	ttwi-ŏ ch'a-gi 뛰어 차기

53

Jump High Kick (WTF)	ttwi-ŏ ol-lyŏ ch'a-gi 뛰어 올려 차기
Junior (WTF)	hu-bae 후배

K

Kick (ITF&WTF)	ch'a-gi or t'ae [Sino-Korean] 차기 or 태
Kick - Backward Stepping (ITF)	ch'a-myŏ tŭ-rŏ o-gi 차 며 들어오기
Kick - Forward Stepping (ITF)	ch'a-myŏ na-ga-gi 차며 나가기
Kick while Grasping (ITF)	put-jap-go ch'a-gi 붙잡고 차기
Kidney	k'ong-p'at 콩팥
Knee	mu-rŭp 무릎
Knee Hollow (WTF)	o-gŭm 오금
Knee Joint	mu-rŭp kwan-jŏl 무릎 관절
Kneel (ITF&WTF) [sit down]	an-jŏ 앉어
Knee Rising Hit (WTF)	mu-rŭp ol-lyŏ ch'i-gi 무릎 올려 치기
Knee Rising Kick (WTF)	mu-rŭp ol-lyŏ ch'a-gi 무릎 올려 차기
Knee Strike (WTF)	mu-rŭp ch'i-gi 무릎 치기
Knee Turning Hit (WTF)	mu-rŭp tol-lyŏ ch'i-gi 무릎돌려 치기

Knee Turning Kick (WTF)	mu-rŭp tol-lyŏ ch'a-gi 무릎돌려 차기
Knife	k'al 칼
Knifehand [see Hand-blade or Edge of the Hand]	son-nal (WTF) or son-k'al (ITF) 손날 or 손칼
Knifehand Block (ITF)	son-k'al mak-ki 손칼 막기
Knifehand Strike (ITF)	son-k'al ttae-ri-gi 손칼 때리기
Knifehand Wedging Block (ITF)	son-k'al he-ch'yŏ mak-ki 손칼 헤쳐 막기
Knuckle Fist (ITF)	son-ga-rak chu-mŏk 손가락 주먹
Knuckle Fist Punch (ITF)	son-ga-rak chu-mŏk tchi-rŭ-gi 손가락 주먹 찌르기
Koguryo Dynasty	Ko-gu-ryŏ shi-dae 고구려시대
Koryo Dynasty	Ko-ryŏ shi-dae 고려 시대

L

Large Hinge (WTF)	k'ŭn tol-tchŏ-gwi 큰 돌쩌귀
Large Hinge Shape (WTF)	k'ŭn tol-tchŏ-gwi hyŏng 큰 돌쩌귀 형
Lead Leg (ITF)	ap-da-ri 앞다리
Lead Leg Kick (ITF)	ap-da-ri ch'a-gi 앞다리 차기
Left	oen 왼

Left Arm	oen p'al
	왼 팔
Left at Ease Stance (WTF)	oen p'yŏn-hi sŏ-gi
	왼 편히 서기
Left Foot	oen pal
	왼 발
Left Hand	oen son
	왼 손
Left-hand Stance (WTF)	oen sŏ-gi
	왼 서기
Left Leg	oen ta-ri
	왼 다리
Left Side [direction]	oen-tchok
	왼 쪽
Leg	ta-ri
	다리
Leg Stretching (ITF)	ta-ri p'yŏ-gi
	다리 펴기
Life Energy	ki
	기
Lifting	tŭl-gi
	들기
Line Up	chul-lo sŏ
	줄로 서
Lips	ip-sul
	입술
Liver	kan-jang
	간장
Long Fist (ITF)	kin chu-mŏk
	긴 주먹
Long Fist Punch (ITF)	kin chu-mŏk tchi-rŭ-gi
	긴 주먹 찌르기

Low

na-jŭn-dae
낮은대

Low Attack (ITF)

na-jŭn-dae kong-gyŏk
낮은대 공격

Low Block (ITF)

na-jŭn-dae mak-ki
낮은대 막기

Low Kick (ITF)

na-jŭn-dae ch'a-gi
낮은대 차기

Low Level

ha-dan
하단

Low Part (WTF)

a-rae pu-bun
아래 부분

Low Punch (ITF)

na-jŭn-dae tchi-rŭ-gi
낮은대 찌르기

Low Section

na-jŭn pu-bun (ITF)
  or a-rae (WTF)
낮은 부분 or 아래

Low Stance (ITF)

nat-ch'wŏ sŏ-gi
낮추어 서기

Low Strike (ITF)

na-jŭn-dae ttae-ri-gi
낮은대 때리기

Low Thrust (ITF)

na-jŭn-dae ttul-ki
낮은대 뚫기

Lower Abdomen

ha-bok-bu
하복부

L-Ready Stance (ITF)

ni-ŭn-ja chun-bi sŏ-gi
니은자 준비 서기

L-Stance (ITF)

ni-ŭn-ja sŏ-gi
니은자 서기

L-Stance High Block (ITF)

ni-ŭn-ja sŏ no-p'ŭn-dae mak-ki
니은자 서 높은대 막기

Luring Block (ITF)

yu-in mak-ki
유인 막기

57

M

Mandible Bone	ha-ak-gol [Sino-Korean] 하악골
Mandibula	t'ŏk kwan-jŏl 턱 관절
Martial Art	mu-sul 무술
Mass	chil-lyang 질량
Master Instructor - Senior Teacher (ITF)	sa-hyŏn 사현
Master Instructor Sir - Senior Teacher Sir (ITF)	sa-hyŏn-nim 사현 님
Mastoid	hu-i-bu 후이부
Match (ITF&WTF)	shi-hap or kyŏ-ru-gi 시합 or 겨루기
Maxilla Bone	sang-ak-gol 상악골
Median Nerve	chung-gan shin-gyŏng 중간 신경
Meditate	mung-nyŏm 묵념
Mid-air Techniques (ITF) [jump-rotating]	ttwi-yŏ tol-myŏ ki-sul 뛰여 돌며 기술
Mid-air Kick (ITF) [jump-rotating]	ttwi-yŏ tol-myŏ ch'a-gi 뛰여 돌며 차기
Mid-air Punch (ITF) [jump-rotating]	ttwi-yŏ tol-myŏ tchi-rŭ-gi 뛰여 돌며 찌르기
Mid-air Thrust (ITF) [jump-rotating]	ttwi-yŏ tol-myŏ ttul-ki 뛰여 돌며 뚫기

Mid-air strike (ITF) [jump-rotating]	ttwi-yŏ tol-myŏ ttae-ri-gi 뛰여 돌며 때리기
Middle (ITF)	ka-un-dae 가운대
Middle Attack (ITF)	ka-un-dae kong-gyŏk 가운대 공격
Middle Block (ITF)	ka-un-dae mak-ki 가운대 막기
Middle Finger	chung-ji 중지
Middle Kick (ITF)	ka-un-dae ch'a-gi 가운대 차기
Middle Knuckle Fist (ITF)	chung-ji chu-mŏk 중지 주먹
Middle Level (ITF)	chung-dan 중단
Middle Punch (ITF)	ka-un-dae tchi-rŭ-gi 가운대 찌르기
Middle Section (ITF)	ka-un-dae pu-bun (ITF) or mom-t'ong (WTF) 가운대 부분 or 몸통
Middle Strike (ITF)	ka-un-dae ttae-ri-gi 가운대 때리기
Middle Thrust (ITF)	ka-un-dae ttul-ki 가운대 뚫기
Mirror	kŏ-ul 거울
Mixed Kicks (WTF)	sŏk-kŏ ch'a-gi 섞어 차기
Model Sparring (ITF)	mo-bŏm mat-sŏ-gi 모범 맞서기
Moral Culture	chŏng-shin su-yang 정신 수양

Motion (ITF)	tong-jak 동작
Mountain	san 산
Mountain Climbing	tŭng-san 등 산
Mountain Pushing (WTF)	t'ae-san mil-gi 태산 밀기
Mountain Shape Block (WTF)	san-t'ŭl mak-ki 산틀 막기
Mountain Shape Cross Block (WTF)	san-t'ŭl ŏt-gal-lyŏ mak-ki 산틀 엇갈려 막기
Movement (ITF)	tong-jak 동작
Multi-direction Kick (WTF)	ta-bang-hyang ch'a-gi 다 방향 차기
Muscle	kŭn-yuk 근육

N

Neck	mok 목
Neck Artery [Carotid]	mok tong-maek 목 동맥
Nerve	shin-gyŏng 신경
Nine [in Native Korean]	a-hop 아홉
Nine [in Sino-Korean]	ku 구
Nine-Shape Block (ITF)	ku-ja mak-ki 구자 막기

Ninth [in Native Korean]	a-hop-tchae 아홉 째
Ninth [in Sino-Korean]	che-ku 제 구
Ninth Degree Black Belt (ITF&WTF)	ku-dan 구 단
Ninth Grade (ITF&WTF) [High White Belt]	ku-gŭp 구 급
No	a-ni-o (formal) 아니오
Nose	k'o 코

O

Oblique Angle Riding Stance (WTF)	mo chu-ch'um sŏ-gi 모 주춤 서기
Oblique Angle Stance (WTF)	mo sŏ-gi 모 서기
Obverse (ITF)	pa-ro 바로
Obverse Punch (ITF)	pa-ro tchi-rŭ-gi 바로 찌르기
Occiput	hu-du-bu 후두부
Occipital Bone	hu-du-gol 후 두골
One [in Native Korean]	ha-na 하나
One [in Sino-Korean]	il 일
One-leg Stance (ITF)	oe-bal sŏ-gi 외발 서기

One-step Sparring (WTF)	han-bŏn kyŏ-ru-gi 한번 겨루기
One-step Sparring (ITF)	il-bo mat-sŏ-gi 일보 맞서기
One-way Three-step Sparring (ITF)	han-tchok sam-bo mat-sŏ-gi 한쪽 삼 보 맞서기
Open Fist (ITF)	p'yŏn chu-mŏk 편 주먹
Open-fist Punch (ITF)	p'yŏn chu-mŏk tchi-rŭ-gi 편 주먹 찌르기
Open Ready Stance (ITF)	p'al-ja chun-bi sŏ-gi 팔 자 준비 서기
Open Stance (ITF)	p'al-ja sŏ-gi 팔자 서기
Opposite Straight Punch (WTF)	pan-dae chi-rŭ-gi 반대 지르기
Outer	pa-kkat 바깥
Outer Block (WTF)	pa-kkat mak-ki 바깥 막기
Outer Downward Kick (WTF)	pa-kkat nae-ryŏ ch'a-gi 바깥 내려 차기
Outer Forearm (WTF) [at wrist]	pa-kkat p'al-mok 바깥 팔목
Outer-forearm Block (WTF)	pa-kkat p'al-mok mak-ki 바깥 팔목 막기
Outer-forearm Face Side Block (WTF)	pa-kkat p'al-mok ŏl-gul yŏp mak-ki 바깥 팔목 얼굴 옆 막기
Outer-forearm Trunk Side Block (WTF)	pa-kkat p'al-mok mom-t'ong yŏp mak-ki 바깥 팔목 몸통 옆 막기

Outside	pa-kkat 바깥
Outside Ankle Joint	pa-kkat pal-mok kwan-jŏl 바깥 발 목 관절
Outside Block (ITF)	pa-kkat mak-ki 바깥 막기
Outside Forearm (ITF)	pa-kkat p'al-mok 바깥 팔목
Outside Open Stance (ITF)	pa-kkat p'al-ja sŏ-gi 바깥 팔자 서기
Outside Tibia [Fibula]	pa-kkat kyŏng-gol 바깥 경골
Outward	pak-kŭ-ro 밖으로
Outward Block (ITF)	pak-kŭ-ro mak-ki 밖으로 막기
Outward Cross-cut (ITF)	pak-kŭ-ro kŭt-gi 밖으로 긋기
Outward Hit (WTF)	pa-kkat ch'i-gi 바깥 치기
Outward Kick (ITF)	pak-kŭ-ro ch'a-gi 밖으로 차기
Outward Strike (ITF)	pak-kŭ-ro ttae-ri-gi 밖으로 때리기
Outward Vertical Kick (ITF)	pak-kŭ-ro se-wŏ ch'a-gi 밖으로 세워 차기
Overlap Backhand (ITF)	p'o-gaen son-dŭng 포갠 손등
Overlapped Hands Ready Stance (WTF)	kyŏp-son chun-bi sŏ-gi 겹 손 준비 서기

P

Paekje Dynasty	Paek-je shi-dae 백제 시대
Palm (ITF) [hand bottom]	son-ba-dak 바닥
Palm Assisting Side Block (WTF)	son-ba-dak kŏ-dŭ-rŏ yŏp mak-ki 손 바닥 거들어 옆 막기
Palm Hand (WTF)	pa-t'ang-son 바탕손
Palm-hand Face Inner Block (WTF)	pa-t'ang-son ŏl-gul an mak-ki 바탕손 얼굴 안 막기
Palm-hand Trunk Block (WTF)	pa-t'ang-son mom-t'ong mak-ki 바탕손 몸통 막기
Palm-hand Trunk Pressing Block (WTF)	pa-t'ang-son mom-t'ong nul-lŏ mak-ki 바탕손 몸통 눌러 막기
Palm-hand Underneath Block (WTF)	pa-t'ang-son a-rae mak-ki 바탕손 아래 막기
Palm-heel (ITF)	pa-t'ang-son 바탕손
Palm-upward Fist (WTF)	che-ch'in chu-mŏk 제친 주먹
Palm-upward Flat-fingertip (WTF)	che-ch'in p'yŏn son-kkŭt 제친 편 손끝
Palm-upward Punch (WTF)	che-ch'yŏ chi-rŭ-gi 제쳐 지르기
Parallel Block (ITF)	na-ran-hi mak-ki 나란히 막기
Parallel Ready Stance (ITF)	na-ran-hi chun-bi sŏ-gi 나란히 준비 서기
Parallel Stance (ITF&WTF)	na- ran-hi sŏ-gi 나란히 서기

Part Mountain Shape Block (WTF)	oe san-t'ŭl mak-ki 외 산 틀 막기
Part Mountain Shape Side Block (WTF)	oe san-t'ŭl yŏp mak-ki 외 산 틀 옆 막기
Patella	sŭl-gae-gol 슬개골
Pattern [Old ITF term]	hyŏng 형
Pattern	t'ŭl (ITF) or p'um-se (WTF) 틀 or 품세
Perseverance	in-nae 인 내
Philosophy	ch'ŏl-hak 철학
Philtrum	in-jung 인중
Pick-shape Kick (ITF)	kok-gwaeng-i ch'a-gi 곡 괭 이 차기
Piercing Kick (ITF)	ch'a-tchi-rŭ-gi 차 찌르기
Pincers Fist (WTF)	chip-ge chu-mŏk 집게 주먹
Pistol	kwŏn-ch'ong 권총
Point of the Chin	mit t'ŏk 밑 턱
Pole	mong-dung-i 몽둥이
Pole Block	mong-dung-i mak-ki 몽둥이 막기
Pole Grasping Block (ITF)	mong-dung-i chap-go mak-ki 몽둥이 잡고 막기

Power	him
	힘
Practice Pants (ITF)	pa-ji
	바지
Practice Shirt (ITF)	chŏ-go-ri
	저고리
Practice Suit (ITF&WTF) [Uniform]	to-bok
	도복
Pre-arranged Free Sparring (ITF)	yak-sok cha-yu mat-sŏ-gi
	약속 자유 맞서기
Pre-arranged Model Sparring (ITF)	yak-sok mo-bŏm mat-sŏ-gi
	약속 모범 맞서기
Pre-arranged One-step Sparring (ITF)	yak-sok il-bo mat-sŏ-gi
	약속 일보 맞서기
Pre-arranged Sparring (WTF)	ma-ch'u-ŏ kyŏ-ru-gi
	마 추어 겨루기
Pre-arranged Sparring (WTF)	yak-sok tae-ryŏn
	약속 대련
Pre-arranged Sparring (ITF)	yak-sok mat-sŏ-gi
	약속 맞서기
Pre-arranged Three-step Sparring (ITF)	yak-sok sam-bo mat-sŏ-gi
	약속 삼 보 맞 서기
Pre-arranged Two-step Sparring (ITF)	yak-sok i-bo mat-sŏ-gi
	약속 이보 맞서기
Press Finger (ITF)	chi-ap
	지압
Pressing Block (ITF&WTF)	nul-lŏ mak-ki
	눌러 막기
Pressing Kick (ITF)	nul-lŏ ch'a-gi
	눌러 차기
Pressing X-Fist Block (ITF)	nul-lŏ kyo-ch'a chu-mŏk mak-ki
	눌러 교차 주먹 막기

Promotion Test	sŭng-kŭp shim-sa 승급 심사
Protective Sparring Equipment	ho-gu 호구
Pubic Region (ITF)	ch'i-bu 치부
Pubis (WTF)	ch'i-gol 치골
Public Service (ITF)	sa-hoe pong-sa 사회 봉사
Pulling the Jaw Punch (WTF)	tang-gyŏ t'ŏk chi-rŭ-gi 당겨 턱 지르기
Punch or Punching (ITF)	tchi-rŭ-gi 찌르기
Punch or Punching (WTF)	chi-rŭ-gi 지르기
Punch - Backward Stepping (ITF)	tchi-rŭ-myŏ tŭ-rŏ o-gi 찌르며 들어 오기
Punch - Forward Stepping (ITF)	tchi-rŭ-myŏ na-ga-gi 찌르며 나가기
Punching Kick (ITF) (Airborne Combination)	tchi-rŭ-myŏ ch'a-gi 찌르며 차기
Punching Technique (WTF)	chu-mŏk ki-sul 주먹 기술
Push Barrel (WTF)	t'ong mil-gi 통 밀기
Push Boulder (WTF)	pa-wi mil-gi 바위 밀기
Pushing	mil-gi 밀기
Pushing-hands Ready Stance (WTF)	t'ong mil-gi chun-bi sŏ-gi 통 밀기 준비 서기

67

Pushing Block (WTF)

he-ch'yŏ mak-ki
헤 쳐 막기

Pushing Block (ITF)

mi-rŏ mak-ki
밀어 막기

Pushing Kick (ITF)

ch'a-mil-gi
차 밀기

Pushing Kick (WTF)

mi-rŏ ch'a-gi
밀어 차기

Pushing Wide-open Block (WTF)

he-ch'yŏ san-t'ŭl mak-ki
헤 쳐 산틀 막기

Push Mountain Shape (WTF)

tae-san mil-gi
태산 밀기

Pushups

mom-t'ong pat-ch'im
몸통 받침

Q

Quadruple Kick (ITF)

sa-jung ch'a-gi
사 중 차기

R

Radial Artery

maek-bak son-mok tong-maek
맥박 손목 동맥

Radial Nerve

yo-gol shin-gyŏng
요골 신경

Radius

yo-gol
요골

Rank (ITF)

gye-gŭp
계급

Rank (WTF)

p'um-gye
품계

Reaction Force (ITF)	pan-dong-nyŏk 반동력
Ready (ITF&WTF)	chun-bi 준비
Ready Stance (ITF&WTF)	chun-bi sŏ-gi 준비 서기
Rear-foot Stance (ITF)	twit-bal sŏ-gi 뒷발 서기
Rear Leg	twit ta-ri 뒷 다리
Recorder (WTF)	ki-rok 기록
Red Color	ppal-gan saek 빨간 색
Red Belt (ITF&WTF)	ppal-gan tti 빨간 띠
Red Belt with a Black Stripe (ITF&WTF)	ppal-gan tti-e kŏ-mŭn sŏn 빨간 띠에 검은 선
Red Contestant (WTF)	hong sŏn-su 홍 선수
Red Contestant Mark (WTF)	hong k'o-nŏ 홍 코너
Referee	chu-shim 주심
Reflex (ITF)	pa-nŭng 반응
Reflex Kick (ITF)	pan-sa ch'a-gi 반사 차기
Repeated Kick (WTF)	kŏ-dŭp ch'a-gi 거듭 차기
Return (ITF&WTF) [to a position]	pa-ro 바로

Reverse (ITF)	pan-dae 반대
Reverse Attention Stance (WTF)	ap-ch'uk mo-a sŏ-gi 앞 축 모아 서기
Reverse Crane Stance (WTF)	o-gŭm sŏ-gi 오금 서기
Reverse Footsword (ITF)	pal-k'al dŭng 발칼 등
Reverse Knifehand (ITF)	son-k'al dŭng 손칼 등
Reverse Punch (ITF)	pan-dae tchi-rŭ-gi 반대 찌르기
Reverse Turning Techniques (ITF)	pan-dae tol-lyŏ ki-sul 반대 돌려 기술
Reverse Turning Kick (ITF)	pan-dae tol-lyŏ ch'a-gi 반대 돌려 차기
Rib [Sino-Korean]	nŭk-gol 늑 골
Right	o-rŭn 오른
Right Arm	o-rŭn p'al 오른 팔
Right at Ease Stance (WTF)	o-rŭn-tchok p'yŏn-hi sŏ-gi 오른쪽 편히 서기
Right Foot	o-rŭn pal 오른 발
Right Hand	o-rŭn son 오른 손
Right-hand Stance (WTF)	o-rŭn sŏ-gi 오른 서기
Right Leg	o-rŭn ta-ri 오른 다리

Right Side [direction]   o-rŭn-tchok
오른 쪽

Righteousness   chŏng-ŭi
정 의

Rise-up Strike (WTF)   ol-lyŏ ch'i-gi
올려 치기

Rising   ol-li-gi
올리기

Rising Block (ITF)   ch'u-kkyŏ mak-ki
추껴 막기

Rising Kick (ITF)   ch'a-ol-li-gi
차 올리기

Rock Pushing (WTF)   pa-wi mil-gi
바위 밀기

Roll or Rolling (ITF)   kul-lŭ-gi
굴르기

Round (WTF)   hwi-jŏn
[in a sparring match]   회전

Rules   kyu-jŏng
규정

S

Salute (ITF&WTF)   kyŏng-nye
경례

Salute the [National] Flag   kuk-ki-e tae-ha-yŏ kyŏng-nye
국기에 대하여 경례

Saw-tooth Wave (ITF)   t'om-nal p'a-do
톱날 파도

Scattered Block (WTF)   he-ch'yŏ mak-ki
헤쳐 막기

School [founding location]   kwan
관

Sciatic Nerve	chwa-gol shin-gyŏng 좌골 신경
Scissors Block (WTF)	ka-wi mak-ki 가위 막기
Scissors Fingertip (WTF)	ka-wi son-kkŭt 가위 손끝
Scissors Fingertip Thrust (WTF)	ka-wi son-kkŭt tchi-rŭ-gi 가위 손끝 찌르기
Scissors Front Kick (WTF)	ka-wi ap ch'a-gi 가위 앞 차기
Scissors Kick (WTF)	ka-wi ch'a-gi 가위 차기
Scissors Pushing Side Kick (WTF)	ka-wi mi-rŏ yŏp ch'a-gi 가위 밀어 옆 차기
Scissors Side Kick (WTF)	ka-wi yŏp ch'a-gi 가위 옆 차기
Scissors Turning Kick (WTF)	ka-wi tol-lyŏ ch'a-gi 가위 돌려 차기
Scooping Block (ITF)	ttŭ-rŏ mak-ki 뜰어 막기
Second [in Native Korean]	tul-tchae 둘 째
Second [in Sino-Korean]	che-i 제 이
Second Degree Black Belt (ITF&WTF)	i-dan 이 단
Second Grade (ITF&WTF) [Low Red Belt]	i-gŭp 이 급
Second Degree Junior Black Belt (WTF)	i-pum 이 붐
Section of the Body (ITF)	mom-ttung pun or mom pu-bun 몸뚱 분 or 몸 부분

Self Control	kŭk-ki 극기
Self Defense	ho-shin-sul 호신술
Semi-free Sparring (ITF)	pan-ja-yu mat-sŏ-gi 반자유 맞서기
Senior (WTF)	sŏn-bae 선배
Seven [in Native Korean]	il-gop 일곱
Seven [in Sino-Korean]	ch'il 칠
Seventh [in Native Korean]	il-gop-tchae 일곱 째
Seventh [in Sino-Korean]	che-ch'il 제 칠
Seventh Degree Black Belt (ITF&WTF)	ch'il-dan 칠 단
Seventh Grade (ITF&WTF) [High Yellow Belt]	ch'il-gŭp 칠 급
Shifting (ITF)	om-gyŏ 옮겨
Shifting the body by moving both feet (ITF)	mi-kkŭ-rŏm pal 미끄럼 발
Shifting Feet Quickly - Stepping (ITF)	cha-jŭn-bal om-gyŏ ti-di-gi 잦은발 옮겨 디디기
Shifting Feet Quickly (ITF) [Dodging]	cha-jŭn-bal 잦은발
Shilla Dynasty	Shil-la shi-dae 신라 시대
Shin	chŏng-gang-i 정강이

Shin Counter Block (WTF)	chŏng-gang-i pa-da mak-ki 정강이 받아 막기
Shoulder	ŏ-kkae 어깨
Shoulder Joint	ŏ-kkae kwan-jŏl 어깨 관절
Shout	ki-hap 기합
Side	yŏp 옆
Side [flank, lateral] (ITF)	ch'ŭk-myŏn 측면
Side Back Strike (ITF)	yŏp twit ttae-ri-gi 옆 뒷 때리기
Side Back Thrust (ITF)	yŏp twit ttul-ki 옆 뒷 뚫기
Side Block (ITF&WTF)	yŏp mak-ki 옆 막기
Side Checking Kick (ITF)	yŏp ch'a-mŏm-ch'u-gi 옆 차 멈추기
Side Cross-cut (ITF)	yŏp kŭt-gi 옆 긋기
Side Downward Strike (ITF)	yŏp nae-ryŏ ttae-ri-gi 옆 내려 때리기
Side Elbow (ITF)	yŏp p'al-gup 옆 팔굽
Side Elbow Thrust (ITF)	yŏp p'al-gup ttul-ki 옆 팔굽 뚫기
Side Facing (ITF)	yŏp-mom 옆 몸
Side Fist (ITF)	yŏp chu-mŏk 옆 주먹

Side Foot Sole [bottom] (ITF)   yŏp pal-ba-dak
옆 발 바닥

Side Front Block (ITF)   yŏp ap mak-ki
옆 앞 막기

Side Front Kick (ITF)   yŏp ap ch'a-gi
옆 앞 차기

Side Front Punch (ITF)   yŏp ap tchi-rŭ-gi
옆 앞 찌르기

Side Front Pushing Kick (ITF)   yŏp ap ch'a-mil-gi
옆 앞 차 밀기

Side Front Snap Kick (ITF)   yŏp ap ch'a-pu-su-gi
  [smashing]   옆 앞 차 부수기

Side Front Strike (ITF)   yŏp ap ttae-ri-gi
옆 앞 때리기

Side Front Thrust (ITF)   yŏp ap ttul-ki
옆 앞 뚫기

Side Hit (WTF)   yŏp ch'i-gi
옆 치기

Side Instep   yŏp pal-dŭng
옆 발등

Side Jaw   yŏp t'ŏk
옆 턱

Side Kick (ITF&WTF)   yŏp ch'a-gi
옆 차기

Side Knee   yŏp mu-rŭp
옆 무릎

Side Piercing Kick (ITF)   yŏp ch'a-tchi-rŭ-gi
옆 차 찌르기

Side Punch (ITF)   yŏp tchi-rŭ-gi
옆 찌르기

Side Punch (WTF)   yŏp chi-rŭ-gi
옆 지르기

Side Punching Kick (ITF)
[Airborne Combination]

yŏp tchi-rŭ-myŏ ch'a-gi
옆 찌르며 차기

Side Pushing Kick (ITF)

yŏp ch'a-mil-gi
옆 차 밀기

Side Rising Kick (ITF)

yŏp ch'a-ol-li-gi
옆 차 올리기

Side Strike (ITF)

yŏp ttae-ri-gi
옆 때리기

Side Thrust (ITF)

yŏp ttul-ki
옆 뚫기

Side Thrusting Kick (ITF)

yŏp ch'a-ttul-ki
옆 차 뚫기

Side Turning Kick (ITF)

yŏp tol-lyŏ ch'a-gi
옆 돌려 차기

Side Vertical Punch (ITF)

yŏp se-wŏ tchi-rŭ-gi
옆 세워 찌르기

Sine Wave (ITF)

hwal-dŭng p'a-do
활등 파도

Single Elbow Strike (ITF)

oe p'al-gup ttae-ri-gi
외 팔굽 때리기

Single Elbow Thrust (ITF)

oe p'al-gup ttul-ki
외 팔 굽 뚫기

Single Finger Spear (ITF)
[Thrust]

han son-ga-rak ttul-ki
한 손가락 뚫기

Single Fingertip (WTF)

han son-kkŭt
한 손끝

Single Fingertip Thrust (WTF)

han son-kkŭt tchi-rŭ-gi
한 손끝 찌르기

Single Fist (ITF)

oe chu-mŏk
외 주먹

Single Hand-blade Block (WTF)

han son-nal mak-ki
한 손날 막기

Single Hand-blade Face
   Inner Block (WTF)

han son-nal ŏl-gul an mak-ki
한 손날 얼굴 안 막기

Single Hand-blade Face
   Outer Block (WTF)

han son-nal ŏl-gul
  pa-kkat mak-ki
한 손날 얼굴 바깥 막기

Single Hand-blade Face
   Twist Block (WTF)

han son-nal ŏl-gul
  pi-t'ŭ-rŏ mak-ki
한 손날 얼굴　비틀어 막기

Single Hand-blade Trunk
   Block (WTF)

han son-nal mom-t'ong mak-ki
한 손날 몸통 막기

Single Hand-blade Trunk (WTF)
   Inner Block

han son-nal mom-t'ong
  an mak-ki
한 손날　몸통 안 막기

Single Hand-blade Underneath
   Side Block (WTF)

han son-nal a-rae yŏp mak-ki
한 손날　아래 옆 막기

Single Hand-blade Underneath
   Twist Block (WTF)

han son-nal a-rae
  pi-t'ŭ-rŏ mak-ki
한 손날　아래 비틀어 막기

Single-hand Wide-open
   Block (WTF)

oe san-t'ŭl mak-ki
외 산틀 막기

Single-hand Wide-open
   Block and Side Kick (WTF)

oe san-t'ŭl yŏp ch'a-gi
외 산틀 옆 차기

Single line Kicks (WTF)

il-ch'a ch'a-gi
일 차 차기

Single Side Elbow Strike (ITF)

oe yŏp p'al-gup ttae-ri-gi
외 옆 팔굽 때리기

Single Side Elbow Thrust (ITF)

oe yŏp p'al-gup ttul-ki
외 옆 팔굽 뚫기

Single Stepping (ITF)

il-bo om-gyŏ ti-di-gi
일보 옮겨 디디기

Single Straight Forearm (ITF)

oe sŏn p'al-mok
외 선 팔목

77

Single Straight Forearm Block (ITF)	oe sŏn p'al-mok mak-ki
	외 선 팔목 막기
Single Straight Knifehand (ITF)	oe sŏn son-k'al
	외 선 손칼
Single Straight Knifehand Block (ITF)	oe sŏn son-k'al mak-ki
	외 선 손칼 막기
Sir	nim
	님
Sit down	an-jŏ
	앉어
Sitting Ready Stance (ITF)	an-nŭn chun-bi sŏ-gi
	앉는 준비 서기
Sitting Stance (ITF)	an-nŭn sŏ-gi
	앉는 서기
Sitting Stance Punch (ITF)	an-nŭn sŏ tchi-rŭ-gi
	앉는 서 찌르기
Six [in Native Korean]	yŏ-sŏt
	여섯
Six [in Sino-Korean]	yuk
	육
Sixth [in Native Korean]	yŏ-sŏt-tchae
	여섯 째
Sixth [in Sino-Korean]	che-yuk
	제 육
Sixth Degree Black Belt (ITF&WTF)	yuk-dan
	육 단
Sixth Grade (ITF&WTF) [Low green Belt]	yuk-gŭp
	육 급
Skip Kick (ITF)	tŭ-rŏ-ka-myŏ ch'a-gi
	들어가며 차기
Skipping Techniques (ITF)	tŭ-rŏ-ka-myŏ ki-sul
	들어가며 기술

Skip Punch (ITF)	tŭ-rŏ-ka-myŏ tchi-rŭ-gi 들어가며 찌르기
Skip Thrust (ITF)	tŭ-rŏ-ka-myŏ ttul-ki 들어가며 뚫기
Skip Strike (ITF)	tŭ-rŏ-ka-myŏ ttae-ri-gi 들어가며 때리기
Skull	tu-gae-gol 두개골
Slide or Sliding (ITF)	mi-kkŭl-gi 미끌기
Sliding the feet to cover long distances (ITF)	o-myŏ mi-kkŭl-gi 오며 미끌기
Slow Motion (ITF)	nŭ-rin tong-jak 느린 동작
Small Hinge (WTF)	cha-gŭn tol-tchŏ-gwi 작은 돌쩌귀
Small Hinge Shape (WTF)	cha-gŭn tol-tchŏ-gwi hyŏng 작은 돌쩌귀 형
Small of the Back	kyŏng-ch'u 경추
Smashing	pu-su-gi 부수기
Snap Kick (ITF) [smashing]	ch'a-pu-su-gi 차 부수기
Solar Plexus	myŏng-ch'i 명치
Sorry	mi-an ham-ni-da 미안 합니다
Sparring (ITF)	mat-sŏ-gi or tae-ryŏn 맞서기 or 대련
Sparring (WTF)	shi-hap 시 합

Sparring System (ITF)	mat-sŏ-gi che-do 맞서기 제도
Spear Hand (ITF)	p'yŏn son-kkŭt 편 손끝
Speed	sok-do 속도
Speed and Reflex (ITF)	sok-do-wa pa-nŭng 속도와 반응
Spinal Chord (WTF) [nerve]	ch'ŏk-ju shin-gyŏng 척주 신경
Spine	ch'ŏk-ju 척주
Spiral Punch (WTF)	tol-lyŏ chi-rŭ-gi 돌려 지르기
Spleen	pi-jang 비장
Sponge Pad (ITF)	sŭ-p'on-ji pe-gae 스폰지 베개
Spot Block (ITF)	kŭ-ja-ri mak-ki 그자리 막기
Spot Kick (ITF)	kŭ-ja-ri ch'a-gi 그자리 차기
Spot Punch (ITF)	kŭ-ja-ri tchi-rŭ-gi 그자리 찌 르기
Spot Strike (ITF)	kŭ-ja-ri ttae-ri-gi 그자리 때리기
Spot Thrust (ITF)	kŭ-ja-ri ttul-gi 그자리 뚫기
Spot Turning (ITF)	kŭ-ja-ri tol-gi 그자리 돌기
Spring-up Punch (WTF)	so-sŭm chi-rŭ-gi 솟음 지르기

Staff [Pole]	mong-dung-i 몽둥이
Stamping Front Kick (WTF)	kul-lŏ ap ch'a-gi 굴러 앞 차기
Stamping Kick (ITF)	ch'a-pap-gi 차 밟기
Stamping Kick (WTF)	kul-lŏ ch'a-gi 굴러 차기
Stamping Motion (ITF)	ku-rŭ-nŭn tong-jak 구 르는 동작
Stamping Side Kick (WTF)	kul-lŏ yŏp ch'a-gi 굴러 옆 차기
Stamping Turning Kick (WTF)	kul-lŏ tol-lyŏ ch'a-gi 굴러 돌려 차기
Stance (ITF&WTF)	sŏ-gi or ku-bi 서기 or 굽이
Start	shi-jak 시작
Static Stability (ITF)	chŏng-jŏk an-jŏng 정적 안정
Stepping (ITF)	ti-di-gi 디디기
Stepping and Shifting (ITF)	om-gyŏ ti-di-gi 옮겨 디디기
Stepping and Shifting Foot Changing (ITF)	om-gyŏ ti-di-myŏ cha-jŭn-bal 옮겨 디디며 잦은발
Stepping and Shifting Turn (ITF)	om-gyŏ ti-di-myŏ tol-gi 옮겨 디디며 돌기
Sternum	hyung-gol 흉골
Stop	kŭ-man or chŏng-ji 그만 or 정지

81

Straight	sŏn 선
Straight Elbow (ITF)	sŏn p'al-gup 선 팔굽
Straight Elbow Thrust (ITF)	sŏn p'al-gup ttul-ki 선 팔굽 뚫기
Straight Fingertip (ITF)	sŏn son-kkŭt 선 손끝
Straight Forearm (ITF)	sŏn p'al-mok 선 팔목
Straight Forearm Block (ITF)	sŏn p'al-mok mak-ki 선 팔목 막기
Straight Kick (ITF)	tchi-gŏ ch'a-gi 찍어 차기
Straight Punch (WTF)	pa-ro chi-rŭ-gi 바로 지르기
Straw Pad (ITF)	chip pe-gae 짚 베개
Stretching (ITF)	p'yŏ-gi 펴기
Stretch Kick (WTF)	ppŏ-dŏ ch'a-gi 뻗어 차기
Strike - Backward Stepping (ITF)	ttae-ri-myŏ tŭ-rŏ o-gi 때리며 들어오기
Strike - Forward Stepping (ITF)	ttae-ri-myŏ na-ga-gi 때리며 나가기
Strike or Striking Technique (ITF)	ttae-ri-gi 때리기
Strike or Striking Technique (WTF)	ch'i-gi 치기
Strong	kang-han 강한

Student	che-ja (ITF)
	제자
or	su-ryŏn-saeng (WTF)
	수련생
Student / Instructor Relationship (ITF)	sa-je ji-do
	사제 지도
Swallow-shape Neck Hit (WTF)	che-bi-p'um mok ch'i-gi
	제비품 목 치기
Swallow-shape Neck Strike (WTF)	che-bi-p'um mok ch'i-gi
	제비품 목 치기
Swallow-shape Jaw Hit (WTF)	che-bi-p'um t'ŏk ch'i-gi
	제비품 턱 치기
Sweeping Kick (ITF)	ssŭ-rŏ ch'a-gi
	쓸어 차기
Sub-Referee	pu-shim
	부심
System of Ranking (ITF)	tan-gŭp che-do
	단 급 제도

T

Taekwon-Do	T'ae-kwŏn-Do
	태권도
Target Block (WTF)	p'yo-jŏk mak-ki
	표적 막기
Target Kick (WTF)	p'yo-jŏk ch'a-gi
	표적 차기
Target Punch (WTF)	p'yo-jŏk chi-rŭ-gi
	표적 지르기
Target Strike (WTF)	p'yo-jŏk ch'i-gi
	표적 치기

Technique (ITF&WTF)	ki-sul or tong-jak 기술 or 동작
Temple	no-ri 놀이
Temporal Bone	ch'ŭk-du-gol 측두골
Temporo-mandibular Joint	kwan-ja-no-ri 관자 놀이
Ten [in Native Korean]	yŏl 열
Ten [in Sino-Korean]	ship 십
Tendon	him-jul 힘줄
Tenets (ITF)	chŏng-shin 정 신
Tenth [in Native Korean]	yŏl-tchae 열 째
Tenth [in Sino-Korean]	che-ship 제 십
Tenth Degree Black Belt (ITF&WTF)	ship-dan 십 단
Tenth Grade (ITF&WTF) [Low White Belt]	ship-gŭp 십 급
Test for Rank Promotion	shim-sa 심사
Thenar [thumb knuckle web]	ŏm-ji-gu 엄지구
Theory of Power (ITF)	hi-mŭi wŏl-li 힘의 원리

Third [in Native Korean]	se-tchae 세 째
Third [in Sino-Korean]	che-sam 제 삼
Third Degree Black Belt (ITF&WTF)	sam-dan 삼 단
Third Degree Junior Black Belt (WTF)	sam-pum 삼 품
Third Grade (ITF&WTF) [High Blue Belt]	sam-gŭp 삼 급
Thrashing Kick (WTF)	hu-ryŏ ch'a-gi 후려 차기
Three [in Native Korean]	set 셋
Three [in Sino-Korean]	sam 삼
Three-direction Kick (ITF)	sam-bang ch'a-gi 삼 방 차기
Three-step Sparring (ITF)	sam-bo mat-sŏ-gi 삼 보 맞서기
Throat	mok-gu-mŏng 목구멍
Throw or Throwing (ITF)	tŏn-ji-gi 던지기
Thrust - Backward Stepping (ITF)	ttu-rŭ-myŏ tŭ-rŏ o-gi 뚫으며 들어 오기
Thrust - Forward Stepping (ITF)	ttu-rŭ-myŏ na-ga-gi 뚫으며 나가기
Thrust or Thrusting (ITF)	ttul-ki 뚫기
Thrust or Thrusting (WTF)	tchi-rŭ-gi 찌르기

85

Thrusting Kick (ITF)	ch'a-ttul-ki 차 뚫기
Thumb	ŏm-ji son-ga-rak 엄지 손가락
Thumb Joint	ŏm-ji kwan-jŏl 엄지 관절
Thumb Knuckle Fist (ITF)	ŏm-ji chu-mŏk 엄지 주먹
Thumb Knuckle Punch (ITF)	ŏm-ji chu-mŏk tchi-rŭ-gi 엄지 주먹 찌르기
Thumb Ridge (ITF)	ŏm-ji pa-t'ang 엄지 바탕
Tibia	kyŏng-gol 경 골
Tibial Nerve	kyŏng-gol shin-gyŏng 경골 신경
Tiger Stance (WTF)	pŏm sŏ-gi 범 서기
Timer	gye-shi 계시
Tip	kkŭt 끝
Toe	pal-ga-rak 발 가락
Toe Edge (ITF)	pal-ga-rak-nal 발 가락날
Toes	pal-kkŭt 발 끝
Toward - "A"	"A" -bang "A" 방
Toward - "B"	"B" -bang "B" 방

Toward - "C"   "C" -bang
"C" 방

Toward -"D"   "D" -bang
"D" 방

Training   su-ryŏn
수련

Training Aids (ITF)   tal-lyŏn-gu
단련 구

Training Equipment (ITF)   su-ryŏn chang-bi
수련 장비

Training Hall (ITF&WTF)   to-jang
도장

Training Schedule (ITF)   su-ryŏn gye-hoek-p'yo
수련 계획표

Travel   yŏ-haeng
여행

Triple Attack (ITF)   sam-jung kong-gyŏk
삼 중 공 격

Triple Kick (ITF)   sam-jung ch'a-gi
삼 중 차기

Triple Punch (ITF)   sam-jung tchi-rŭ-gi
삼 중 찌르기

Triple Stepping (ITF)   sam-bo om-gyŏ ti-di-gi
삼 보 옮겨 디디기

Triple Strike (ITF)   sam-jung ttae-ri-gi
삼 중 때리기

Triple Thrust (ITF)   sam-jung ttul-ki
삼 중 뚫기

Trunk of the Body
  [Middle Section - (WTF)] mom-t'ong
몸 통

Trunk Block (WTF)   mom-t'ong mak-ki
몸통 막기

Trunk Inner Block (WTF)   mom-t'ong an mak-ki
몸통 안 막기

Trunk Outer Block (WTF)   mom-t'ong pa-kkat mak-ki
몸통 바깥 막기

Trunk Outer Hit (WTF)   mom-t'ong pa-kkat ch'i-gi
몸통 바깥 치기

Trunk Punch (WTF)   mom-t'ong chi-rŭ-gi
몸통 지르기

Trunk Pushing Block (WTF)   mom-t'ong he-ch'yŏ mak-ki
몸통 헤쳐 막기

Trunk Side Block (WTF)   mom-t'ong yŏp mak-ki
몸통 옆 막기

Trunk Twist Block (WTF)   mom-t'ong pi-t'ŭ-rŏ mak-ki
몸통 비틀어 막기

Trust   shin-yong
신용

Tug and Hit (WTF)   tang-gyŏ ch'i-gi
당겨 치기

Tug and Jaw Hit (WTF)   tang-gyŏ t'ŏk ch'i-gi
당겨 턱 치기

Tug and Punch (WTF)   tang-gyŏ chi-rŭ-gi
당겨 지르기

Turn Around (ITF&WTF)   twi-ro to-ra
뒤로 돌아

Turning   tol-gi
돌기

Turning Kick (ITF&WTF)   tol-lyŏ ch'a-gi
돌려 차기

Turning Punch (ITF)   tol-lyŏ tchi-rŭ-gi
돌려 찌르기

Turtle Ship   kŏ-buk-sŏn
거북선

Twin Backfist (ITF)	ssang dŭng chu-mŏk 쌍 등 주먹
Twin Backhand (ITF)	ssang son-dŭng 쌍 손등
Twin Elbow (ITF)	ssang p'al-gup 쌍 팔굽
Twin Elbow Thrust (ITF)	ssang p'al-gup ttul-ki 쌍 팔굽 뚫기
Twin Fist (ITF)	ssang chu-mŏk 쌍 주먹
Twin-fist on the Waist (WTF)	tu-ju-mŏk hŏri 두주먹 허리
Twin-fist Palm-upward Punch (WTF)	tu-ju-mŏk che-ch'yŏ chi-rŭ-gi 두주먹 제쳐 지르기
Twin Forearm Block (ITF)	ssang p'al-mok mak-ki 쌍 팔목 막기
Twin Knifehand (ITF)	ssang son-k'al 쌍 손칼
Twin Knifehand Block (ITF)	ssang son-k'al mak-ki 쌍 손칼 막기
Twin Knifehand Strike (ITF)	ssang son-k'al ttae-ri-gi 쌍 손칼 때리기
Twin Palm Rising Block (ITF) [hand bottom]	ssang son-ba-dak ch'u-kkyŏ mak-ki 쌍 손바닥 추껴 막기
Twin Reverse Knifehand Strike (ITF)	ssang son-k'al dŭng ttae-ri-gi 쌍 손칼 등 때리기
Twin Side Back Elbow Thrust (ITF)	ssang yŏp twit p'al-gup ttul-ki 쌍 옆 뒷 팔굽 뚫기
Twin Side Elbow Thrust (ITF)	ssang yŏp p'al-gup ttul-ki 쌍 옆 팔굽 뚫기
Twin Side Fist (ITF)	ssang yŏp chu-mŏk 쌍 옆 주먹

Twin Straight Forearm (ITF)	ssang sŏn p'al-mok 쌍 선 팔목
Twin Straight Forearm Block (ITF)	ssang sŏn p'al-mok mak-ki 쌍 선 팔목 막기
Twin Straight Knifehand (ITF)	ssang sŏn son-k'al 쌍 선 손칼
Twin Straight Knifehand Block (ITF)	ssang sŏn son-k'al mak-ki 쌍 선 손칼 막기
Twin-foot Kick (ITF)	ssang-bal ch'a-gi 쌍 발 차기
Twist Block (WTF)	pi-t'ŭ-rŏ mak-ki 비틀어 막기
Twisting Kick (ITF)	pi-t'ŭ-rŏ ch'a-gi 비틀어 차기
Twist Kicking (WTF)	pi-t'ŭ-rŏ ch'a-gi 비틀어 차기
Twist Punch (WTF)	tol-lyŏ chi-rŭ-gi 돌려 지르기
Two [in Native Korean]	tul 둘
Two [in Sino-Korean]	i 이
Two-direction Kick (ITF)	i-bang ch'a-gi 이 방 차기
Two-step Sparring (ITF)	i-bo mat-sŏ-gi 이 보 맞서기
Two-way Three-step Sparring (ITF)	yang-tchok sam-bo mat-sŏ-gi 양 쪽 삼보 맞서기

U

U-letter-Shape Punch (WTF)	U-ja chi-rŭ-gi U-자 지르기
Ulna	ch'ŏk-gol 척
Ulnar Nerve	ch'ŏk-gol shin-gyŏng 척골 신경
Umbilicus	pae-kkob 배 꼽
Umpire (ITF)	shim-p'an 심판
Umpire Classification (ITF)	shim-p'an pu-ryu 심판 부류
Under	mit or a-rae 밑 or 아래
Under Fist (ITF)	mit chu-mŏk 밑 주먹
Under Forearm (ITF&WTF) [at wrist]	mit p'al-mok 밑 팔목
Underneath Block (WTF)	a-rae mak-ki 아래 막기
Underneath Pull-out (WTF)	mi-t'ŭ-ro ppae-gi 밑으로 빼기
Underneath Pushing Block (WTF)	a-rae he-ch'yŏ mak-ki 아래 헤쳐 막

Underneath Punch (WTF)	a-rae chi-rŭ-gi
	  or nae-ryŏ chi-rŭ-gi
	아래 지르기
	  or 내려 지르기

Underneath Side Block (WTF)	a-rae yŏp mak-ki 아래 옆 막기
Underneath Twist Block (WTF)	a-rae pi-t'ŭ-rŏ mak-ki 아래 비틀어 막기

Upper	wi 위
Upper Abdomen	sang-bok-bu 상 복부
Upper and Back Elbow Strike (ITF)	wi twit p'al-gup ttae-ri-gi 위 뒷 팔굽 때리기
Upper Arm	p'al-juk-ji 팔죽지
Upper Back	kyŏn-gap 견갑
Upper Elbow	wi p'al-gup 위 팔굽
Upper Elbow Strike (ITF)	wi p'al-gup ttae-ri-gi 위 팔굽 때리기
Upper Neck	wit mok 윗 목
Upset Fingertip (ITF)	twi-ji-bŭn son-kkŭt 뒤집은 손끝
Upset Flat Fingertip (ITF)	ŏpŭn p'yŏn son-kkŭt 엎은 편 손끝
Upset Punch (ITF)	twi-ji-bŏ tchi-rŭ-gi 뒤집어 찌르기
Upward	ol-lyŏ or wi-ro 올려 or 위로
Upward Block (ITF)	ol-lyŏ mak-ki 올려 막기
Upward Kick (ITF)	ol-lyŏ ch'a-gi 올려 차기
Upward Pull-out (WTF)	wi-ro ppae-gi 위로 빼기
Upward Punch (ITF)	ol-lyŏ tchi-rŭ-gi 올려 찌르기

U-Shape Block (ITF)	mong-dung-i mak-ki
	몽둥이 막기
or	ti-gŭt-ja mak-ki
	디귿 자 막기
U-Shape Grasp (ITF)	mong-dung-i chap-gi
	몽둥이 잡기
or	ti-gŭt-ja put-jap-gi
	디귿 자 붙잡기
U-Shape Grasping Block (ITF)	mong-dung-i chap-gi mak-ki
	몽둥이 잡기 막기
U-Shape Punch (ITF)	ti-gŭt-ja tchi-rŭ-gi
	디귿 자 찌르기
U-Shape Punching Kick (ITF)	ti-gŭt-ja tchi-rŭ-myŏ ch'a-gi
	디귿 자 찌르며 차기
U-Shape Trunk Punch (WTF)	mom-t'ong U-ja chi-rŭ-gi
	몸통 U-자 지그기

V

Vertical Fist (WTF)	se-un chu-mŏk
	세운 주먹
Vertical Flat-fingertip (WTF)	se-un p'yŏn son-kkŭt
	세운 편 손끝
Vertical Kick (ITF)	se-wŏ ch'a-gi
	세워 차기
Vertical Punch (ITF)	se-wŏ tchi-rŭ-gi
	세워 찌르기
Vertical Punch (WTF)	se-wŏ chi-rŭ-gi
	세워 지르기
Vertical Stance (ITF)	su-jik sŏ-gi
	수직 서기
Virtue	mi-dŏk
	미덕

Vital Point Attacking (ITF)	kŭp-so tchi-rŭ-gi 급소 찌르기
Vital Spots (ITF)	kŭp-so 급소

W

Waist	hŏ-ri 허리
Waist Block (ITF)	hŏ-ri mak-ki 허리 막기
Walking Ready Stance (ITF)	kŏn-nŭn chun-bi sŏ-gi 걷는 준비 서기
Walking Stance (ITF)	kŏn-nŭn sŏ-gi 걷는 서기
Walking Stance Obverse Punch (ITF)	kŏn-nŭn sŏ pa-ro tchi-rŭ-gi 걷는 서 바로 찌르기
Walking Stance Reverse Punch (ITF)	kŏn-nŭn sŏ pan-dae tchi-rŭ-gi 걷는 서 반대 찌르기
Warning (WTF) [minus-1]	kyŏng-go [ha-na] 경고 (하나)
Warrior Ready Stance (ITF)	mu-sa chun-bi sŏ-gi 무사 준비 서기
Way	Do 도
Weak	ya-kan 약한
Wedging Block (ITF)	he-ch'yŏ mak-ki 헤쳐 막기
Weight (WTF)	ch'e-gŭp 체급
White Color	hin saek 흰 색

White Belt (ITF&WTF)	hin tti
	흰 띠
White Belt with a Yellow Stripe (ITF&WTF)	hin tti-e no-ran sŏn
	흰 띠에 노란 선
Wide-open Block (WTF)	san-t'ŭl mak-ki
	산틀 막기
Windpipe	sum-t'ong
	숨통
Wing Punch (WTF)	nal-gae chi-rŭ-gi
	날개 지르기
Wing Spreading (WTF)	nal-gae p'yŏ-gi
	날개 펴기
Wisdom	chi-hye
	지혜
World-wide	se-gye-jŏk
	세계 적
World Taekwon-Do Federation (WTF)	Se-gye T'ae-kwŏn-Do Yŏn-maeng
	세계 태권도 연맹
Wrist	p'al-mok or son-mok
	팔목 or 손목
Wrist Block (WTF)	p'al-mok mak-ki
	팔목 막기
Wrist Joint	son-mok kwan-jŏl
	손목 관절
W-Shape Block (ITF)	san mak-ki
	산 막기

X

X-Backhand (ITF)	kyo-ch'a son-dŭng 교차 손 등
X-Fist (ITF)	kyo-ch'a chu-mŏk 교차 주먹
X-Fist Block (ITF)	kyo-ch'a chu-mŏk mak-ki 교차 주먹 막기
X-Fist Rising Block (ITF)	kyo-ch'a chu-mŏk ch'u-kkyŏ mak-ki 교차 주먹 추껴 막기
X-Knifehand (ITF)	kyo-ch'a son-k'al 교차 손칼
X-Knifehand Block (ITF)	kyo-ch'a son-k'al mak-ki 교차 손칼 막기
X-Knifehand Rising Block (ITF)	kyo-ch'a son-k'al ch'u-kkyŏ mak-ki 교차 손 칼 추껴 막기
X-Ready Stance (ITF)	kyo-ch'a chun-bi sŏ-gi 교차 준비 서기
X-Stance (ITF)	kyo-ch'a sŏ-gi 교차 서기

Y

Yell (ITF&WTF)	ki-hap 기합
Yellow Color	no-ran saek 노란 색
Yellow Belt (ITF&WTF)	no-ran tti 노란 띠
Yellow Belt with a Green Stripe (ITF&WTF)	no-ran tti-e ch'o-rok sŏn 노란 띠에 초록 선

Yes	ye or ne
	예 or 네
Yi Dynasty	I-jo shi-dae
	이조 시대
Yoke Hit (WTF)	mǒng-e ch'i-gi
	멍에 치기
Yoke Pull-out (WTF)	mǒng-e ppae-gi
	멍에 빼기

Chapter 3
(제 3 장)

Korean- English Dictionary
han-yŏng sajŏn
(한 영 사 전)

This chapter can be used to find the meaning of a specific Korean term used in martial arts. It has been designed to give an English translation for a specific Korean term, as well as to offer a more extensive definition, identify some root verbs and their meanings, and - in some cases - refer to the Chinese origin of terms. This information adds a unique perspective on specific techniques and profoundly enhances one's understanding. Therefore, for most terms we have provided extensive definitions to provide clarity and completeness.

This chapter is arranged in English alphabetical order according to Romanized Korean. Since Romanized Korean also contains letters the English language does not have, some modifications have been made to the English alphabetical order. Symbols and Roman letter combinations have been used to represent single Korean letters as described in the Appendices A through D. Each term in this chapter is presented in a modified English alphabetical order according to this Korean Romanization. This order is as follows: a, b (also see "p"), ch, ch', d (also see "t"), g (also see "k"), h, i, j (also see "ch"), k, k', m, n, o, ŏ, p, pp, p', s, ss, t, tch, tt, t', u, ŭ, ŭi, wa, wi, wŏ, ya, ye, yo, yŏ, yu, and yi. (The martial artist should note that this is not in the order of the Korean alphabet.)

a 아

a-gwi-son	Arc Fist (WTF) [the space between the thumb and the fingers]
a-hop	Nine [in Native Korean]
a-hop-tchae	Ninth [in Native Korean]
an	Inner, inside, interior
an-bu	Eye Region
an ch'i-gi	Inward Hit (WTF)
an-gu	Eyeball
a-ni-o	No

an-jŏ	Kneel or Sit Down [an-jŏ is derived from the root verb an-da (앉다) meaning to sit on one's knees, to sit down, or to a seat]
an-jŏng	Stable [an-jŏng is derived from the verb an-jŏng-ha-da (안정하다), meaning to be (become) stabilized, to be settled, or to settle]
an kyŏng-gol	Inner Tibia
an mak-ki	Inner-Block (WTF)
an mak-ki	Inside Block (ITF)
an-myŏn	Face Area [Sino-Korean]
an nae-ryŏ ch'a-gi	Inner Downward Kick (WTF)
an-nŭn	Sit [an-nŭn is derived from the root verb an-da (앉다), meaning to sit on one's knees, to sit down, or to take a seat]
an-nŭn chun-bi sŏ-gi	Sitting Ready Stance (ITF)
an-nŭn sŏ-gi	Sitting Stance (ITF)
an-nŭn sŏ tchi-rŭ-gi	Sitting Stance Punch (ITF)
An-nyŏng ha-se-yo ?	Good morning, Good afternoon, Good evening, or How are you? [informal-polite-honorific form of greeting used any time of day]
An-nyŏng ha-shim-ni-kka ?	Good morning, Good afternoon, Good evening, or How are you? [formal, polite-honorific form of greeting used any time of day]
An-nyŏng-hi chu-mu-se-yo .	Good night. [informal, polite-honorific]
An-nyŏng-hi chu-mu-ship-shi-o .	Good night. [formal, polite-honorific]
An-nyŏng-hi ka-se-yo .	Good bye. [to person (s) who are leaving] [informal, polite-honorific]

An-nyŏng-hi ka-ship-shi-o .	Good bye. [to person (s) who are leaving] [formal, polite-honorific]
An-nyŏng-hi gye-se-yo .	Good bye. [to person (s) who are staying] [informal, polite]
An-nyŏng-hi gye-ship-shi-o .	Good bye. [to person (s) who are staying] [formal, polite]
an pal-mok kwan-jŏl	Inner Ankle Joint
an p'al-mok	Inner Forearm at the wrist (ITF&WTF)
an p'al-mok kŏ-dŭ-rŏ mom-t'ong mak-ki	Inner-forearm Assisting Trunk Block (WTF)
an p'al-mok mak-ki	Inner-forearm Block (WTF)
an p'al-mok mom-t'ong he-ch'yŏ mak-ki	Inner-forearm Trunk Pushing Block (WTF)
an p'al-mok mom-t'ong pa-kkat mak-ki	Inner-forearm Trunk Outer Block (WTF)
an p'al-mok mom-t'ong pi-t'ŭ-rŏ mak-ki	Inner-forearm Trunk Twist Block (WTF)
an p'al-mok ŏl-gul pa-kkat mak-ki	Inner-forearm Face Outer Block (WTF)
an p'al-mok ŏl-gul pi-t'ŭ-rŏ mak-ki	Inner-forearm Face Twist Block (WTF)
an p'al-ja sŏ-gi	Inner Open Stance (ITF)
an p'al-mok	Inner Forearm (ITF)
an-tchok	Inside Area, the inside, the inner part, or the lanes on inside of a track (ITF)
an-tchok hŏ-bŏk-da-ri	Inside Thigh (ITF)
an-tchok chu-ch'um sŏ-gi	Inward Riding Stance (WTF)
an-tchok sŏ-gi	Inward Stance (WTF)
a-nŭ-ro	Inward, toward the inside, in, within, or inside of

a-nŭ-ro ch'a-gi	Inward Kick (ITF)
a-nŭ-ro kŭt-gi	Inward Cross-cut (ITF)
a-nŭ-ro mak-ki	Inward Block (ITF)
a-nŭ-ro se-wŏ ch'a-gi	Inward Vertical Kick (ITF)
a-nŭ-ro ttae-ri-gi	Inward Strike (ITF)
ap	Front, the fore (part), forward, in front of, before, or ahead
ap-chu-ch'um sŏ-gi	Forward Riding Stance (WTF)
ap chu-mŏk	Forefist (ITF)
ap ch'a-mil-gi	Front Pushing Kick (ITF)
ap ch'a-mŏm-ch'u-gi	Front Checking Kick (ITF)
ap ch'a-ol-li-gi	Front Rising Kick (ITF)
ap ch'a-pu-su-gi	Front Snap Kick (ITF)
ap ch'a-tchi-rŭ-gi	Front Piercing Kick (ITF)
ap ch'a-gi	Front Kick (ITF&WTF)
ap ch'i-gi	Front Hit (WTF)
ap-ch'uk	Front-sole (WTF)
ap-ch'uk mo-a sŏ-gi	Reverse Attention Stance (WTF)
ap ta-ri	Lead Leg or Front Leg (ITF)
ap ta-ri ch'a-gi	Lead Leg Kick or Front Leg Kick (ITF)
ap kko-a sŏ-gi	Forward Cross Stance (WTF)
ap-kkum-ch'i	Ball of the Foot
ap ku-bi	Forward Inflection Stance (WTF)
ap mak-ki	Front Block (ITF)
ap nae-ryŏ ttae-ri-gi	Front Downward Strike (ITF)
ap p'al-gup	Front Elbow (ITF)
ap p'al-gup ttae-ri-gi	Front Elbow Strike (ITF)

ap p'al-gup ttul-ki	Front Elbow Thrust (ITF)
ap sŏ-gi	Forward Stance (WTF)
ap tchi-rŭ-gi	Front Punch (ITF)
ap tchi-rŭ-myŏ ch'a-gi	Front Punching Kick (ITF)
ap ttae-ri-gi	Front Strike (ITF)
a-pŭ-ro i-bo om-gyŏ ti-di-myŏ tol-gi	Forward Double Step-turning (ITF)
a-pŭ-ro om-gyŏ ti-di-myŏ tol-gi	Forward Step-turning (ITF)
a-rae	Low Section, the bottom, the foot, the base, the lower part, the underside, or underneath (WTF)
a-rae chi-rŭ-gi	Underneath Punch (WTF)
a-rae he-ch'yŏ mak-ki	Underneath Pushing Block (WTF)
a-rae pa-da mak-ki	Foot-blade Underneath Counter Block (WTF)
a-rae mak-ki	Underneath Block (WTF)
a-rae pi-t'ŭ-rŏ mak-ki	Underneath Twist Block (WTF) [low counter block]
a-rae pu-bun	Low Part (WTF)
a-rae yŏp mak-ki	Underneath Side Block (WTF)

b ㅂ

(In Han-gŭl, ㅂ is usually represented by a"p", in martial arts, the following terms are traditionally listed as a "b" - also see other terms listed under "p")

- bal	Foot [when used as the last or medial syllable in a word]
- bang	-Direction [as in Toward - "A", Toward the East, Toward the front] (ITF)

- bo	A Step, a Pace [when used as the last syllable in a word]

ch ㅈ

cha-gŭn	Small [cha-gŭn is derived from the verb chak-da (작다), meaning to be small, to be little, tiny, to be of small size, to be petty, to be trifling, to be trivial, to be young, to be insignificant, to be low, to be narrow-minded, or to be small-minded]
cha-gŭn tol-tchŏ-gwi	Small Hinge (WTF)
cha-gŭn tol-tchŏ-gwi hyŏng	Small Hinge Shape (WTF)
cha-gyŏk-jŭng	Certificate
cha-jŭn	Quickly [cha-jŭn is derived from the verb chat-da (잦다), meaning to be frequent or to be incessant]
cha-jŭn-bal	Shifting Feet Quickly [dodging] (ITF)
cha-jŭn-bal om-gyŏ ti-di-gi	Shifting Feet Quickly While Stepping (ITF)
chap-gi	Grab (ITF) [chap-gi is derived from the verb chap-da (잡 다), meaning to catch, to get, to take, to seize, to hold, to grasp, to grip, or to clutch]
chap-go ch'a-gi	Holding Kick (WTF)
chap-go ap ch'a-gi	Holding Front Kick (WTF)
chap-go yŏp ch'a-gi	Holding Side Kick (WTF)
chap-go tol-lyŏ ch'a-gi	Holding Turning Kick (WTF)
cha-yu mat-sŏ-gi	Free Sparring (ITF)
cha-yu tae-ryŏn	Free Sparring (WTF)

che-	Number __ [e.g. #4], or __ th [e.g., 4th] - [used in making a Sino-Korean cardinal number into a Sino-Korean ordinal number]
che-ch'il	Seventh [in Sino-Korean]
che-ch'in	Upside Down [che-ch'in is derived from the verb che-ch'i-da (제치 다) to turn over (down), to turn upside down, or to lay (a thing) face down]
che-ch'in chu-mŏk	Palm-upward Fist (WTF)
che-ch'in p'yŏn son-kkŭt	Palm-upward Flat-fingertip (WTF)
che-ch'yŏ	Upside Down [che-ch'yŏ is derived from the verb che-ch'i-da (제치 다) to turn over (down), to turn upside down, or to lay (a thing) face down]
che-ch'yŏ chi-rŭ-gi	Palm-upward Punch (WTF)
che-do	che-do is defined as a system, an institution, organization, or order
che-i	Second [in Sino-Korean]
che-il	First [in Sino-Korean]
che-ja	Student, a disciple, a pupil, or an apprentice (ITF)
che-bi-p'um	Swallow-shape [che-pi (제비)) is defined as a Swallow; p'um (품) is defined as a shape or an appearance]
che-bi-p'um mok ch'i-gi	Swallow-shape Neck Strike (WTF)
che-bi-p'um t'ŏk ch'i-gi	Swallow-shape Jaw Hit (WTF)
che-ku	Ninth [in Sino-Korean]
che-o	Fifth [in Sino-Korean]
che-p'al	Eighth [in Sino-Korean]
che-sa	Fourth [in Sino-Korean]
che-sam	Third [in Sino-Korean]

che-ship	Tenth [in Sino-Korean]
che-yuk	Sixth [in Sino-Korean]
chi-hye	Wisdom [chi-hye is defined as wisdom, intelligence, wits, sagacity, or resourcefulness]
chi-ap	Press Finger (ITF) [chi-ap is defined as finger pressure]
Chi-Do Kwan	Korean Martial Art school founded by Yun Gae P'yung in 1946
chil-lyang	Mass (ITF), quantity of matter
chip pe-gae	Straw Pad (ITF)
chip-ge	chip-ge is defined as a pair of tongs, tweezers, forceps, pincers, nippers, or pliers
chip-ge chu-mŏk	Pincers Fist (WTF)
chip-ge-son	Finger Pincers (ITF)
chip-jung	Concentration (WTF), convergence, centralization, or gathering to center
chi-rŭ-gi	Punching (WTF) [chi-rŭ-gi is derived from the verb chi-rŭda (지르다), meaning to kick, to give a kick, to beat, to hit, to knock, to strike, or to give a blow]
Chi-T'ae p'um-se	WTF pattern practiced by 5th Degree [Representing coming out of the Earth]
cho-jŏl	Control [cho-jŏl is derived from the verb cho-jŏl-ha-da (조절하다), meaning to control, regulate, adjust, or govern]
Cho-sŏn shi-dae	Choson Dynasty (1392 - 1910)
Choi Hong Hi, Chang-gun	Choi Hong Hi, General [The Father of Taekwon-Do] (born November 9, 1918)

chŏ-go-ri	Practice Shirt (ITF), traditional Korean jacket
ch'ŏk-ju	Spine
chŏng-ji	Stop [chŏng-ji is derived from the verb chŏng-ji-ha-da (정지하다), meaning to stop, to interrupt, or to suspend]
chŏng-jŏk	Static [chŏng-jŏk is derived from the verb chŏng-jŏk-ha-da (정적하다), meaning to be still, to be silent, or to be quiet]
chŏng-jŏk an-jŏng	Static Stability (ITF)
chŏng-gang-i	Shin
chŏng-gang-i pa-da mak-ki	Shin Counter Block (WTF)
chŏng-shin	Tenets (ITF), mind, spirit, soul, will, intention, mentality, or motive
chŏng-shin su-yang	Moral Culture (ITF)
chŏng-ŭi	Righteousness, justice, or right
chu	a post or support beam - originating from the Chinese term 柱 (pronounced in Chinese as *zhu*)
chu-ch'um	Sliding (ITF) [chu-ch'um is derived from the verb chu-ch'um-ga-ri-da (주춤거리다), meaning to shrink (fall, hold) back, to flinch, to wince, to hesitate, to hang a leg, to be shy, to be at a loss, or to be indecisive]
chul-lo-sŏ	Line Up [chul-lo-sŏ literally means to stand in a line]
chu-mŏk	Fist (ITF&WTF)
chu-mŏk ki-sul	Punching Technique (WTF)

chun-bi	Ready (ITF&WTF), preparation, (preliminary) arrangements, or readiness
chun-bi sŏ-gi	Ready Stance (ITF&WTF)
chung	chung is defined as the center or middle and originates from the Chinese term 中 (pronounced in Chinese as *zhong)*
chung-dan	Middle Level (ITF)
chung-gan	chung-gan is defined as the middle, in between, midway, or half-way
chung-gan shin-gyŏng	Median Nerve (WTF)
chung-ji	Middle Finger
chung-ji chu-mŏk	Middle Knuckle Fist (ITF)
chung-nyŏk chung-shim	Center of Gravity (ITF) [chung-nyŏk is defined as a Gravitational Force; and chung-shim is defined as balance or the Center of Gravity]
chung-shim	Balance, the center, the middle, or the pivot
chu-shim	Referee, or umpire
chŭk-shi kong-gyŏk	Instantaneous Attack (ITF), [chŭk-shi is defined as being at once, immediately, instantaneously, or without delay]
chwa-gol shin-gyŏng	Sciatic Nerve

ch' ㅊ

ch'a-gi	Kicking (ITF&WTF) [ch'a-gi is derived from the verb ch'a-da (차다), meaning to kick or to give a kick]
ch'a mil-gi	Pushing Kick (ITF)
ch'a mŏm-ch'u-gi	Checking Kick (ITF)

110

ch'a-myŏ na-ga-gi	Kick - Forward Stepping (ITF)
ch'a-myŏ tŭ-rŏ o-gi	Kick - Backward Stepping (ITF)
Ch'ang-Hŏn	Penname of General Choi Hong Hi, and the name given to the patterns system created by him for Taekwon-Do (ITF) - initiated in 1945 [originated from the Chinese set of characters 蒼軒 (pronounced in Chinese as *Cang Xuan* and meaning "blue" and "airy and bright room" respectively)]
Ch'ang-Mu Kwan	Korean Martial Art school founded by In Yun P'yung in 1946
ch'a ol-li-gi	Rising Kick (ITF)
ch'a pap-gi	Stamping Kick (ITF)
ch'a pu-su-gi	Smashing Kick (ITF)
ch'a tchi-rŭ-gi	Piercing Kick (ITF)
ch'a ttul-ki	Thrusting Kick (ITF)
ch'a-ryŏt	Attention (ITF&WTF)
ch'a-ryŏt sŏ-gi	Attention Stance (ITF&WTF)
ch'et-da-ri chi-rŭ-gi	Fork-shape Punch (WTF) [ch'et-da-ri is defined as the leg shaped supports for a sieve, kind of like a fork]
ch'e-gŭp	Weight (WTF) [for competition]
ch'i-bu	Pubic Region (ITF), the private parts
ch'i-gi	Strike or Hit (WTF) [ch'i-gi is derived from the verb ch'i-da (치 다), meaning to strike, to hit, to give a blow, to thrash, to beat, to knock, to slug, to slap, to flog, to whip, to smack, to smite, to wallop, to whack, or to pound]
ch'i-gol	Pubis (WTF), or pubic bone

ch'il	Seven [in Sino-Korean] - originating from the Chinese term for seven, 七 (pronounced in Chinese as *qi*)
ch'il-dan	Seventh Degree Black Belt (ITF&WTF)
ch'il-gŭp	Seventh Grade (ITF&WTF) [High Yellow Belt]
Ch'oi-Yŏng t'ŭl	ITF pattern practiced by 3rd Degree [Named after General Ch'oi Yŏng, Premier and Commander-in-Chief of the Armed forces during the 14th Century Koryo Dynasty. Ch'oi Yŏng was greatly respected for his loyalty, patriotism and humility]
ch'o-jŏm	Focus Point (ITF)
ch'o-jŏm pang-p'ae	Focus Shield (ITF)
ch'ong-gŏm	Bayonet
ch'o-rok saek	Green Color
ch'o-rok tti	Green Belt (ITF&WTF)
ch'o-rok tti-e p'u-rŭn sŏn	Green Belt with a Blue Stripe (ITF&WTF)
ch'ŏk-ch'u	Spine
ch'ŏk-ch'u shin-gyŏng	Spinal Chord (nerve), or spinal column
ch'ŏk-gol	Ulna, originating from the Chinese term 恥骨 (pronounced in Chinese as *zhou-gu*)
ch'ŏk-gol shin-gyŏng	Ulnar Nerve
ch'ŏl-hak	Philosophy
Ch'ŏng-Do Kwan	Korean Martial Art school [Civilian] founded by founded by General Choi Hong Hi in 1954 with the help of Nam Tae Hi

ch'ŏng k'o-nŏ	Blue Contestant Mark (WTF) [ch'ŏng is defined as Blue; k'o-nŏ means Corner]
ch'ŏng sŏn-su	Blue Contestant (WTF)
Ch'ŏn-Ji t'ŭl	ITF pattern practiced by 9th Grade [Chon-Ji literally means "the Heaven the Earth." Interpreted as the creation of the world or the beginning of human history]
Ch'ŏn-Kwŏn p'um-se	WTF pattern practiced by 6th Degree [Representing the "Sky"]
Ch'ŏn ma-ne-yo	That's all right - You're welcome - Not at all (informal, polite)
ch'ŏt	ch'ŏt (첫) is defined as the first, a new, a maiden, the starting, or the beginning
ch'ŏt-dan	Beginning Black Belt (ITF&WTF)
ch'ŏt-pum	Beginning Junior Black Belt (WTF)
ch'ŏt-tchae	First [in Native Korean]
ch'u-k'yŏ	Rising [ch'u-k'yŏ is derived from the verb ch'u-k'i-da (추키다), meaning to lift (hold) up]
ch'u-k'yŏ mak-ki	Rising Block (ITF)
Ch'ung-Jang t'ŭl	ITF pattern practiced by 2nd Degree [Pseudonym given to General Kim Duk Ryang who lived during the Yi Dynasty in the 14th century]
Ch'ung-Mu t'ŭl	ITF pattern practiced by 1st Grade [Represents the posthumous title, meaning Loyalty and Valor, given to the great Yi Dynasty Admiral Yi Sun Shin (1545-1598), who invented the first armored battleship (kobukson) in 1592]

113

Ch'ung-Mu Kwan	Korean Martial Art school founded by Lee Won Kuk in 1945
ch'ŭk-du-gol	Temporal Bone
ch'ŭk-myŏn	Side (ITF), flank, or the lateral face

d ㄷ

(In Han-gŭl, ㄷ is usually represented by a "t", in martial arts, the following terms are traditionally listed as a "d" - also see other terms listed under "t")

-dan	Degree [Black Belt Ranking], a rank, a grade, or a class (ITF&WTF) [also see tan under ㄷ]
Dan-Gun t'ŭl	ITF pattern practiced by 8th Grade [Named after the holy Dan-Gun, the legendary founder of Korea in the year 2,333 B.C.]
-Do	Art, the way, the road, the path, teachings, doctrines, or the truth - originated from the Chinese term 道 (pronounced in Chinese as *dao*)
Do-San t'ŭl	ITF pattern practiced by 7th Grade [Pseudonym of the patriot Ahn Chang Ho (1876-1938), who devoted his entire life to furthering the education of Korea and it's independence movement]

g ㄱ

(In Han-gŭl, ㄱ is usually represented by a "k", in martial arts, the following terms are traditionally listed as a "g" - also see other terms listed under "k")

-gu	A tool or an implement
-gŭp	Grade - Colored Belt Ranking (ITF&WTF) [also see kŭp under ㄱ]

Gye-Baek t'ŭl	ITF pattern practiced by 1st Degree [Named after Gye Baek, a great general in the Paekje Dynasty (660 A.D.)]
gye-gŭp	Rank [belt color or dan/gup level]
gye-shi	Timer (WTF), time keeper [gye-shi is derived from the verb gye-shi-ha-da (계시하다), meaning to clock or time]
gye-sok	Continue (WTF), continuation [gye-sok is derived from the verb gye-sok-ha-da (계속하다), meaning to continue, to maintain, to go on with, or to keep up]

h ㅎ

ha	ha is defined as the lower end and originates from the Chinese term 下 (pronounced in Chinese as *xia*)
ha-ak-gol	Mandible Bone (WTF) [ha-ak-gol originates from the Chinese term 下巴骨 (pronounced in Chinese as *xia-ba-gu*)]
ha-ban-shin	Foot Parts (ITF) [ha-ban-shin literally means low body parts]
ha-bok-bu	Lower Abdomen (ITF)
ha-dan	Low Level (ITF)
hae-san	Dismissed [hae-san is derived from the verb hae-san-ha-da (해산하다), meaning to breakup, to disperse, to dissolve, to disorganize, to disband, to liquidate, or to wind up]
hak-da-ri	Crane Leg
hak-da-ri kŭm-gang mak-ki	Crane Diamond Block (WTF)

115

hak-da-ri sŏ-gi	Crane Stance (WTF)
hak-da-ri tchi-rŭ-gi	Crane Thrust (WTF)
hak-da-ri tol-tchŏ-gwi	Crane Stance Hinge (WTF)
han-	han, when used as a suffix means to have one of a given item, or single [in Native Korean]
ha-na	One [in Native Korean]
han-bŏn	han-bŏn is defined as being once, one time, or one round
han-bŏn kyŏ-ru-gi	One-step Sparring (WTF)
han son-ga-rak	Forefinger (ITF)
han son-ga-rak ttul-ki	Single Finger Spear (Thrust) (ITF)
han son-kkŭt	Single Fingertip (WTF)
han son-kkŭt tchi-rŭ-gi	Single Fingertip Thrust (WTF)
han son-nal mak-ki	Single Hand-blade Block (WTF)
han son-nal a-rae pi-t'ŭ-rŏ mak-ki	Single Hand-blade Underneath Twist Block (WTF)
han son-nal mom-t'ong mak-ki	Single Hand-blade Trunk Block (WTF)
han son-nal ŏl-gul pa-kkat mak-ki	Single Hand-blade Face Outer Block (WTF)
han son-nal ŏl-gul an mak-ki	Single Hand-blade Face Inner Block (WTF)
han son-nal mom-t'ong mak-ki	Single Hand-blade Trunk Block (WTF)
han son-nal mom-t'ong an mak-ki	Single Hand-blade Trunk Inner Block (WTF)
han son-nal ŏl-gul pi-t'ŭ-rŏ mak-ki	Single Hand-blade Face Twist Block (WTF)
han son-nal a-rae yŏp mak-ki	Single Hand-blade Underneath Side Block (WTF)

Han-Su p'um-se	WTF pattern practiced by 7th Degree [Representing the adaptability and flexibility of "Water"]
han-tchok sam-bo mat-sŏ-gi	One-way Three-step Sparring (ITF)
ha-nŭl-son sŏ-gi	Heaven Hand Stance (ITF) [ha-nŭl is defined as the sky, the heaven, or the air]
Hap-Ki-Do	Korean Martial Art founded by Choi Yong Shul in 1940
he-ch'yŏ	Wedging or Pushing [he-ch'yŏ is derived from the verb he-ch'i-da (헤치다), meaning to make one's way through, to push aside, scatter, disperse, breakup, pull apart, or plow one's way through]
he-ch'yŏ mak-ki	Wedging Block (ITF)
he-ch'yŏ mak-ki	Pushing Block (WTF)
he-ch'yŏ san-t'ŭl mak-ki	Pushing Wide-open Block (WTF)
him	Force or Power
hi-mŭi wŏl-li	Theory of Power (ITF)
him-jul	Tendon
hin saek	White Color
hin tti	White Belt (ITF&WTF)
hin tti-e no-ran sŏn	White Belt with a Yellow Stripe (ITF&WTF)
ho-gu	Protective Sparring Equipment
ho-hŭp	Breathing [ho-hŭp is derived from the verb ho-hŭp-ha-da (호흡하다), meaning to breath or draw one's breath]
ho-hŭp cho-jŏl	Breath Control (ITF)

ho-mi son-kkŭt	Angle Fingertip (ITF) [ho-mi is defined as a weeding hoe]
hon-hap	Combination (ITF) [hon-hap is derived from the verb hon-hap-ha-da (혼 합 하 다), meaning to mix, to mingle, to blend, to compound, to intermix, or to commingle]
hon-hap ch'a-gi	Combination Kick (ITF)
hon-hap kong-gyŏk	Combination Attack (ITF)
hong k'o-nŏ	Red Contestant Mark (WTF) [hong is defined as red or crimson; k'o-nŏ means Corner]
hong sŏn-su	Red Contestant (WTF)
ho-shin-sul	Self Defense Technique (ITF) [ho-shin is derived from the verb ho-shin-ha-da (호신하다), meaning to protect oneself, to defend oneself, or to preserve oneself]
hŏ-ri	Waist (ITF)
hŏ-ri mak-ki	Waist Block (ITF)
hu-bae	Junior (WTF) [hu-bae is defined as one's junior, or of a younger generation]
hu-du-bu	Occiput (ITF)
hu-du-gol	Occipital Bone (WTF)
hu-i-bu	Mastoid (ITF)
hu-ryŏ ch'a-gi	Thrashing Kick (WTF) [hu-ryŏ is derived from the verb hu-ri-da (후리 다), meaning to beat at, to pummel, to flail, to shave off, to mow, or to cut down]
hwal-dŭng p'a-do	Sine Wave (ITF) [hwal-dŭng is defined as the back of a bow (archery)]
hwang-so mak-ki	Bull Block (WTF)

Hwa-rang t'ŭl	ITF pattern practiced by 2nd Grade [Named after the hwa-rang youth group which eventually became the actual driving force for the unification of the three kingdoms of Korea during the 1st Century A.D.]
Hwa-rang Do	Hwa-rang Code of Ethics as well as a Korean Martial Art school restarted by Joo Bang Lee and Joo Sang Lee in 1960
hwi-jŏn	A round in a sparring match (WTF) [hwi-jŏn is derived from the verb hwi-jŏn-ha-da (회 전하다), meaning to fight (a battle), to encounter, to meet, or to engage (the enemy)]
hyang	Direction
hyŏng	Old ITF term for patterns [hyŏng is defined as a shape or how something looks]
hyung-gol	Sternum

i 이

i	Two [in Sino-Korean] originating from the Chinese term for two, 二 (pronounced in Chinese as *er*)
i-bang ch'a-gi	Two-direction Kick (ITF)
i-bo mat-sŏ-gi	Two-step Sparring (ITF)
i-bo om-gyŏ ti-di-gi	Double Stepping (ITF)
i-bo om-gyŏ ti-di-myŏ tol-gi	Double Stepping Turn (ITF)
i-dan	Second Degree Black Belt (ITF&WTF)
i-gŭp	Second Grade (ITF&WTF) [Low Red Belt]

119

I-jo shi-dae	Yi Dynasty (1392 - 1910) - literally means the "Yi ruling period"
i-jung	Double
i-jung ap ch'a-pu-su-gi	Double Front Snap Kick (smashing) (ITF)
i-jung ch'a-gi	Double Kick (ITF)
i-jung kong-gyŏk	Double Attack (ITF)
i-jung ttae-ri-gi	Double Strike (ITF)
il	One [in Sino-Korean] - originating from the Chinese term for one, —— (pronounced in Chinese as *yi*)
il-bo mat-sŏ-gi	One-step Sparring (ITF)
il-bo om-gyŏ ti-di-gi	Single Stepping (ITF)
il-dan	First Degree Black Belt (ITF&WTF)
il-gop	Seven [in Native Korean]
il-gop-tchae	Seventh [in Native Korean]
il-gŭp	First Grade (ITF&WTF) [High Red Belt]
il-ja ch'a-gi	Single Line Kicks (WTF) [il-ja means "linear-shaped" as in the shape of the Chinese character for one, —— (pronounced in Chinese as *yi*)]
il-pum	First Degree Junior Black Belt (WTF)
Il-Yŏ p'um-se	WTF pattern practiced by 8th Degree [Representing the "Oneness" of mind (spirit) and body (material)]
i-ma	Forehead
in-ga-mi	Humanity
in-ji chu-mŏk	Fore-knuckle Fist (ITF)
in-jung	Philtrum (ITF), the perpendicular furrow of the upper lip

in-nae	Perseverance (ITF) [in-nae is derived from the verb in-nae-ha-da (인내하다) meaning to endure, to put up with, to bear patiently, to persevere (in), or to be patient with - originating from the Chinese term 忍耐 (pronounced in Chinese as *ren-nai*)]
i-ŏ-jin tong-jak	Connecting Motion (ITF) [i-ŏ-jin is derived from the verb i-ŏ-jin-ha-da (이어지다), meaning to get joined on, to be continued, or to be linked]
ip-sul	Lips
i-pum	Second Degree Junior Black Belt (WTF)

j ㅈ

(In Han-gŭl, ㅈ is usually represented by a "ch", in martial arts, the following terms are traditionally listed as a "j" - also see other terms listed under "ch")

-ja	-ja, as a suffix, means shape, character, letter, or ideograph
Ji-Do Kwan	Korean Martial Art school founded by Yun Gae Byang in 1953
Ju-ch'e t'ŭl	ITF pattern practiced by 2nd Degree [Represents the philosophical idea that is rooted in Baek-du Mountain, that man is the master of everything and decides everything. The pattern diagram is in the shape of the Chinese character 山 (pronounced in Chinese as *shan*), meaning hill, mountain, or range and therefore represents Baek-du Mountain]

Jung-Gŭn t'ŭl   ITF pattern practiced by 4th Grade [Named after the patriot Ahn Jung Gŭn (1879-1910), who assassinated Ito, Hiro-Bumi, the first Japanese Governor-General of Korea]

-jŭng   a certificate

k ㄱ

kal-lyŏ   Break (WTF) [kal-lyŏ is derived from the verb kal-lida (갈 리 다), meaning to be divided (into), split, branch off, diverge (from), ramify, or to be forked]

kam-jŏm [ha-na]   Deduction [minus-1] (WTF) [kam-jŏm is from the verb kam-jŏm-ha-da (감점 하다), meaning to give (a person) a demerit mark or to make a cut in marks]

kam-sa ham-ni-da   Thank you (formal, polite-honorific) [Sino-Korean]

ka-myŏ   Going [ka-myŏ is derived from the verb ka-da (가다), meaning to go, to proceed, or to travel]

kan-jang   Liver

kang-han   Strong [kang-han is derived from the verb kang-ha-da (강 하 다), meaning to be strong, powerful, or mighty]

ka-ra-t'e   Karate [Generic term of Japanese empty-hand Martial Art]

ka-ri-u-gi   Covering (ITF) [ka-ri-u-gi is derived from the verb ka-ri-u-da (가리우 다), meaning to screen, or to obstruct]

ka-sŭm   Chest

ka-un-dae	Middle or Center
ka-un-dae ch'a-gi	Middle Kick (ITF)
ka-un-dae kong-gyŏk	Middle Attack (ITF)
ka-un-dae mak-ki	Middle Block (ITF)
ka-un-dae pu-bun	Middle Section (ITF)
ka-un-dae tchi-rŭ-gi	Middle Punch (ITF)
ka-un-dae ttae-ri-gi	Middle Strike (ITF)
ka-un-dae ttul-ki	Middle Thrust (ITF)
ka-wi ap ch'a-gi	Scissors Front Kick (WTF)
ka-wi ch'a-gi	Scissors Kick (WTF)
ka-wi mak-ki	Scissors Block (WTF)
ka-wi mi-rŏ yŏp ch'a-gi	Scissors Pushing Side Kick (WTF)
ka-wi son-kkŭt	Double Finger Spear (ITF) or Scissors Fingertip (WTF)
ka-wi son-kkŭt tchi-rŭ-gi	Scissors Fingertip Thrust (WTF)
ka-wi tol-lyŏ ch'a-gi	Scissors Turning Kick (WTF)
ka-wi yŏp ch'a-gi	Scissors Side Kick (WTF)
ki	Life energy, spirits, energy, strength, vitality, vigor, breath, wind, natural passion, or life force - originating from the Chinese term 氣 (pronounced in Chinese as *qi*)
ki-bon	Basic - basic foundation, beginning
ki-bon chun-bi sŏ-gi	Basic Ready Stance (WTF)
ki-bon yŏn-sŭp	Fundamental Exercises
ki-hap	Yell or Shout (ITF&WTF), concentration of spirit, willpower, gathering together all energy, or breathing in harmony
kin chu-mŏk	Long Fist (ITF)

kin chu-mŏk tchi-rŭ-gi	Long Fist Punch (ITF)
ki-rok	Recorder [ki-rok is derived from the verb ki-rok-ha-da (기록하 다), meaning to record, to write down, to put (place) on record, to register]
ki-sul	Technique (ITF&WTF), art, ability, or skill
ki-yŏk-ja tchi-rŭ-gi	Angle Punch (ITF)[ki-yŏk-ja literally means "ki-yŏk-Shaped", after the first letter in the Korean alphabet, ㄱ]
Ko-Dang t'ŭl	Retired ITF pattern practiced by 2nd Degree [Pseudonym of the patriot Cho Man Shik, who dedicated his life to the Korean Independence Movement and to the education of his people]
Ko-gu-ryŏ shi-dae	Koguryo Dynasty (37 B.C. - 668 A.D.), one of the "Three Kingdoms" of ancient Korea
ko-jŏng sŏ-gi	Fixed Stance (ITF) [ko-jŏng is derived from the verb ko-jŏng-ha-da fixed (고정하다), meaning to be fixed, tied (locked) up, to fix, to settle, or to solidify]
kok-gwaeng-i ch'a-gi	Pick-shape Kick (ITF) [kok-gwaeng-i is defined as a hoe, pick, or pickax]
kol	Bone - originating from the Chinese term 骨 (pronounced in Chinese as *gu*)
Ko-map sŭm-ni-da	Thank you (formal, polite-honorific) [Native Korean]
kom-son	Bear Hand (ITF&WTF)
kon-bong	Club (weapon)
kong-gi pang-p'ae	Air Shield (ITF) [kong-gi is defined as air; and pang-p'ae is defined as a shield or a buckler]

kong-gyŏk	Attack, assault, onslaught, or raid
kong-gyŏk ki-sul	Attack Techniques (WTF)
kong-gyŏk pu-wi	Attacking Tools (ITF)
kong-gyŏk-ki	Attack Techniques (ITF)
kong-jung mo-dŭm-bal ch'a-gi	Flying Twin-foot Closed Kick (WTF)
kong-jung yŏn-sok ch'a-gi	Flying Consecutive Kick (WTF) [kong-jung is defined as in the air, in the sky, or in space]
Ko-ryŏ shi-dae	Koryo Dynasty (918 A.D. - 1392)
Ko-ryŏ p'um-se	WTF pattern practiced by 1st Grade [Representing the Koryo Dynasty (918 A.D. - 1392) of ancient Korea]
kŏ-buk-sŏn	Turtle Ship - an iron clad warship shaped like a turtle, invented by Admiral Yi Shun Shin in 1592 [kŏ-buk means a tortoise, a terrapin, or a sea turtle; and sŏn (when used as a suffix) means a ship or a vessel]
kŏ-dŭp ch'a-gi	Repeated Kick (WTF) [kŏ-dŭp is derived from the verb kŏ-dŭp-ha-da (거듭하다) meaning to repeat or to do again]
kŏ-dŭ-rŏ	Assisting [kŏ-dŭ-rŏ is derived from the verb kŏ-dŭl-da (거들다), meaning to give help, assist, lend a helping hand]
kŏ-dŭ-rŏ a-rae mak-ki	Assisting Underneath Block (WTF)
kŏ-dŭ-rŏ mak-ki	Assisting Block (WTF)
kŏ-dŭ-rŏ mom-t'ong mak-ki	Assisting Trunk Block (WTF)
kŏ-dŭ-rŏ ŏl-gul mak-ki	Assisting Face Block (WTF)
kŏdŭ-rŏ ŏl-gul yŏp mak-ki	Assisting Face Side Block (WTF)
kŏ-dŭ-rŏ ŏl-gul pa-kkat ch'i-gi	Assisting Face Outer Hit (WTF)

kŏ-dŭ-rŏ son-nal mak-ki	Assisting Hand-blade Block (WTF)
kŏl-ch'ŏ	Hooking [kŏl-ch'ŏ is derived from the verb kŏl-ch'i-da (걸 치 다), meaning to extend (over), to spread (over), to range (from A to B), to cover, or reach]
kŏl-ch'ŏ ch'a-gi	Hooking Kick (ITF)
kŏl-ch'ŏ mak-ki	Hooking Block (ITF)
kŏl-gi	Tackling [kŏl-gi is derived from the verb kŏl-da (걸다), meaning to hang-up, to hook, to suspend, to put-up, or to set-up]
kŏ-mŭn saek	Black Color
kŏ-mŭn tti	Black Belt (ITF&WTF)
kŏn-nŭn	Walking [kŏn-nŭn is derived from the verb kŏ-da (걷다), meaning to walk, to go on foot, to step, or to hike]
kŏn-nŭn chun-bi sŏ-gi	Walking Ready Stance (ITF)
kŏn-nŭn sŏ pan-dae chi-rŭ-gi	Walking Stance Reverse Punch (ITF)
kŏn-nŭn sŏ pa-ro tchi-rŭ-gi	Walking Stance Obverse Punch (ITF)
kŏn-nŭn sŏ-gi	Walking Stance (ITF)
kŏ-rŏ	Hook [kŏ-rŏ is derived from the verb kŏl-da (걸 다), meaning to hook, to hang (a thing on a peg), to suspend, to put up, or set up]
kŏ-rŏ ch'a-gi	Hook Kick (ITF)
kŏ-rŏ tchi-rŭ-gi	Hooking Punch (ITF)
kŏ-ul	Mirror [training aid]
ku	Nine [in Sino-Korean] - originating from the Chinese term for nine, 九 (pronounced in Chinese as *jiu*)

ku-bi — Inflection (WTF) [ku-bi is derived from the verb ku-p'i-da (굽히다), meaning to turn, to curve, to bend, or to stoop]

ku-bu-ryŏ — Bending [ku-bu-ryŏ is from the verb ku-bu-ri-da (구부리다), meaning to bend (one's back), stoop, curve, crook (one's elbow), or bow (one's knee)]

ku-bu-ryŏ chun-bi sŏ-gi — Bending Ready Stance (ITF)

ku-bu-ryŏ sŏ-gi — Bending Stance (ITF)

ku-dan — Ninth Degree Black Belt (ITF&WTF)

ku-gŭp — Ninth Grade (ITF&WTF) [High White Belt]

ku-ja mak-ki — Nine-Shape Block (ITF) [ku-ja literally means "九-Shaped", named after the Chinese character for nine, 九 (pronounced in Chinese as *jiu*)]

kuk-ki — Flag (national)

kuk-ki-e tae-ha-yŏ — Face the (national) Flag

kuk-ki-e tae-ha-yŏ kyŏng-nye — Salute the (national) Flag

kuk-je — International

Kuk-je T'ae-kwŏn-Do Yŏn-maeng — International Taekwon-Do Federation (ITF) (formed on March 22, 1966)

Kuk-ki-wŏn — World Headquarters of the World Taekwon-Do Federation

kul-lŏ — Stamping [kul-lŏ is derived from the verb ku-rŭ-da (구르다), meaning to stamp on (the floor), tread noisily, pound, or to roll (over)]

kul-lŏ ap ch'a-gi — Stamping Front Kick (WTF)

kul-lŏ ch'a-gi — Stamping Kick (WTF)

kul-lŏ tol-lyŏ ch'a-gi — Stamping Turning Kick (WTF)

kul-lŏ yŏp ch'a-gi	Stamping Side Kick (WTF)
kul-lŭ-gi	Rolling (ITF) [kul-lŭ-gi is derived from the verb ku-rŭ-da (구르다), meaning to stamp on (the floor), tread noisily, to pound, or to roll (over)]
ku-p'in	Bending [ku-p'in is derived from the verb ku-p'i-da (굽히다), meaning to turn, to curve, to bend, or to stoop]
ku-p'in son-mok	Bow Wrist (WTF)
ku-p'in son-mok ŏl-gul mak-ki	Bow Wrist Face Block (WTF)
ku-p'in son-mok mom-t'ong mak-ki	Bow Wrist Trunk Block (WTF)
ku-rŭ-nŭn	Stamping [ku-rŭ-nŭn is derived from the verb ku-rŭ-da (구 르다), meaning to stamp (on the floor), tread noisily, to pound, or to roll (over)]
ku-rŭ-nŭn tong-jak	Stamping Motion (ITF)
ku-sŏng	Composition (ITF), [ku-sŏng is derived from the verb ku-sŏng-ha-da (구성하다), meaning to organize, to constitute, form, compose, or make up]
kŭ-ja-ri ch'a-gi	Spot Kick (ITF)
kŭ-ja-ri mak-ki	Spot Block (ITF)
kŭ-ja-ri tchi-rŭ-gi	Spot Punch (ITF)
kŭ-ja-ri tol-gi	Spot Turning (ITF)
kŭ-ja-ri ttae-ri-gi	Spot Strike (ITF)
kŭ-ja-ri ttul-ki	Spot Thrust (ITF)

kŭk-ki	Self Control (ITF) [kŭk-ki is derived from the verb kŭk-ki-ha-da (극기 하다), meaning to control (conquer) oneself, to be master of one's self - originating from the Chinese term 克己 (pronounced in Chinese as *ke-ji*)]
kŭ-man	Stop [kŭ-man is derived from the verb kŭ-man-du-da (그만두다), meaning to stop, cease, quit, or discontinue]
kŭm-gang	kŭm-gang is defined as a Diamond
kŭm-gang ap tchi-rŭ-gi	Diamond Forward Punch (WTF)
kŭm-gang mak-ki	Diamond Block (WTF) [named for the Diamond Mountains 금강 산 (kŭm-gang-san)]
kŭm-gang mom-t'ong mak-ki	Diamond Trunk Block (WTF)
Kŭm-Gang p'um-se	WTF pattern practiced by 1st Degree [Meaning "Diamond"]
kŭm-gang yŏp tchi-rŭ-gi	Diamond Side Punch (WTF)
kŭn-yuk	Muscle
kŭp	Grade - Colored Belt Ranking (ITF&WTF)
kŭp-jŭng	Grade Certificate
kŭp-so	Vital Spots (ITF)
kŭp-so tchi-rŭ-gi	Vital Point Attacking (ITF)
kŭt-gi	Cross-cut (ITF) [kŭt-gi is derived from the verb kŭt-da (긋 다), meaning to draw, to mark, or to strike]
kwan	One's ancestral home, family seat, or the founding location of a school system, and originates from the Chinese term 食官 (pronounced in Chinese as *guan*)

kwang-dae ppyŏ	Cheek Bone
Kwang-Gae t'ŭl	ITF pattern practiced by 1st Degree [Named after the famous Korean King Kwang Gae Tae Wang (375-418), who regained all the previously lost territories including the greater part of Manchuria. The pattern diagram is in the shape of the Chinese character 土 (pronounced in Chinese as *tu*), meaning earth, ground, or soil and therefore represents the recovery of the lost territory]
kwan-jang	Grand Master (WTF)
kwan-jang nim	Grand Master Sir (WTF)
kwan-ja-nori	Temporo-mandibular Joint
kwan-jŏl	Joint
kwi	Ear
kwŏn	Fist - originating from the Chinese term for fist, 拳 (pronounced in Chinese as *quan*)
kwŏn-bŏp	Chinese Martial Art (Boxing)
kwŏn-ch'ong	Pistol
kyo-ch'a	"X" or Crossing [kyo-ch'a is derived from the verb kyo-ch'a-ha-da (교 차하 다), meaning to cross (each other), or to intersect (each other)]
kyo-ch'a chu-mŏk	X-Fist (ITF)
kyo-ch'a chu-mŏk ch'u-k'yŏ mak-ki	X-Fist Rising Block (ITF)
kyo-ch'a chu-mŏk mak-ki	X-Fist Block (ITF)
kyo-ch'a chun-bi sŏ-gi	X-Ready Stance (ITF)
kyo-ch'a son-dŭng	X-Backhand (ITF)

kyo-ch'a son-k'al	X-Knifehand (ITF)
kyo-ch'a son-k'al ch'u-k'yŏ mak-ki	X-Knifehand Rising Block (ITF)
kyo-ch'a son-k'al mak-ki	X-Knifehand Block (ITF)
kyo-ch'a sŏ-gi	X-Stance (ITF)
kyŏ-dŭ-rang-i	Armpit
kyŏk-p'a-gi	Breaking [kyŏk-p'a-gi is derived from the verb kyŏk-p'a-ha-da (격 파하 다), meaning to defeat, to destroy, to beat out, to crush, or to smash up]
kyŏl-hu	Adam's Apple
kyŏm-son	Humility [kyŏm-son is derived from the verb kyŏm-son-ha-da (겸손하다), meaning to be modest, to be diffident, to be humble, to be unassuming, or to humble ones self]
kyŏn-gap	Upper Back, shoulder blade, shoulder, or scapula
kyŏng-bu	Cervical Bundle
kyŏng-ch'u	Small of the Back
kyŏng-gi	Competition (ITF) [kyŏng-gi is derived from the verb kyŏng-gi-ha-da (경기하다), meaning to have a contest (game) or to play a game(match)]
kyŏng-go [ha-na]	Warning (WTF) [minus-1] [kyŏng-go is derived from the verb kyŏng-go-ha-da (경고하다), meaning to warn (a person) against (of), to give a warning, or to caution against]
kyŏng-gol	Cervical Vertebrae (WTF), the neck bone, or a hard bone
kyŏng-gol	Tibia (ITF), the shin bone
kyŏng-gol shin-gyŏng	Tibial Nerve

131

kyŏng-nye	Bow [kyŏng-nye is derived from the verb kyŏng-nye-ha-da (경례하다), meaning to bow or to make a salute]
kyŏng-nye cha-se	Bowing Posture (ITF)
kyŏp-son chun-bi sŏ-gi	Overlapped Hands Ready Stance (WTF) [kyŏp-son is derived from the verb kyŏp-ch'i-da (겹치다), meaning to pile or heap up, put one upon another, overlap]
kyŏ-ru-gi	Bout or Match [kyŏ-ru-gi is derived from the verb kyŏ-ru-da (겨루다), meaning to pit (one's skill) against, to vie (with), to rival (another in something), to compete, contend, to struggle, or to strive (with another for)]
kyŏ-rum-se sŏ-gi	Fighting Stance (WTF)
kyŏt-dŭl-gi	Assisting [kyŏt-dŭl-gi is derived from the verb kyŏt-dŭl-da (곁들다), meaning to lend (give) a hand (to a person), to give a helping hand, to help, to assist, aid, to take the part of, or to side with]
kyŏt-da-ri sŏ-gi	Assisting Stance (WTF)
kyu-jŏng	Rules
kyun-hyŏng	Equilibrium

kk ㄲ

kko-a	Cross or Twist [kko-a is derived from the verb kko-da (꼬 다), meaning to twisted or to twine]
kko-a sŏ-gi	Cross Stance (WTF)
kko-gi	Crossing (ITF) [kko-gi is form the verb kko-da (꼬다), meaning to cross, to twist, or to twine]

kkŭ-rŏ	Pulling [kkŭ-rŏ is derived from the verb kkŭl-da (끌다), meaning to pull, draw, give a pull, haul, tug, tow, or to jerk]
kkŭ-rŏ ol-li-gi	Drawing Up (WTF)
kkŭt	End or Tip (ITF)

k' ㅋ

k'al	Knife, a sword, a saber, a blade
k'o	Nose
k'ong-p'at	Kidney
k'ŭn tol-tchŏ-gwi	Large Hinge (WTF)
k'ŭn tol-tchŏ-gwi hyŏng	Large Hinge Shape (WTF)

m ㅁ

maek-bak	Pulse
maek-bak son-mok tong-maek	Radial Artery
magŭ-myŏ na-ga-gi	Block - Forward Stepping (ITF)
magŭ-myŏ tŭ-rŏ o-gi	Block - Backward Stepping (ITF)
mak-ki	Block or Blocking (ITF&WTF) [mak-ki is derived from the verb mak-da (막 다), meaning to block, to obstruct, to stop, to check, or to intercept]
mak-ki pu-wi	Blocking Tools (ITF)
mak-ki tae	Blocking Apparatus (ITF)
mat-ba-da kong-gyŏk	Head-on Attack (ITF) [mat-ba-da is derived from the verb mat-ba-da (맞받다), meaning to receive (face) head-on, to respond at once, to crash head-on, or to crash into each other]

133

ma-ch'u-ŏ kyŏ-ru-gi	Pre-arranged Sparring (WTF) [ma-ch'u-ŏ is derived from the verb ma-ch'u-da (마 추다), meaning to order, to order from, to give an order for, or to place an order with]
mat-sŏ-gi	Sparring (ITF) [mat-sŏ-gi is derived from the verb mat-sŏ-da (맞서다), meaning to stand against or opposite each other, to face or confront each other, to pit oneself against]
mat-sŏ-gi che-do	System of Sparring (ITF)
me chu-mŏk	Hammer-fist (WTF)
mi-an ham-ni-da	I am sorry.
mi-dŏk	Virtue [mi-dŏk is defined as virtue, a noble attribute, a good trait, or a grace of character]
mi-gan	Bridge of the Nose
mi-gol	Coccyx
mi-kkŭl-gi	Sliding (ITF) [mi-kkŭl-gi is derived from the verb mi-kkŭ-rŏ-chi-da (미끄러지다) meaning to slide, to glide, to slip, or to skid]
mi-kkŭ-rŏm	Sliding [mi-kkŭ-rŏm is derived from the verb mi-kkŭ-rŏ-chi-da (牽喘 測 meaning to slide, to glide, to slip, or to skid]
mi-kkŭ-rŏm pal	Shifting the body by moving both feet (ITF)
mi-kkŭ-rŭm-bal-lo tchi-rŭ-myŏ na-ga-gi	Forward Sliding Punch (ITF)
mi-kkŭ-rŭm-bal-lo tchi-rŭ-myŏ tŭrŏ-o-gi	Backward Sliding Punch (ITF)

mil-gi	Pushing (ITF&WTF) [mil-gi is derived from the verb mil-da (밀다), meaning to push, to shove, to thrust, to jostle, or give a push]
mi-rŏ ch'a-gi	Pushing Kick (WTF)
mi-rŏ mak-ki	Pushing Block (ITF)
mit	Under
mit chu-mŏk	Under Fist (ITF)
mit p'al-mok	Under Forearm at the wrist (ITF&WTF)
mit t'ŏk	Point of the Chin (ITF)
mi-t'ŭ-ro	Down or Downward
mi-t'ŭ-ro ppae-gi	Underneath Pull-out (WTF)
mo	Angle, Edge, or Corner
mo-a	Gathering or Close [mo-a is from the verb mo-i-da (모이다), meaning to be all together, to be in a body, or to be "en masse"]
mo-a chun-bi sŏ-gi	Close Ready Stance (ITF)
mo-a sŏ-gi	Close Stance (ITF&WTF)
mo-bŏm	A model, example, pattern, or paragon
mo-bŏm mat-sŏ-gi	Model Sparring (ITF)
mo chu-ch'um sŏ-gi	Oblique Angle Riding Stance (WTF) Close Attention Stance (WTF)
mo-dŭm-bal	Drawing the Feet together (ITF)
mo-dŭm-bal ch'a-gi	Joint-feet Kick (WTF)
mo-dŭm son-kkŭt	Combined All-fingertip (WTF)
mo-dŭm son-kkŭt ch'i-gi	Combined All-fingertip Hit (WTF)
mok	Neck
mok-gu-mŏng	Throat

mok tong-maek	Neck Artery (Carotid)
mom	The Body
mom nat-ch'u-gi	Body Dropping (ITF)
mom pu-bun	Section of the Body
mom tol-lyŏ ch'a-gi	Body Turning Kick (WTF)
mom-ttung	A Body or a Frame
mom-ttung pun	Section of the Body (ITF)
mom-t'ong	Trunk, trunk of the body, the bulk of one's body, or the middle of the body or middle section (WTF)
mom-t'ong an mak-ki	Trunk Inner Block (WTF)
mom-t'ong chi-rŭ-gi	Trunk Punch (WTF)
mom-t'ong he-ch'yŏ mak-ki	Trunk Pushing Block (WTF)
mom-t'ong mak-ki	Trunk Block (WTF)
mom-t'ong pa-ch'im	Pushups (ITF)
mom-t'ong pa-kkat ch'i-gi	Trunk Outer Hit (WTF)
mom-t'ong pa-kkat mak-ki	Trunk Outer Block (WTF)
mom-t'ong pi-t'ŭ-rŏ mak-ki	Trunk Twist Block (WTF)
mom-t'ong pu-wi	Body - Middle Section (WTF)
mom-t'ong U-ja chi-rŭ-gi	U-Shape Trunk Punch (WTF) - as in the English letter "U"
mom-t'ong yŏp mak-ki	Trunk Side Block (WTF)
mong-dung-i	Pole or Staff (ITF), a stick, a club, or a cudgel
mong-dung-i chap-gi	Pole Grasp (ITF)
mong-dung-i chap-go mak-ki	Pole Grasping Block or U-Shape Grasping Block (ITF)

mong-dung-i mak-ki	Pole Block (U-Shape Block) (ITF)
mo sŏ-gi	Oblique Angle Stance (WTF)
mo-ŭn	Combined [mo-ŭn is derived from the verb mo-ŭ-da (모으다), meaning to gather, to get (things, people) together, to collect, or to make a collection of]
mo-ŭn se p'yŏn son-kkŭt	Combined Three Flat-fingertip (WTF)
mo-ŭn se son-kkŭt tchi-rŭ-gi	Combined Three-fingertip Thrust (WTF)
mo-ŭn se son-kkŭt ch'i-gi	Combined Three-fingertip Hit (WTF)
mo-ŭn tu p'yŏn son-kkŭt	Combined Two Flat-fingertip (WTF)
mo-ŭn tu-son-kkŭt tchi-rŭ-gi	Combined Two-fingertip Thrust (WTF)
mo-ŭn tu-son-kkŭt ch'i-gi	Combined Two-fingertip Hit (WTF)
mŏng-e ch'i-gi	Yoke Hit (WTF)
mŏng-e ppae-gi	Yoke pull-out (WTF)
mŏm-ch'u-gi	Checking (ITF) [mŏm-ch'u-gi is derived from the verb mŏm-ch'u-da (멈추다), meaning to stop, to cease, to put a stop to, or to halt]
mŏm-ch'wo mak-ki	Checking Block (ITF)
mŏ-ri	Head
Mu-Dŭk Kwan	Korean Martial Art school founded by Hwang Ki in 1945
mung-nyŏm	Meditation or silent prayer
Mun-Mu t'ŭl	ITF pattern practiced by 4th Degree [Named for the 30th king of the Shilla Dynasty, Mun Mu (661 A.D. - 680 A.D.). According to his will, his body was placed in the sea where his soul could forever defend his land against the Japanese]

mu-rŭp	Knee
mu-rŭp kwan-jŏl	Knee Joint
mu-rŭp ol-lyŏ ch'a-gi	Knee Rising Kick (WTF)
mu-rŭp ol-lyŏ ch'i-gi	Knee Rising Hit (WTF)
mu-rŭp ch'i-gi	Knee Strike (WTF)
mu-rŭp tol-lyŏ ch'a-gi	Knee Turning Kick (WTF)
mu-rŭp tol-lyŏ ch'i-gi	Knee Turning Hit (WTF)
mu-sa chun-bi sŏ-gi	Warrior Ready Stance (ITF) [mu-sa is defined as a warrior, a soldier, or a knight]
mu-sul	Military (martial) Arts
myŏng-ch'i	Solar Plexus

n ㄴ

naeng-su ma-ch'al	Cold Showers and Baths [naeng-su means cold water; and ma-ch'al is derived from the verb ma-ch'al-ha-da (마찰하다), meaning to rub or to chafe (the skin)]
nae-ryŏ	Downward [nae-ryŏ is derived from the verb nae-ri-da (내리다), meaning to descend, come (go) down, or to fall]
nae-ryŏ chi-rŭ-gi	Underneath Punch (WTF)
nae-ryŏ ch'a-gi	Downward Kick (ITF&WTF)
nae-ryŏ ch'i-gi	Downward Strike (WTF)
nae-ryŏ kyo-ch'a chu-mŏk mak-ki	Downward X-Fist Block (ITF)
nae-ryŏ kyo-ch'a mak-ki	Downward X-Block (ITF)
nae-ryŏ kyo-ch'a son-k'al mak-ki	Downward X-Knifehand Block (ITF)

nae-ryŏ mak-ki	Downward Block (ITF)
nae-ryŏ tchi-rŭ-gi	Downward Punch (ITF)
nae-ryŏ ttae-ri-gi	Downward Strike (ITF)
nae-ryŏ ttul-ki	Downward Thrust (ITF)
na-ga ch'a-gi	Hook Kick (WTF) [na-ga is derived from the verb na-ga-da (나 가 다), meaning to step out, to go forward, to go out, to get out, or to take a way out]
na-ga-gi	Forward Stepping (ITF)
na-jŭn-dae	Low (ITF) [na-jŭn-dae is derived from the verb nat-da (낮 다), meaning to be low]
na-jŭn-dae kong-gyŏk	Low Attack (ITF)
na-jŭn-dae ch'a-gi	Low Kick (ITF)
na-jŭn-dae mak-ki	Low Block (ITF)
na-jŭn pu-bun	Low Section (ITF)
na-jŭn-dae tchi-rŭ-gi	Low Punch (ITF)
na-jŭn-dae ttae-ri-gi	Low Strike (ITF)
na-jŭn-dae ttul-ki	Low Thrust (ITF)
nal	Edge, a blade
nal-gae chi-rŭ-gi	Wing Punch (WTF)
nal-gae p'yŏ-gi	Wing Spreading (WTF)
na-ran-hi	A line, a row, or side by side
na-ran-hi chun-bi sŏ-gi	Parallel Ready Stance (ITF)
na-ran-hi mak-ki	Parallel Block (ITF)
na-ran-hi sŏ-gi	Parallel Stance (WTF)
nat-ch'u-gi	Ducking (ITF) [nat-ch'u-gi is derived from the verb nat-ch'u-da (낮추다), meaning to lower, to let (bring) down, or to drop]

nat-ch'wŏ sŏ-gi	Low Stance (ITF)
ne	Yes
net	Four [in Native Korean]
ne-tchae	Fourth [in Native Korean]
-nim	Sir, father, honorable master, mister, esquire [a suffix attached to a title expressing respect]
ni-ŭn-ja	ni-ŭn-ja literally means "ni-ŭn-Shaped", after the second consonant in the Korean alphabet, ㄴ
ni-ŭn-ja chun-bi sŏ-gi	L-Ready Stance (ITF)
ni-ŭn-ja sŏ-gi	L-Stance (ITF)
ni-ŭn-ja sŏ no-p'ŭn-dae mak-ki	L-Stance High Block (ITF)
no-p'i	High [no-p'i is derived from the verb nop-da (높다), meaning to be high, to be lofty, to be tall, or to be elevated]
no-p'i ch'a-gi	High Kick (ITF)
no-p'i pi-t'ŭ-rŏ ch'a-gi	High Twisting Kick (ITF)
no-p'ŭn-dae	High (ITF) [no-p'ŭn-dae is derived from the verb nop-da (높다) to be high, to be lofty, to be tall, or to be elevated]
no-p'ŭn-dae kong-gyŏk	High Attack (ITF)
no-p'ŭn-dae mak-ki	High Block (ITF)
no-p'ŭn-dae p'al-gup ttae-ri-gi	High Elbow Strike (ITF)
no-p'ŭn-dae p'al-gup ttul-ki	High Elbow Thrust (ITF)
no-p'ŭn pu-bun	High Section (ITF)
no-p'ŭn-dae tchi-rŭ-gi	High Punch (ITF)
no-p'ŭn-dae ttae-ri-gi	High Strike (ITF)

no-p'ŭn-dae ttul-ki	High Thrust (ITF)
no-ran saek	Yellow Color
no-ran tti	Yellow Belt (ITF&WTF)
no-ran tti-e ch'o-rok sŏn	Yellow Belt with a Green Stripe (ITF&WTF)
nŏ-mŏ	Crossing Over [nŏ-mŏ is derived from the verb nŏm-da (넘 다), meaning to cross, to go across (over), to go or get beyond, to clear, or to hurdle]
nul-lŏ	Pressing [nul-lŏ is derived from the verb nul-li-da (눌 리 다), meaning to be pushed or to be pressed]
nul-lŏ ch'a-gi	Pressing Kick (ITF)
nul-lŏ kyo-ch'a chu-mŏk mak-ki	Pressing X-Fist Block (ITF)
nul-lŏ mak-ki	Pressing Block (ITF&WTF)
nun	Eye
nu-wŏ	Laying or Ground [nu-wŏ is derived from the verb nup-da (눕 다), meaning to lie down, to lay one's self down, to recline, to lie reclined, or to stretch out]
nu-wŏ ch'a-gi	Ground Kick (ITF)
nu-wŏ ki-sul	Ground Technique (ITF)
nu-wŏ mu-rŭp ku-bu-ri-gi	Ground Knee Bending (ITF)
nu-wŏ ta-ri-kko-gi	Ground Leg Crossing (ITF)
nu-wŏ pal ki-sul	Ground Foot Technique (ITF)
nu-wŏ p'i-ha-gi	Ground Dodging (ITF)
nu-wŏ son ki-sul	Ground Hand Technique (ITF)
nu-wŏ tchi-rŭ-gi	Ground Punch (ITF)
nu-wŏ ttae-ri-gi	Ground Strike (ITF)

nu-wŏ ttul-ki	Ground Thrust (ITF)
nŭk-gol	Rib [Sino-Korean]
nŭk-gol shin-gyŏng	Intercostal Nerve
nŭ-rin tong-jak	Slow Motion (ITF) [nŭ-rin is derived from the verb nŭ-ri-da (느리다), meaning to be slow]

O 오

o	Five [in Sino-Korean] - originating from the Chinese term for five, 五 (pronounced in Chinese as *wu*)
o-dan	Fifth Degree Black Belt (ITF&WTF)
O-Do Kwan	Korean Martial Art school (Military) founded by General Choi Hong Hi in 1954 with the help of Nam Tae Hi
oe-	Single, one, lone, or sole
oe chu-mŏk	Single Fist (ITF)
oe pal sŏ-gi	One-Leg Stance (ITF)
oe p'al-gup ttae-ri-gi	Single Elbow Strike (ITF)
oe p'al-gup ttul-ki	Single Elbow Thrust (ITF)
oe san-t'ŭl mak-ki	Single-hand Wide-open Block (WTF)
oe san-t'ŭl mak-ki	Part Mountain Shape Block (WTF)
oe san-t'ŭl yŏp mak-ki	Part Mountain Shape Side Block (WTF)
oe san-t'ŭl yŏp ch'a-gi	Single-hand Wide-open Block and Side Kick (WTF)
oe sŏn p'al-mok	Single Straight Forearm (ITF)
oe sŏn p'al-mok mak-ki	Single Straight Forearm Block (ITF)
oe sŏn son-k'al	Single Straight Knifehand (ITF)
oe sŏn son-k'al mak-ki	Single Straight Knifehand Block (ITF)

oe yŏp p'al-gup ttae-ri-gi	Single Side Elbow Strike (ITF)
oe yŏp p'al-gup ttul-ki	Single Side Elbow Thrust (ITF)
oen	Left
oen p'al	Left Arm
oen pal	Left Foot
oen p'yŏn-hi sŏ-gi	Left at Ease Stance (WTF)
oen son	Left Hand
oen sŏ-gi	Left-hand Stance (WTF)
oen ta-ri	Left Leg
oen-tchok	Left Side (direction)
oen-tchok-ŭ-ro to-nŭn	Counter Clockwise (turn) (ITF)
o-gi	Coming [o-gi is derived from the verb o-da (오다), meaning to come, to arrive (at), to reach, to show up, to turn up, or to appear]
o-gŭm	Knee Hollow (WTF) or Fossa of the Knee (ITF), the crook inside of, the curve of, or hollow of the knee
o-gŭm sŏ-gi	Reverse Crane Stance (WTF)
o-gŭp	Fifth Grade (ITF&WTF) [High Green Belt]
o-gŭ-ryŏ sŏ-gi	Crouched Stance (ITF) [o-gŭ-ryŏ is derived from the verb o-gŭ-ri-da (오그리다), meaning to curl (ones body) up, to crouch, to huddle, or to lower]
o-ja sŏ-gi	Inverted "T"-Shape Stance (WTF) [o-ja literally means "ㅗ -Shaped", after the Han-gŭl vowel, ㅗ , pronounced as "O"]

ol-li-gi	Rising (ITF) [ol-li-gi is derived from the verb ol-li-da (올리다), meaning to raise, to lift up, to put up, or to elevate]
ol-lyŏ	Upward (ITF) [ol-lyŏ is derived from the verb ol-li-da (올리다), meaning to raise, to lift up, to put up, or to elevate]
ol-lyŏ ch'a-gi	Upward Kick (ITF)
ol-lyŏ ch'i-gi	Rise-up Strike (WTF)
ol-lyŏ mak-ki	Upward Block (ITF)
ol-lyŏ tchi-rŭ-gi	Upward Punch (ITF)
om-gyŏ	Shifting [om-gyŏ is derived from the verb om-gi-da (옮기다), meaning to move (to), to remove (to), to transfer, to shift (home)]
om-gyŏ ti-di-gi	Stepping and Shifting (ITF)
om-gyŏ ti-di-myŏ cha-jŭn-bal	Stepping and Shifting Foot Changing (ITF)
om-gyŏ ti-di-myŏ tol-gi	Stepping and Shifting Turn (ITF)
o-myŏ	Cover a distance [o-myŏ is derived from the verb o-da (오다), meaning to come (at), to arrive, to reach, to show up, to turn up, or to appear]
o-myŏ mi-kkŭl-gi	Sliding the feet to cover distances (ITF)
on-	on- as a prefix, is defined as the whole, the entire, the complete, the perfect, the total, full, or all
on-mom	Full Facing (ITF)
o-rŭm	Correct [o-rŭm is derived from the verb or-da (옳다), meaning to be right, to be rightful, to be proper, to be reasonable, to be just, to be correct, to be true, to be exact, to be accurate, to be honest, or to be truthful]

o-rŭn-	Right
o-rŭn p'al	Right Arm
o-rŭn pal	Right Foot
o-rŭn son	Right Hand
o-rŭn sŏ-gi	Right-hand Stance (WTF)
o-rŭn ta-ri	Right Leg
o-rŭn-tchok	Right Side (direction)
o-rŭn-tchok p'yŏn-hi sŏ-gi	Right at Ease Stance (WTF)
o-rŭn-tchok-ŭ-ro to-nŭn	Clockwise (turn) (ITF)

ŏ 어

ŏ-kkae	Shoulder
ŏ-kkae kwan-jŏl	Shoulder Joint
ŏl-gul	Face [ŏl-gul is defined as a face, facial features, the face area, or high section (WTF)]
ŏl-gul an mak-ki	Face Inner Block (WTF)
ŏl-gul ap ch'a ol-lyŏ mak-ki	Face Front-sole Rising Block (WTF)
ŏl-gul ap ch'i-gi	Face Front Hit (WTF)
ŏl-gul chi-rŭ-gi	Face Punch (WTF)
ŏl-gul he-ch'yŏ mak-ki	Face Pushing Block (WTF)
ŏl-gul mak-ki	Face Block (WTF)
ŏl-gul ŏt-gal-lyŏ mak-ki	Face Cross Block (WTF)
ŏl-gul pa-kkat mak-ki	Face outer Block (WTF)
ŏl-gul pi-t'ŭ-rŏ mak-ki	Face Twist Block (WTF)
ŏl-gul pu-wi	Face Parts (WTF)

145

ŏl-gul yŏp ch'a-ol-lyŏ mak-ki	Face Foot-blade Rising Block (WTF)
ŏl-gul yŏp mak-ki	Face Side Block (WTF)
ŏm-ji chu-mŏk	Thumb Knuckle Fist (ITF)
ŏm-ji chu-mŏk tchi-rŭ-gi	Thumb Knuckle Punch (ITF)
ŏm-ji-gu	Thenar (Thumb Knuckle web)
ŏm-ji kwan-jŏl	Thumb Joint
ŏm-ji pa-t'ang	Thumb Ridge
ŏm-ji son-ga-rak	Thumb
ŏng-dŏng-i kwan-jŏl	Hip Joint
ŏ-pŭn	Facing Down [ŏ-pŭn is derived from the verb ŏp-da (엎 다), meaning to upset, to overturn, to turn over, to turn upside down, or to put face down]
ŏ-pŭn p'yŏn son-kkŭt	Upset Flat-fingertip (WTF)
ŏ-pŭn son-kkŭt	Flat Fingertip (ITF)
ŏt-gal-lyŏ	Crossing [ŏt-gal-lyŏ is derived from the verb ŏt-gal-li-da (엇갈 리다), meaning to cross (each other), or to miss each other on the road]
ŏt-gal-lyŏ a-rae mak-ki	Cross Underneath Block (WTF)
ŏt-gal-lyŏ mak-ki	Cross Block (WTF)

p ㅂ

pa-ch'im	Holding Up [pa-ch'im is derived from the verb pa-ch'i-da (받 치 다), meaning to prop up, support, bolster, or hold up]
pa-da	Counter [pa-da is derived from the verb pa-da (받 다), meaning to receive (an action), to accept, or to take]
pa-da ch'a-gi	Counter Kick (ITF)

146

Paek-je shi-dae	Paekje Dynasty (18 B.C. - 663 A.D.) - one of the "Three Kingdoms" of ancient Korea
paek-jŏl-bul-gul	Indomitable Spirit [paek-jŏl-bul-gul is derived from the verb paek-jŏl-bul-gul-hi-da (백절불굴하다), meaning to be undefeatible, to be unbending, to be unflinching, or to be indomitable - originating from the Chinese term 百折不屈 (pronounced in Chinese as *bai-zhe-bu-chu*)]
pae-kkob	Umbilicus
pa-ji	Practice Pants (ITF), Korean traditional baggy pants worn by men
pa-kkat	Outside, Outer (ITF), or exterior
pa-kkat ch'i-gi	Outward Hit (WTF)
pa-kkat kyŏng-gol	Outside Tibia (Fibula)
pa-kkat mak-ki	Outside Block (ITF) or Outer Block (WTF)
pa-kkat p'al-mok	Outer Forearm at the wrist
pa-kkat p'al-mok mak-ki	Outer-forearm Block (WTF)
pa-kkat p'al-mok mom-t'ong yŏp mak-ki	Outer-forearm Trunk Side Block (WTF)
pa-kkat p'al-mok ŏl-gul yŏp mak-ki	Outer-forearm Face Side Block (WTF)
pa-kkat nae-ryŏ ch'a-gi	Outer Downward Kick (WTF)
pa-kkat pal-mok kwan-jŏl	Outside Ankle Joint
pa-kkat p'al-ja sŏ-gi	Outside Open Stance (ITF)
pa-kkat p'al-mok	Outside Forearm (ITF)
pa-kku-gi	Alternating [pa-kku-gi is derived from the verb pa-kku-da (바꾸다), meaning to change, to alter, to modify, to convert, or to vary]

pak-kǔ-ro	Outward
pak-kǔ-ro ch'a-gi	Outward Kick (ITF)
pak-kǔ-ro kǔt-gi	Outward cross-cut (ITF)
pak-kǔ-ro mak-ki	Outward Block (ITF)
pak-kǔ-ro se-wǒ ch'a-gi	Outward Vertical Kick (ITF)
pak-kǔ-ro ttae-ri-gi	Outward Strike (ITF)
pal	Foot
pal ap ol-lyǒ ch'a-gi	Front Rising Kick (WTF), literally meaning front foot rising kick
pal-ba-dak	Foot Sole (ITF), foot bottom
pal-dǔng	Instep, foot-back
pal-ga-rak	Toe
pal-ga-rak-nal	Toe Edge
pal ki-sul	Foot Techniques (ITF&WTF)
pal kǒl-gi	Foot Tackling (ITF)
pal-k'al	Footsword (ITF)
pal-k'al dǔng	Reverse Footsword (ITF)
pal-kkum-ch'i	Heel (back of the foot)
pal-kkǔt	Toes
pal mat-sǒ-gi	Foot Sparring (ITF)
pal-mok	Ankle
pal-mok kwan-jǒl	Ankle Joint
pal-lal	Foot-blade (WTF), Edge of the Foot or Footsword (ITF)
pal-lal dǔng	Foot-blade Back (WTF)
pal twi-ch'uk	Back Heel
pal twi-kkum-ch'i	Foot Back Sole (Heel) (ITF) or Heel of the Foot (WTF)

pal tŭl-gi	Foot Lifting (ITF)
pam chu-mŏk	Chestnut Fist (WTF)
pan-dae	Reverse (ITF), opposition [pan-dae is derived from the verb pan-dae-ha-da (반대하다), meaning to be against, to be opposed to, to object to, or to be hostile to]
pan-dae chi-rŭ-gi	Opposite Straight Punch (WTF)
pan-dae tchi-rŭ-gi	Reverse Punch (ITF)
pan-dae tol-lyŏ ch'a-gi	Reverse Turning Kick (ITF)
pan-dae tol-lyŏ ki-sul	Reverse Turning Techniques (ITF)
pan-dal	A Half Moon or a Crescent
pan-dal ch'a-gi	Crescent Kick (ITF)
pan-dal ch'a-gi	Dichotomy Kick (WTF)
pan-dal tchi-rŭ-gi	Crescent Punch (ITF)
pan-dal ttae-ri-gi	Crescent Strike (ITF)
pan-dal-son	Arc Hand (ITF)
pan-dal-son ch'u-k'yŏ mak-ki	Arc-hand Rising Block (ITF)
pan-dong-nyŏk	Reaction Force (ITF)
-pang	Direction
pang-hyang pa-kku-gi	Change Direction (WTF)
pan-gyŏk	Counter Attack (ITF)
pang-ŏ	Defense (ITF) [pang-ŏ is derived from the verb pang-ŏ-ha-da (방어하다), meaning to defend, to bulwark, to shield, to protect oneself (against), or to safeguard (against)]
pang-ŏ-gi	Defensive Techniques (ITF)
pan-ja-yu mat-sŏ-gi	Semi-free Sparring (ITF)

pan-mom	Half Facing (ITF)
pan-sa ch'a-gi	Reflex Kick (ITF) [pan-sa is derived from the verb pan-sa-ha-da (반사하다), meaning to reflect or to reverberate]
pan tol-lyŏ ch'a-gi	Half Turning Kick (ITF), or Arc Kick (WTF)
pa-nŭng	Reflex (ITF), reaction, response
pap-gi	Smashing Technique [pap-gi is derived from the verb pap-da (밟 다), meaning to step (on) or to tread (on)]
pan-shin	pan-shin is defined as one side of the body or half of the body
pa-ro	Obverse (ITF), at once, immediately, directly, just exactly, precisely, right, rightly, honestly, correctly, properly, or straight, or return to a position (ITF&WTF)
pa-ro chi-rŭ-gi	Straight Punch (WTF)
pa-ro tchi-rŭ-gi	Obverse Punch (ITF)
pat-ch'i-gi	Holding (ITF) [pat-ch'i-gi is derived from the verb pat-ch'i-da (받 치 다), meaning to support, to prop (bolster) up, or to hold up]
pa-t'ang	pa-t'ang is defined as the bottom, the base, or the foundation
pa-t'ang-son	Palm Heel (ITF)
pa-t'ang-son	Palm Hand (WTF)
pa-t'ang-son a-rae mak-ki	Palm-hand Underneath Block (WTF)
pa-t'ang-son mom-t'ong mak-ki	Palm-hand Trunk Block (WTF)
pa-t'ang-son mom-t'ong nul-lŏ mak-ki	Palm-hand Trunk Pressing Block (WTF)

pa-t'ang-son ŏl-gul an mak-ki	Palm-hand Face Inner Block (WTF)
pa-wi	A rock, any piece of stone, or a crag
pa-wi mil-gi	Rock Pushing, Push Boulder (WTF)
pe-gae	Pad [pe-gae literally means a pillow, a bolster, or an air cushion]
pi-gol	Fibula (WTF)
pi-jang	Spleen (ITF)

pi-t'ŭ-rŏ	Twisting [pi-t'ŭ-rŏ is derived from the
	  verb pi-t'ŭl-da (비 틀다), meaning to
	  twist, to wrench, to screw, or contort]

pi-t'ŭ-rŏ ch'a-gi	Twist Kick (WTF) or Twisting Kick (ITF)
pi-t'ŭ-rŏ mak-ki	Twist Block (WTF)
po chu-mŏk	Covering Fist (WTF) [po is defined as a small wrapping cloth]
po chu-mŏk chun-bi sŏ-gi	Covered-fist Ready Stance (WTF)
pok-bu	Abdomen
pong	Staff (pole)
pŏm sŏ-gi	Tiger Stance (WTF)
pu-bun	A part, a portion, a section, a piece, or a fragment
pu-ri	Suddenness or Unexpectedness
pu-ryu	A class, a kind, or a category
pu-sa-bŏm	Assistant Instructor, Vice Teacher (ITF)
pu-sa-bŏm-nim	Assistant Instructor Sir, Vice Teacher Sir (ITF)
pu-sang	Injury or a wound
pu-shim	Judge, a sub-umpire, or sub-referee

151

pu-su-gi	Smashing (ITF) [pu-su-gi is derived from the verb pu-su-da (부수다), meaning to smash, to break, to destroy, or to demolish]
put-ja-ba mak-ki	Grasping Block (ITF) [put-ja-ba is derived from the verb put-jap-da (붙잡다), meaning to seize, to grasp, to catch, to hold, or to take (catch hold of)]
put-jap-go ch'a-gi	Grasp and Kick or Kick while Grasping (ITF)
pu-wi	A part or a region

pp 배

ppae-gi	Pull-out (WTF) [ppae-gi is derived from the verb ppae-da (빼다), meaning to take (pull) out, to draw, or to extract]
ppal-gan saek	Red Color
ppal-gan tti	Red Belt (ITF&WTF)
ppal-gan tti-e kŏ-mŭn sŏn	Red Belt with a Black Stripe (ITF&WTF)
ppa-rŭn tong-jak	Fast Motion (ITF) [ppa-rŭn is derived from the verb ppa-rŭ-da (빠르다), meaning to be fast, to be rapid, to be swift, to be speedy, to be quick (agile, sharp and alert)]
ppŏ-dŏ ch'a-gi	Stretch Kick (WTF) [ppŏ-dŏ is derived from the verb ppŏt-da (뻗다), meaning to stretch out]
ppyŏ	Bone

p' 교

p'a-do	Wave (ITF) [p'a-do is defined as a wave, a billow, a surge, a breaker, or a ripple]
p'al	Arm
p'al	Eight [in Sino-Korean] - originating from the Chinese term for eight, 八 (pronounced in Chinese as *ba*)
p'al-dan	Eighth Degree Black Belt (ITF&WTF)
p'al-gup	Elbow (bottom), Forearm near the Elbow
p'al-gup ap ch'i-gi	Elbow Front Strike (WTF)
p'al-gup ch'i-gi	Elbow Strike (WTF)
p'al-gup kwan-jŏl	Elbow Joint
p'al-gup nae-ryŏ ch'i-gi	Elbow Downward Strike (WTF)
p'al-gup nae-ryŏ ttae-ri-gi	Elbow Downward Strike (ITF)
p'al-gup ol-lyŏ ch'i-gi	Elbow Rise-up Strike (WTF)
p'al-gup p'yo-jŏk ch'i-gi	Elbow Target Strike (WTF)
p'al-gup tol-lyŏ ch'i-gi	Elbow Turning Strike (WTF)
p'al-gup ttae-ri-gi	Elbow Strike (ITF)
p'al-gup twi ch'i-gi	Elbow Back Strike (WTF)
p'al-gup yŏp ch'i-gi	Elbow Side Strike (WTF)
p'al-gŭp	Eighth Grade (ITF&WTF) [Low Yellow Belt]
P'al-gwae	P'al-gwae means the 8-Diagrams - originating from the Chinese term 八卦 (pronounced in Chinese as *ba gua*) representing the eight divination symbols in the Chinese Book of Changes (i-ching)

P'al-gwae ch'il-jang p'um-se	WTF P'al-gwae pattern practiced by 3rd Grade - representing "Mountain" (the immovable, stable, firmness, solemn majesty, and tranquillity), and depicting one of the eight divination symbols in the Chinese Book of Changes (i-ching)
P'al-gwae i-jang p'um-se	WTF P'al-gwae pattern practiced by 8th Grade - representing "Joyfulness" (strength of mind, inner firmness and outer gentleness), and depicting one of the eight divination symbols in the Chinese Book of Changes (i-ching)
P'al-gwae il-jang p'um-se	WTF P'al-gwae pattern practiced by 9th Grade - representing "Heaven" (the sun, the light and symbolizing the source of the creation of all things in the universe), and depicting one of the eight divination symbols in the Chinese Book of Changes (i-ching)
P'al-gwae o-jang p'um-se	WTF P'al-gwae pattern practiced by 5th Grade - representing "Wind" (mighty force, strength, flexibility, calmness), and depicting one of the eight divination symbols in the Chinese Book of Changes (i-ching)
P'al-gwae p'al-jang p'um-se	WTF P'al-gwae pattern practiced by 2nd Grade - representing "Earth" (the source of life, the root, and also the beginning and the end), and depicting one of the eight divination symbols in the Chinese Book of Changes (i-ching)
P'al-gwae sa-jang p'um-se	WTF P'al-gwae pattern practiced by 6th Grade - representing "Thunder and Lightning" (great power and dignity), and depicting one of the eight divination symbols in the Chinese Book of Changes (i-ching)

P'al-gwae sam-jang p'um-se	WTF P'al-gwae pattern practiced by 7th Grade - representing "Fire" and the sun (brightness, light and heat), and depicting one of the eight divination symbols in the Chinese Book of Changes (i-ching)

P'al-gwae sam-jang
  p'um-se
    WTF P'al-gwae pattern practiced by 7th Grade - representing "Fire" and the sun (brightness, light and heat), and depicting one of the eight divination symbols in the Chinese Book of Changes (i-ching)

P'al-gwae yuk-jang
  p'um-se
    WTF P'al-gwae pattern practiced by 4th Grade - representing "Water" (signifying incessant flow, formless flexibility, and softness), and depicting one of the eight divination symbols in the Chinese Book of Changes (i-ching)

p'al-gwa-da-ri
    Extremities [p'al-gwa-da-ri literally means arm-and-leg]

p'al-ja
    p'al-ja literally means "8-Shaped", named after the Chinese character for eight, 八 (pronounced in Chinese as *ba*)

p'al-ja chun-bi sŏ-gi
    Open Ready Stance (ITF)

p'al-ja sŏ-gi
    Open Stance (ITF)

p'al-juk-ji
    Upper Arm

p'al- kkum-ch'i
    Elbow or forearm near the elbow

p'al-mok
    Forearm near the wrist [p'al-mok is defined as the forearm blade near the wrist]

p'al-mok he-ch'yŏ mak-ki
    Forearm Wedging Block (ITF)

p'al-mok mak-ki
    Wrist Block (WTF)

p'i-ha-gi
    Dodging (ITF&WTF)[p'i-ha-gi is derived from the verb p'i-ha-da (피하다), meaning to shrink, to evade, to side-step, dodge, or to duck]

p'i-ha-myŏ ch'a-gi
    Dodging Kick (ITF)

p'i-ha-myŏ ki-sul
    Dodging Technique (ITF&WTF)

p'i-ha-myŏ kong-gyŏk
    Dodging Attack (ITF)

p'i-ha-myŏ tchi-rŭ-gi	Dodging Punch (ITF)
p'i-ha-myŏ ttae-ri-gi	Dodging Strike (ITF)
p'i-ha-myŏ ttul-ki	Dodging Thrust (ITF)
p'il-sŭng	Certain (sure and unfailing) Victory
p'o-gaen son-dŭng	Overlap Backhand (ITF)[p'o-gaen is derived from the verb p'o-gae-da (포개 다), meaning to pile up, to heap up, to put one upon another, to lay one on top of the other, or to stack]
P'o-Ŭn t'ŭl	ITF pattern practiced by 1st Degree [Pseudonym of the loyal subject and famous poet Chong Mong Chu (1337-1392), whose poem, "I Would Not Serve a Second Master Though I Might be Crucified a Hundred Times", is well known in Korea]
p'um	Shape, appearance, looks, the way a thing looks or behaves
p'um-gye	Rank or Grade (WTF)
p'um-se	WTF Term for Patterns [p'um-se originates from p'um (품) which is defined as shape, appearance, looks, the way a thing looks or behaves]
p'u-rŭn saek	Blue Color
p'u-rŭn tti	Blue Belt (ITF&WTF)
p'u-rŭn tti-e ppal-gan sŏn	Blue Belt with a Red Stripe (ITF&WTF)
p'yŏ-gi	Stretching [p'yŏ-gi is derived from the verb p'yŏ-da (펴다), meaning to stretch (out), to spread (out), to open, to smooth out, to straighten, to unroll, to uncoil, or to unfold]
p'yo-jŏk	A Target or a mark
p'yo-jŏk chi-rŭ-gi	Target Punch (WTF)

p'yo-jŏk ch'a-gi	Target Kick (WTF)
p'yo-jŏk ch'i-gi	Target Strike (WTF)
p'yo-jŏk mak-ki	Target Block (WTF)
p'yŏn	p'yŏn is derived from the verb p' yŏ-da (펴다), meaning to spread (out), to open, to unfold, to stretch (out), to smooth out, to straighten, to unroll, or to uncoil
p'yŏn chu-mŏk	Open-fist (ITF) or Flat-fist (WTF)
p'yŏn chu-mŏk pan-dae chi-rŭ-gi	Flat-fist Reverse Straight Punch (WTF)
p'yŏn chu-mŏk pan-dae se-wŏ chi-rŭ-gi	Flat-fist Reverse Straight Vertical Punch (WTF)
p'yŏn chu-mŏk pa-ro chi-rŭ-gi	Flat-fist Straight Punch (WTF)
p'yŏn chu-mŏk pa-ro se-wŏ chi-rŭ-gi	Flat-fist Straight Vertical Punch (WTF)
p'yŏn chu-mŏk tchi-rŭ-gi	Open-fist Punch (ITF)
p'yŏn son-kkŭt	Spear Hand (ITF), Flat Fingertip (WTF)
p'yŏn son-kkŭt ap tchi-rŭ-gi	Flat Fingertip Front Thrust (WTF)
p'yŏn son-kkŭt che-ch'yŏ chi-rŭ-gi	Flat-fingertip Palm Upward Punch (WTF)
p'yŏn son-kkŭt che-ch'yŏ tchi-rŭ-gi	Flat-fingertip Palm Upward Thrust (WTF)
p'yŏn son-kkŭt ŏ-p'ŭn tchi-rŭ-gi	Flat-fingertip Flat Thrust (WTF)
p'yŏn son-kkŭt se-wŏ tchi-rŭ-gi	Flat-fingertip Erect Thrust (WTF)
p'yŏn son-kkŭt se-wŏ chi-rŭ-gi	Flat-fingertip Vertical Punch (WTF)

P'yŏng-Wŏn p'um-se	WTF pattern practiced by 3rd Degree [Representing a vast "plain" or moorland]
p'yŏn-hi	p'yŏn-hi is derived from the verb p'yŏn-ha-da (편하다), meaning to be comfortable, to be easy, to be untroubled, or to be free of care
p'yŏn-hi sŏ-gi	At Ease Stance (WTF)

S 人

sa	Four [in Sino-Korean] - originating from the Chinese term for four, 四 (pronounced in Chinese as *si*)
sa-bang	4-direction
sa-bang ch'a-gi	Four-direction Kick (ITF)
sa-bang hyang ch'a-gi	Four-direction Kick (WTF)
sa-bŏm	Instructor (ITF&WTF), teacher, coach, or a model to others
sa-bŏm-nim	Instructor Sir - Teacher Sir (ITF&WTF)
sa-bŏm-nim kke	Face the Instructor (ITF&WTF)
sa-bŏm pu-ryu	Instructor Classification (ITF)
sa-dan	Fourth Degree Black Belt (ITF&WTF)
-saeng	a student of something
sa-gŭp	Fourth Grade (ITF&WTF) [Low Blue Belt]
sa-hoe pong-sa	Public Service
sa-hyŏn	Master Instructor - Senior Teacher (ITF)
sa-hyŏn-nim	Master Instructor Sir - Senior Teacher Sir (ITF)
sa-je-ji-do	Student / Instructor Relationship (ITF)

sa-ju mak-ki | Four-direction Block (ITF)
(ITF exercise practiced by 10th Grade)

sa-ju tchi-rŭ-gi | Four-direction Punch (ITF)
(ITF exercise practiced by 10th Grade)

sa-ju ttul-ki | Four-direction Thrust (ITF)
(ITF exercise practiced by 2nd Grade)

sa-jung ch'a-gi | Quadruple Kick (ITF)

sam | Three [in Sino-Korean] - originating
from the Chinese term for three, 三
(pronounced in Chinese as *san*)

sam-bang ch'a-gi | Three-direction Kick (ITF)

sam-bo mat-sŏ-gi | Three-step Sparring (ITF)

sam-bo om-gyŏ ti-di-gi | Triple Stepping (ITF)

sam-dan | Third Degree Black Belt (ITF&WTF)

sam-gŭp | Third Grade (ITF&WTF)
[High Blue Belt]

Sam-Il t'ŭl | ITF pattern practiced by 3rd Degree
[Denotes the historical date of the
Korean Independence Movement which
began throughout the country on
March 1, 1919 (thus, the terms "sam"
representing (3) March; and "il"
representing the first day (1)]

sam-jung ch'a-gi | Triple Kick (ITF)

sam-jung kong-gyŏk | Triple Attack (ITF)

sam-jung tchi-rŭ-gi | Triple Punch (ITF)

sam-jung ttae-ri-gi | Triple Strike (ITF)

sam-jung ttul-ki | Triple Thrust (ITF)

sam-pum | Third Degree Junior Black Belt (WTF)

san | Mountain - originating from the Chinese
character 山 (pronounced in Chinese
as *shan*)

A Martial Artist's Guide to Korean Terms

san mak-ki	W-Shape Block (ITF) or Mountain Block (WTF)
sang	sang is defined as the upper part, the top, the head, or the high end, and originates from the Chinese term 上 (pronounced in Chinese as *shang*)
sang-ak-gol	Maxilla Bone
sang-ban-shin	Hand Parts (ITF)
sang-bak-gol	Humerous, upper arm bone, brachium
sang-bok-bu	High or Upper Abdomen
sang-dan	High Level (ITF)
Sang-Mu Kwan	Korean Martial Art school founded by Ro P'yung Chik in 1953
sang-wan shin-gyŏng	Brachial Plexus [sang-wan is defined as the upper arm or brachium]
san-t'ŭl mak-ki	Wide-open Block (WTF), or Mountain Shape Block
san-t'ŭl ŏt-gal-lyŏ mak-ki	Mountain Shape Cross Block (WTF)
sa-sŏn sŏ-gi	Diagonal Stance (ITF) [sa-sŏn is defined as an oblique line or a slant line]
Sa-sŏng	Grand Master (ITF)
Sa-sŏng-nim	Grand Master Sir (ITF)
sa-t'a-gu-ni	Groin
se-gye-jŏk	World-wide, international, or all over the world
Se-gye T'ae-kwŏn-Do Yŏn-maeng	World Taekwon-Do Federation (WTF) (formed on May 28, 1973)

Se-jong t'ŭl	ITF pattern practiced by 5th Degree [Named after the greatest Korean king, Se-jong (1397-1450), who invented, Han-gŭl, the Korean alphabet in 1443. The pattern diagram is in the shape of the Chinese character 王 (pronounced in Chinese as *wang*), meaning king or ruler and therefore represents king]
set	Three [in Native Korean]
se-tchae	Third [in Native Korean]
se-wŏ	Vertical [se-wŏ is derived from the verb se-u-da (세우다), meaning to stand, to make a stand, make erect, or to raise]
se-wŏ ch'a-gi	Vertical Kick (ITF)
se-wŏ chi-rŭ-gi	Erected-fist (vertical) Punch (WTF)
se-wŏ tchi-rŭ-gi	Vertical Punch (ITF)
se-un	Vertical [se-un is derived from the verb se-u-da (세우다), meaning to stand, to make a stand, make erect, or to raise]
se-un chu-mŏk	Vertical Fist (WTF)
se-un p'yŏn son-kkŭt	Vertical Flat-fingertip (WTF)
shi-bŏm	Demonstration (ITF) [shi-bŏm is derived from the verb shi-bŏm-ha-da (시범하다), meaning to set an example or show (give) a good example]
shi-hap	Bout or Match (ITF) or Sparring (WTF), a game, a match, a contest, a bout, a fight, a tournament, or a meet
shi-jak	Commence (ITF), Start or Begin (WTF) [shi-jak is derived from the verb shi-jak-ha-da (시작하다), meaning to begin, to commence, to start, to go into, or to launch]

161

shil-kyŏk	Disqualification, loss of ones rights [shil-kyŏk is derived from the verb shilkyŏk-ha-da (실격 하 다), meaning to be disqualified]
Shil-la shi-dae	Shilla Dynasty (57 B.C. - 935 A.D.) - one of the "Three Kingdoms" of ancient Korea.
Shil-lye ham-ni-da	Pardon me. Excuse me.
shim-jang	Heart
shim-p'an	Umpire (ITF) [shim-p'an is derived from the verb shim-p'an-ha-da (심판하다), mea ning to referee (a game), to act as an umpire, or to judge]
shim-p'an pu-ryu	Umpire Classification (ITF)
shim-sa	Test for Rank Promotion (ITF&WTF) [shim-sa is derived from the verb shim-sa-ha-da (심사하다), meaning to judge, to examine, to inspect, to investigate, or to screen]
-shin	-shin means body and is derived from the word shin-ch'e (신체)
shin-yong	Trust [shin-yong is derived from the verb shin-yong-ha-da (신용하다) meaning to trust, to confide in, to place confidence in, or to give credence to]
shin-ch'uk	Flexibility [shin-ch'uk is derived from the verb shin-ch'uk-ha-da (신 축 하 다), meaning to expand and contract]
shin-gyŏng	Nerve
ship	Ten [in Sino-Korean] - originating from the Chinese term for ten, 十 (pronounced in Chinese as *shi*)

Ship-Jin p'um-se	WTF pattern practiced by 4th Degree [Representing long living things such as mountain, sun, water, stones, clouds, and the "Decimal" system]
ship-dan	Tenth Degree Black Belt (ITF&WTF)
ship-gŭp	Tenth Grade (ITF&WTF) [Low White Belt]
shi-dae	A dynasty, an age, a period, an era, a time, or an epoch
so-gim	Fake (ITF) [so-gim is derived from the verb so-ki-da (속이다), meaning to deceive, to cheat, to take in, to trick, to swindle, to defraud, to play a trick (on a person), or to impose on]
sok-do	Speed [sok-do is derived from the verb sok-ha-da (속하다), meaning to be fast, to be quick, to be rapid, to be swift or speedy]
sok-do-wa pa-nŭng	Speed and Reflex (ITF)
son	Hand
son-ba-dak kŏ-dŭ-rŏ yŏp mak-ki	Palm Assisting Side Block (WTF)
son-dŭng	Hand-back (WTF), Backhand (ITF)
son-ga-rak chu-mŏk	Knuckle Fist (ITF)
son-ga-rak chu-mŏk tchi-rŭ-gi	Knuckle Fist Punch (ITF)
son-ga-rak kwan-jŏl	Finger Joint
son-ga-rak pa-dak	Finger Belly (bottom) (ITF)
son ki-sul	Hand Techniques (ITF)
son-k'al	Knifehand (ITF)
son-k'al he-ch'yŏ mak-ki	Knifehand Wedging Block (ITF)
son-k'al mak-ki	Knifehand Block (ITF)

son-k'al ttae-ri-gi	Knifehand Stike (ITF)
son-k'al dŭng	Reverse Knifehand (ITF)
son-k'al pa-t'ang	Base of Knifehand (ITF)
son-kkŭt	Fingertip
son-mok	Wrist
son-mok kwan-jŏl	Wrist Joint (ITF)
son-mok dŭng	Bow Wrist (ITF)
son-mok dŭng mak-ki	Bow Wrist Block (ITF)
son-nal	Hand-blade or Knifehand (WTF), or the edge of the hand (Knifehand edge) (ITF)
son-nal a-rae he-ch'yŏ mak-ki	Hand-blade Underneath Pushing Block (WTF)
son-nal a-rae mak-ki	Hand-blade Underneath Block (WTF)
son-nal a-rae ŏt-gal-lyŏ mak-ki	Hand-blade Underneath Cross Block (WTF)
son-nal kŭm-gang mak-ki	Hand-blade Diamond Block (WTF)
son-nal mom-t'ong he-ch'yŏ mak-ki	Hand-blade Trunk Pushing Block (WTF)
son-nal mom-t'ong mak-ki	Hand-blade Trunk Block (WTF)
son-nal mom-t'ong yŏp mak-ki	Hand-blade Trunk Side Block (WTF)
son-nal oe san-t'ŭl mak-ki	Hand-blade Single-hand Wide-open Block (WTF)
son-nal tŭng	Hand-blade Back (WTF)
son-nal tŭng a-rae mak-ki	Hand-blade Back Underneath Block (WTF)
son-nal tŭng mom-t'ong mak-ki	Hand-blade Back Trunk Block (WTF)

son-nal tŭng mom-t'ong he-ch'yŏ mak-ki	Hand-blade Back Trunk Pushing Block (WTF)
son-nal tŭng ŏl-gul mak-ki	Hand-blade Back Face Block (WTF)
son-nal tŭng san-t'ŭl mak-ki	Hand-blade Back Wide-open Block (WTF)
son-ba-dak	Palm (hand bottom)
so-sŭm chi-rŭ-gi	Spring-up Punch (WTF) [so-sŭm is derived from the verb sot-da (솟다), meaning to gush (spring) out (forth), to flow out, or to well out]
sŏ-gi	Stance (ITF&WTF) [sŏ-gi is derived from the verb sŏ-da (서 다), meaning to stand up, to rise to one's feet, or to get on to one's feet]
sŏk-kŏ ch'a-gi	Mixed Kicks (WTF) [sŏk-kŏ is derived from the verb sŏkk-da (섞다), meaning to mix, to mingle, or to blend]
sŏn-bae	Senior (WTF), superior, elder, old timer
sŏn	Straight, a line, or a route
sŏn p'al-gup	Straight Elbow (ITF)
sŏn p'al-gup ttul-ki	Straight Elbow Thrust (ITF)
sŏn p'al-mok	Straight Forearm (ITF)
sŏn p'al-mok mak-ki	Straight Forearm Block (ITF)
sŏn son-kkŭt	Straight Fingertip (ITF)
sŏn-su	Contestant (WTF), a player, an athlete, or a champion
Sŏ-San t'ŭl	ITF pattern practiced by 5th Degree [Pseudonym of the great monk Choi Hyong Ung (1520-1604), who lived during the Yi Dynasty, and organized a corps of monk soldiers to repulse the Japanese pirates in 1592]

Su-Bak-Gi	Ancient Korean Martial Art (935 A.D. - 1392 A.D.)
su-jik sŏ-gi	Vertical Stance (ITF) [su-jik is defined as perpendicular or vertical]
sum-t'ong	Windpipe
sŭng-kŭp shim-sa	Promotion Test [sŭng-kŭp is defined as a promotion, a advancement, a raise, or a preferment]
su-p'yŏng	Level, Even, or Horizontal
su-p'yŏng p'ado	Horizontal Wave (ITF)
su-p'yŏng p'al-gup ttae-ri-gi	Horizontal Elbow Strike (ITF)
su-p'yŏng p'al-mok	Horizontal Forearm (ITF)
su-p'yŏng p'al-mok mak-ki	Horizontal Forearm Block (ITF)
su-p'yŏng tchi-rŭ-gi	Horizontal Punch (ITF)
su-p'yŏng ttae-ri-gi	Horizontal Strike (ITF)
sup'yŏng ttae-ri-myŏ ch'a-gi	Horizontal Striking Kick (ITF)
su-p'yŏng ttul-ki	Horizontal Thrust (ITF)
su-ryŏn	Training, practice, culture, discipline, or drill
su-ryŏn chang-bi	Training Equipment (ITF)
su-ryŏn gye-hoek-p'yo	Training Schedule (ITF)
su-ryŏn-saeng	Student (WTF)
su-yang	Culture [su-yang is derived from the verb su-yang-ha-da (수양하다), meaning to improve oneself (one's mind), to cultivate, or to train]
sŭl-gae-gol	Patella, the knee-pan, knee-cap, or the patella

sŭ-p'on-ji pe-gae	Sponge Pad (ITF)
swae-gol	Clavicle or upper collar bone
swi-ŏt	At Ease (ITF&WTF) [swi-ŏt is derived from the verb swi-da (쉬 다), meaning to rest, to take a rest, to have a rest, or to relax]

SS 从

ssang	A Pair, a Couple, a Brace, or a Twin
ssang-bal ch'a-gi	Twin-foot Kick (ITF)
ssang chu-mŏk	Twin Fist (ITF)
ssang dŭng chu-mŏk	Twin Backfist (ITF)
ssang p'al-gup	Twin Elbow (ITF)
ssang p'al-gup ttul-ki	Twin Elbow Thrust (ITF)
ssang p'al-mok mak-ki	Twin Forearm Block (ITF)
ssang son-dŭng	Twin Backhand (ITF)
ssang son-k'al	Twin Knifehand (ITF)
ssang son-k'al dŭng ttae-ri-gi	Twin Reverse Knifehand Strike (ITF)
ssang son-k'al mak-ki	Twin Knifehand Block (ITF)
ssang son-k'al ttae-ri-gi	Twin Knifehand Strike (ITF)
ssang son-ba-dak ch'u-k'yŏ mak-ki	Twin Palm Rising Block (ITF)
ssang sŏn p'al-mok	Twin Straight Forearm (ITF)
ssang sŏn p'al-mok mak-ki	Twin Straight Forearm Block (ITF)
ssang sŏn son-k'al	Twin Straight Knifehand (ITF)
ssang sŏn son-k'al mak-ki	Twin Straight Knifehand Block (ITF)
ssang yŏp chu-mŏk	Twin Side Fist (ITF)
ssang yŏp p'al-gup ttul-ki	Twin Side Elbow Thrust (ITF)

ssang yŏp twit p'al-gup ttul-ki	Twin Side Back Elbow Thrust (ITF)
ssŭ-rŏ ch'a-gi	Sweeping Kick (ITF) [ssŭ-rŏ is derived from the verb ssŭr-da (쓸다), meaning to sweep]

t ㄷ

ta-bang-hyang ch'a-gi	Multi-direction Kick (WTF) [ta-bang is defined as many-direction, and hyang is also defined as direction]
tae-bi	Guard or Guarding (ITF) [tae-bi is derived from the verb tae-bi-ha-da (대비하다), meaning to provide (for, against), to prepare (oneself for), to be ready (for), to make preparation (for, against)]
tae-bi mak-ki	Guarding Block (ITF)
tae ch'ong-gŏm	Defense Against a Bayonet (ITF)
Tae-dan-hi ko-map sŭm-ni-da.	Thank you very much. (formal, polite-honorific)
tae-ha-yŏ	tae-ha-yŏ is derived from the verb tae-ha-da (대하다), meaning to face, to confront, to be opposite of, or to be over against]
tae kon-bong	Defense Against a Club (ITF)
tae kwŏn-ch'ong	Defense Against a Pistol (ITF)
tae mong-dung-i	Defense Against a Pole (ITF)
tae mu-gi	Defense Against an Armed Opponent (ITF) [mu-gi is defined as arms, a weapon, or ordnance]
tae pu-ri kong-gyŏk	Defense Against a Sudden Attack (ITF)

tae-ryŏn	Sparring (ITF) [tae-ryŏn is derived from the verb tae-rim-ha-da (다 림 하 다), meaning to be opposed to each other, to be confronted with, to be pitted against, or to stand face to face]
tae-shin-mun	Skull
tae tand-o	Defense Against a Dagger (ITF)
tae-t'wi-gol	Femur, Thigh Bone
tal-lyŏn	Forging (ITF) [tal-lyŏn is derived from the verb tal-lyŏn-ha-da (단련하다), meaning to temper or to forge]
tal-lyŏn chu	Forging Post (ITF)
tal-lyŏn ppaek	Forging Bag (ITF)
tal-lyŏn-gu	Training Aids (ITF)
tan	Degree [Black Belt Ranking], a rank, a grade, or a class (ITF&WTF)
tan-do	Dagger
tang-gyŏ	Tug [tang-gyŏ is derived from the verb tang-gi-da (당 기 다), meaning to pull, to draw, to tug, or to haul]
tang-gyŏ chi-rŭ-gi	Tug and Punch (WTF)
tang-gyŏ ch'i-gi	Tug and Hit (WTF)
tang-gyŏ t'ŏk chi-rŭ-gi	Tug the Jaw Punch (WTF)
tang-gyŏ t'ŏk ch'i-gi	Tug and Jaw Hit (WTF)
Tang-Su-Do Mu-Duk Kwan	Korean Martial Art school founded by Hwang Ki from Mu-Duk Kwan founded in 1945
tan-gŭp che-do	System of Ranking (ITF)
tan-jŭng	Degree Certificate
ta-ri	Leg
ta-ri-p'yŏ-gi	Leg Stretching (ITF)

ta-shi	Again
ta-sŏt	Five [in Native Korean]
ta-sŏt-tchae	Fifth [in Native Korean]
ti-di-gi	Stepping (ITF) [ti-di-gi is derived from the verb ti-di-da (디디다), meaning to step on or to tread (on)]
ti-gŭt -ja	ti-gŭt -ja literally means "ti-gŭt-Shaped", after the third consonant in the Korean alphabet, ㄷ
ti-gŭt-ja mak-ki	ㄷ -Shape Block (ITF) - [as in the English letter "U"-Shape]
ti-gŭt-ja put-jap-gi	ㄷ -Shape grasp (ITF) - [as in the English letter "U"-Shape]
ti-gŭt-ja tchi-rŭ-gi	ㄷ -Shape Punch (ITF) - [as in the English letter "U"-Shape]
ti-gŭt-ja tchi-rŭ-myŏ ch'a-gi	ㄷ -Shape Punching Kick (ITF) - [as in the English letter "U"-Shape]
to-bok	Practice Suit, Uniform (ITF), Taoist garb
to-jang	Training Hall (ITF&WTF), drill hall, gymnasium, or Buddhist preaching court
tol-gi	Turning (ITF&WTF) [tol-gi is derived from the verb tol-da (돌 다), meaning to go round, to turn, to spin, to gyrate, to revolve, or to rotate]
tol-tchŏ-gwi	Hinge
tol-li-myŏ	Turning [tol-li-myŏ is derived from the verb tol-li-da (돌 리다), meaning to turn, to revolve, to roll, or to spin]
tol-li-myŏ mak-ki	Circular Block (ITF)

tol-lyŏ	Turning [tol-lyŏ is from the verb tol-li-da (돌 리 다), meaning to turn, to revolve, to roll, or to spin]
tol-lyŏ chi-rŭ-gi	Spiral or Twist Punch (WTF)
tol-lyŏ ch'a-gi	Turning Kick (ITF&WTF)
tol-lyŏ tchi-rŭ-gi	Turning Punch (ITF)
tong-jak	Movement (ITF), motion, technique, or actions
tong-jŏk an-jŏng	Dynamic Stability (ITF)[tong-jŏk is defined as dynamic or kinetic]
tong-maek	Artery or Arterial
to-su-dal-lyŏn	Calisthenics (Empty handed training) (ITF)
tŏn-ji-gi	Throwing (ITF) [tŏn-ji-gi is derived from the verb tŏn-ji-da (던 지 다), meaning o throw, to fling, to hurl, to cast, to toss, or to pitch]
tu-	Two [in Native Korean]
tu-ju-mŏk che-ch'yŏ chi-rŭ-gi	Twin-fist Palm-upward Punch (WTF)
tu-ju-mŏk hŏ-ri	Twin-fist on the Waist (WTF)
tu-ju-mŏk hŏ-ri chun-bi sŏ-gi	Fists on the Waist Ready Stance (WTF)
tu-ju-mŏk tchi-rŭ-gi	Double-fist Punch (ITF)
tu-gae-gol	Skull
tul	Two [in Native Korean]
tul-tchae	Second [in Native Korean]
tu-p'al-mok	Double Forearm (ITF)
tu-p'al-mok mak-ki	Double Forearm Block (ITF)
tu-ban-dal-son mak-ki	Double Arc-hand Block (ITF)

tu-son-dŭng	Double Backhand (ITF)
tu-son-ga-rak	Double Finger (ITF)
tu-son-ga-rak ttul-ki	Double Finger Spear (Thrust) (ITF)
tu yŏp p'al-gup	Double Side Elbow (ITF)
tu yŏp p'al-gup ttul-ki	Double Side Elbow Thrust (ITF)
tŭl-gi	Lifting [tŭl-gi is derived from the verb tŭl-da (들다), meaning to raise, to lift (up), to hold up, to put (a thing) on, to hoist, or to heave]
tŭng	Back
tŭng chu-mŏk	Backfist (ITF&WTF)
tŭng chu-mŏk kŏ-dŭ-rŏ ŏl-gul ap ch'i-gi	Backfist Assisting Face Front Hit (WTF)
tŭng chu-mŏk ŏl-gul ap ch'i-gi	Backfist Face Front Hit (WTF)
tŭng chu-mŏ-k ŏl-gul pa-kkat ch'i-gi	Backfist Face Outer Hit (WTF)
tŭng chu-mŏk ttae-ri-gi	Backfist Strike (ITF)
tŭng p'al-mok	Back of Forearm at Wrist
tŭng son-mok tong-maek	Back Wrist Artery
tŭng-san	Mountain climbing
tŭ-rŏ-ka-myŏ	Move Into [tŭ-rŏ-ka-myŏ is derived from the verb tŭ-rŏ-ka-da (들어 가다), meaning to enter, to go in (into), to get in (into), to step (walk) in]
tŭ-rŏ-ka-myŏ ch'a-gi	Skip Kick (ITF)
tŭ-rŏ-ka-myŏ ki-sul	Skipping Techniques (ITF)
tŭ-rŏ-ka-myŏ tchi-rŭ-gi	Skip Punch (ITF)
tŭ-rŏ-ka-myŏ ttae-ri-gi	Skip Strike (ITF)
tŭ-rŏ-ka-myŏ ttul-ki	Skip Thrust (ITF)

tŭ-rŏ-o-gi	Backward Stepping (ITF)
twi	Back
twi chi-rŭ-gi	Back Punch (WTF)
twi ch'i-gi	Back Hit (WTF)
twi-ch'uk	Back Sole, Back Heel
twi-ch'uk him-jul	Achilles Tendon
twi-ch'uk mo-a sŏ-gi	Attention Stance (WTF) [twi-ch'uk mo-a means "heels close together"]
twi-ch'uk yak-jŏm	Achilles Heel [yak-jŏm (약점) is defined as a weak point (spot or side), a vulnerable point, a defect, a weakness, a flaw, a disadvantage, or as one's blind side]
twi-ji-bŏ	Turning Over [twi-ji-bŏ is derived from the verb twi-jib-da (뭐집다), meaning to turn over, to turn (a coat) inside out, to turn wrong side out, to turn upside down, to turn up (a card), or to turn out (a pocket)]
twi-ji-bŏ tchi-rŭ-gi	Upset Punch (ITF)
twi-ji-bŭn son-kkŭt	Upset Fingertip (ITF)
twi-kkum-ch'i	Back Sole (heel area) (ITF)
twi ol-lyŏ ch'a-gi	Backward Lifting Kick (WTF)
twi-ro to-ra	Turn Around, About Face (ITF&WTF)
twi-ro i-bo om-gyŏ ti-di-myŏ tol-gi	Backward Double Step-turning (ITF)
twi-ro-om-gyŏ ti-di-myŏ tol-gi	Backward Step-turning (ITF)
twit	Back
twit-bal sŏ-gi	Rear-foot Stance (ITF)
twit ch'a-gi	Back Kick (ITF&WTF)

twit ch'a-mil-gi	Back Pushing Kick (ITF)
twit ch'a-pu-su-gi	Back Snap Kick (smashing) (ITF)
twit ch'a-tchi-rŭ-gi	Back Piercing Kick (ITF)
twit ta-ri	Rear Leg or Back Leg
twit kko-a sŏ-gi	Backward Cross Stance (WTF)
twit ku-bi	Back Inflection Stance (WTF)
twit kyŏng-gol	Back Tibia (Achilles tendon area)
twit p'al-gup	Back Elbow
twit p'al-gup ttae-ri-gi	Back Elbow Strike (ITF)
twit p'al-gup ttul-ki	Back Elbow Thrust (ITF)
twi ttae-ri-gi	Back Strike (ITF)

tch   쌍

tchi-gŏ ch'a-gi	Straight Kick (ITF) [tchi-gŏ is derived from the verb tchik-da (찍 다), meaning a line drawn with a (vigorous) stroke]
tchi-rŭ-gi	Punch (ITF) or Thrust (WTF)[tchi-rŭ-gi is derived from the verb tchi-rŭda (찌르다), meaning to punch, to thrust, kick, to give, to pierce, stab, to push, to jab (a person) a kick, to knock, to strike, to give (a person) a blow]
tchi-rŭ-myŏ ch'a-gi	Punching Kick (Airborne Combination) (ITF)
tchi-rŭ-myŏ na-ga-gi	Punch - Forward Stepping (ITF)
tchi-rŭ-myŏ tŭ-rŏ o-gi	Punch - Backward Stepping (ITF)
- tchok	Direction, side, or way

tt ㄸ

ttae-ri-gi	Strike (ITF) [ttae-ri-gi is derived from the verb ttae-ri-da (때 리다), meaning to strike, to hit, to give a blow, to thrash, to beat, to knock, to slug, to slap, to flog, to whip, to smack, to smite, to wallop, to whack, or to pound]
ttae-ri-myŏ na-ga-gi	Strike - Forward Stepping (ITF)
ttae-ri-myŏ tŭ-rŏ o-gi	Strike - Backward Stepping (ITF)
tti	Belt, sash, girdle, waist band, or belting
tti saek	Belt Color
ttŏ-rŏ-ji-gi	Fall or Falling (ITF) [ttŏ-rŏ-ji-gi is derived from the verb ttŏ-rŏ-ji-da (떨 어지다), meaning to fall, to drop, to get (have) a fall, to come (go) down, to be down, or to crash]
ttu-rŭ-myŏ na-ga-gi	Thrust - Forward Stepping (ITF)
ttu-rŭ-myŏ tŭ- rŏ o-gi	Thrust - Backward Stepping (ITF)
ttul-ki	Thrust (ITF) [ttul-ki is derived from the verb ttul-da (뚫다), meaning to bore, to drill, to punch, make a hole through, to pierce into, perforate, to cut through, to shoot through, or to penetrate]
ttŭ-rŏ mak-ki	Scooping Block (ITF) [ttŭ-rŏ is derived from the verb ttŭ-da (뜨다), meaning to scoop up or to ladle]
ttwi-gi	Flying or Jumping to Evade (ITF) [ttwi-gi is derived from the verb ttwi-da (뛰다) meaning to run, rush, vault, hop, skip, to jump, to leap, to spring, or to bound]
ttwi-myŏ ap ch'ago pi-t'ŭ-rŏ ch'a-gi	Flying Front and Twisting Kick [jumping] (ITF)
ttwi-myŏ ch'a-gi	Flying Kick [jumping] (ITF)

ttwi-myŏ hon-hap ch'a-gi	Flying Combination Kick [jumping] (ITF)
ttwi-myŏ hon-hap kong-gyŏk	Flying Combination Attack [jumping] (ITF)
ttwi-myŏ i-jung kong-gyŏk	Flying Double Attack [jumping] (ITF)
ttwi-myŏ ka-wi ch'a-gi	Flying Scissors-shape Kick [jumping] (ITF)
ttwi-myŏ ki-sul	Flying Techniques [jumping] (ITF)
ttwi-myŏ pi-t'ŭ-rŏ ch'a-gi	Flying Twisting Kick [jumping] (ITF)
ttwi-myŏ ra-sŏn-shik ch'a-gi	Flying Spiral Kick [jumping] (ITF)
ttwi-myŏ sam-jung kong-gyŏk	Flying Triple Attack [jumping] (ITF)
ttwi-myŏ tchi-rŭ-gi	Flying Punch [jumping] (ITF)
ttwi-myŏ ttae-ri-gi	Flying Strike [jumping] (ITF)
ttwi-myŏ ttul-ki	Flying Thrust [jumping] (ITF)
ttwi-myŏ tu-bal yŏp ch'a mil-gi	Flying Double Foot Side Pushing Kick [jumping] (ITF)
ttwi-myŏ yŏn-sok ch'a-gi	Flying Consecutive Kick [jumping] (ITF)
ttwi-myŏ yŏn-sok kong-gyŏk	Flying Consecutive Attack [jumping] (ITF)
ttwi-myŏ yŏn-sok tchi-rŭ-gi	Flying Consecutive Punch [jumping] (ITF)
ttwi-myŏ yŏn-sok ttae-ri-gi	Flying Consecutive Strike [jumping] (ITF)
ttwi-myŏ yŏn-sok ttul-ki	Flying Consecutive Thrust [jumping] (ITF)
ttwi-ŏ	Jumping [ttwi-ŏ is derived from the verb ttwi-da (뛰다), meaning to jump, to leap, to spring, to bound, to vault, to hop, or to skip]

ttwi-ŏ ch'a-gi	Jump Kick (WTF)
ttwi-ŏ ol-lyŏ ch'a-gi	Jump High Kick (WTF)
ttwi-ŏ nŏ-mŏ ch'a-gi	Flying [jumping] Overhead Kick (ITF)
ttwi-ŏ nŏ-mŏ tchi-rŭ-gi	Flying [jumping] Overhead Punch (ITF)
ttwi-yŏ tol-myŏ ch'a-gi	Mid-air [jump-rotating] Kick (ITF)
ttwi-yŏ tol-myŏ ki-sul	Mid-air [jump-rotating] Techniques (ITF)
ttwi-yŏ tol-myŏ tchi-rŭ-gi	Mid-air [jump-rotating] Punch (ITF)
ttwi-yŏ tol-myŏ ttae-ri-gi	Mid-air [jump-rotating] Strike (ITF)
ttwi-yŏ tol-myŏ ttul-ki	Mid-air [jump-rotating] Thrust (ITF)

t' ㅌ

t'ae	Foot, Jump or Jumping, Kick, or Smash with the Foot [originating from the Chinese term 跆 (pronounced in Chinese as *tai*)]
T'ae-Baek p'um-se	WTF pattern practiced by 2nd Degree [Meaning Big, Bright, Saint Mountain Representing the area around Baek-du mountain]
t'ae-gŭk	The Great Absolute, Large, Big, Eternity [- originating from the Chinese term 太極 (pronounced in Chinese as *tai-ji*), in Chinese philosophy, it is the source of the Yin and the Yang)
T'ae-gŭk ch'il-jang p'um-se	WTF T'ae-gŭk pattern practiced by 3rd Grade - representing "Mountain" (the immovable, stable, firmness, solemn majesty, and tranquillity), and depicting one of the eight divination symbols in the Chinese Book of Changes (i-ching)

177

T'ae-gŭk i-jang p'um-se	WTF T'ae-gŭk pattern practiced by 8th Grade - representing "Joyfulness" (strength of mind, inner firmness and outer gentleness), and depicting one of the eight divination symbols in the Chinese Book of Changes (i-ching)
T'ae-gŭk il-jang p'um-se	WTF T'ae-gŭk pattern practiced by 9th Grade - representing "Heaven" (the sun, the light, symbolizing the source of the creation of all things in the universe), and depicting one of the eight divination symbols in the Chinese Book of Changes (i-ching)
T'ae-gŭk o-jang p'um-se	WTF T'ae-gŭk pattern practiced by 5th Grade - representing "Wind" (mighty force, strength, flexibility, and calmness), and depicting one of the eight divination symbols in the Chinese Book of Changes (i-ching)
T'ae-gŭk p'al-jang p'um-se	WTF T'ae-gŭk pattern practiced by 2nd Grade - representing "Earth" (the source of life, the root, and also the beginning and the end), and depicting one of the eight divination symbols in the Chinese Book of Changes (i-ching)
T'ae-gŭk sa-jang p'um-se	WTF T'ae-gŭk pattern practiced by 6th Grade - representing "Thunder and Lightning" (great power and dignity), and depicting one of the eight divination symbols in the Chinese Book of Changes (i-ching)
T'ae-gŭk sam-jang p'um-se	WTF T'ae-gŭk pattern practiced by 7th Grade - representing "Fire" and the sun (brightness, light and heat), and depicting one of the eight divination symbols in the Chinese Book of Changes (i-ching)

T'ae-gŭk yuk-jang p'um-se	WTF T'ae-gŭk pattern practiced by 4th Grade - representing "Water" (incessant flow, formless flexibility, softness), and depicting one of the eight divination symbols in the Chinese Book of Changes (i-ching)
T'ae-kwŏn-Do	Korean Martial Art named in 1955 by General Choi Hong Hi (the Father of Taekwon-Do), literally meaning Foot-Fist-Way - the term Taekwon-Do was chosen due to its similarity to the term T'ae-Kyŏn, however, the individual words each originate from the Chinese set of characters 跆 拳 道 (pronounced in Chinese as *tai-quan-dao*)
T'ae-Kyŏn	Ancient Korean Martial Art dating back to 37 B.C.
t'ae-san mil-gi	Mountain Pushing (WTF)
T'oi-Gye t'ŭl	ITF pattern practiced by 3rd Grade [Pen name of the noted scholar Yi Hwang (1501-1570), an authority on neo-confucianism." The pattern diagram is in the shape of the Chinese character 士 (pronounced in Chinese as *shi*), meaning scholar, officer, or soldier and therefore represents scholar]
T'ong-Il t'ŭl	ITF pattern practiced by 6th Degree [Denotes the resolution of the unification of Korea which has been divided since 1945]
t'ong mil-gi	Push Barrel (WTF)
t'ong mil-gi chun-bi sŏ-gi	Pushing-hands Ready Stance (WTF)
t'om-nal p'a-do	Saw-tooth Wave (ITF) [t'om-nal is defined as a saw-blade]

t'ŏk	Chin or Jaw
t'ŏk kwan-jŏl	Mandibula
t'ŏk-gŏ-ri	Chin-up
t'ŭl	ITF term for Patterns [t'ŭl is defined as a framework, a frame, or a matrix]
t'ŭl-lim	Incorrect [t'ŭl-lim is derived from the verb t'ŭl-li-da (틀리다), meaning to go wrong (amiss, awry), to become wrong, to be mistaken (erroneous, incorrect, different)]

u 우

U-ja chi-rŭ-gi	U-Shape Punch (WTF) [U-ja literally means "U-Shaped", like the English letter "U"]
um	Negative, feminine, shade, or cloudy - originating from the Chinese term 陰 (pronounced in Chinese as y*in*)]
un-dong	Exercise (ITF), movement, motion, exercise, sports, or athletics

ŭ 으

Ŭl-Ji t'ŭl	ITF pattern practiced by 4th Degree [Named after General Ŭl Ji Mun Dok who successfully defended Korea against a Tang's invasion force of nearly one million soldiers led by Yang Je in 612 A.D.]

180

ŭi 의

Ŭi-Am t'ŭl	ITF pattern practiced by 2nd Degree [Pseudonym of Son Byong Hi, leader of the Korean Independence Movement on March 1, 1919]

wi 위

wi	Upper Part, Upside, Top Side, or Above
wi p'al-gup	Upper Elbow
wi p'al-gup ttae-ri-gi	Upper Elbow Strike (ITF)
wi-ro	Upward
wi-ro ppae-gi	Upward Pull-out (WTF)
wi twit p'al-gup ttae-ri-gi	Upper and Back Elbow Strike (ITF)
wit mok	Upper Neck
wit t'ŏk	Angle of the Mandible (upper jaw)

wŏ 워

Wŏn-Hyo t'ŭl	ITF pattern practiced by 6th Grade [Named after noted monk Wŏn Hyo (617 A.D. - 686 A.D.) who introduced Buddhism to the Shilla Dynasty in the year 686 A.D.]

ya 야

yak-sok	Pre-arranged [yak-sok is derived from the verb yak-sok-ha-da (약속하다), meaning to make an appointment, an engagement, or an agreement]
yak-sok cha-yu mat-sŏ-gi	Pre-arranged Free Sparring (ITF)

yak-sok i-bo mat-sŏ-gi	Pre-arranged Two-step Sparring (ITF)
yak-sok il-bo mat-sŏ-gi	Pre-arranged One-step Sparring (ITF)
yak-sok mat-sŏ-gi	Pre-arranged Sparring (ITF)
yak-sok mo-bŏm mat-sŏ-gi	Pre-arranged Model Sparring (ITF)
yak-sok sam-bo mat-sŏ-gi	Pre-arranged Three-step Sparring (ITF)
yak-sok tae-ryŏn	Pre-arranged Sparring (WTF)
ya-kan	Weak [ya-kan is derived from the verb ya-ka-da (약하다), meaning to be weak, to be frail, to be delicate, to faint, or to be feeble]
yang	Positive, masculine, light, or sunny side of the Yin and Yang - originating from the Chinese term 陽 (pronounced in Chinese as *yang*)
yang-tchok sam-bo mat-sŏ-gi	Two-way Three-step Sparring (ITF)

ye 예

ye	Yes
ye-jol	Etiquette, propriety, decorum, manners
ye-ŭi	Courtesy, politeness, civility - originating from the Chinese term 禮義 (pronounced in Chinese as *li-yi*)

yo 요

yo-gol	Radius
yo-gol shin-gyŏng	Radial Nerve

yŏ 여

yŏ-dŏl — Eight [in Native Korean]

yŏ-dŏl-tchae — Eighth [in Native Korean]

yŏ-haeng — Travel

yŏk-sa — History

yŏl — Ten [in Native Korean]

yŏl-tchae — Tenth [in Native Korean]

yŏm-ch'i — Integrity, a sense of honor, or a sense of shame - originating from the Chinese term 廉恥 (pronounced in Chinese as *lian-chi*)

Yŏn-Gae t'ŭl — ITF pattern practiced by 4th Degree [Named after a famous general during the Koguryo Dynasty, Yŏn Gae So Moon, who forced the Chinese Tang Dynasty to quit it's invasion of Korea in 649 A.D.]

yŏn-maeng — Federation, league, union, confederation, or alliance

yŏn-sok — Continuous (ITF) [yŏn-sok is derived from the verb yŏn-sok-ha-da (연 속하 다), meaning to continue, to be continuous, to last, or to follow one after another]

yŏn-sok ch'a-gi — Consecutive Kick (continuous) (ITF)

yŏn-sok kong-gyŏk — Consecutive Attack (ITF)

yŏn-sok tong-jak — Continuous Motion (ITF)

183

yŏn-sŭp	Exercises (ITF) [yŏn-sŭp is derived from the verb yŏn-sŭp-ha-da (연 습하다), meaning to practice, to carry out, to exercise, or to hold (carry out) maneuvers]
yŏp	Side or Flank
yŏp ap ch'a-mil-gi	Side Front Pushing Kick (ITF)
yŏp ap ch'a-pu-su-gi	Side Front Snap Kick [smashing] (ITF)
yŏp ap ch'a-gi	Side Front Kick (ITF)
yŏp ap mak-ki	Side Front Block (ITF)
yŏp ap tchi-rŭ-gi	Side Front Punch (ITF)
yŏp ap ttae-ri-gi	Side Front Strike (ITF)
yŏp ap ttul-ki	Side Front Thrust (ITF)
yŏp chi-rŭ-gi	Side Punch (WTF)
yŏp chu-mŏk	Side Fist (ITF)
yŏp ch'a-gi	Side Kick (ITF&WTF)
yŏp ch'a-mil-gi	Side Pushing Kick (ITF)
yŏp ch'a-mŏm-ch'u-gi	Side Checking Kick (ITF)
yŏp ch'a-ol-li-gi	Side Rising Kick (ITF)
yŏp ch'a-tchi-rŭ-gi	Side Piercing Kick (ITF)
yŏp ch'a-ttul-ki	Side Thrusting Kick (ITF)
yŏp ch'i-gi	Side Hit (WTF)
yŏp kŭt-gi	Side Cross-cut (ITF)
yŏp mak-ki	Side Block (ITF&WTF)
yŏp mu-rŭp	Side Knee
yŏp nae-ryŏ ttae-ri-gi	Side Downward Strike (ITF)
yŏp pal-dŭng	Side Instep
yŏp p'al-gup	Side Elbow

yŏp p'al-gup ttul-ki	Side Elbow Thrust (ITF)
yŏp pal-ba-dak	Side Foot (bottom) Sole (ITF)
yŏp se-wŏ tchi-rŭ-gi	Side Vertical Punch (ITF)
yŏp tchi-rŭ-gi	Side Punch (ITF)
yŏp tchi-rŭ-myŏ ch'a-gi	Side Punching Kick (ITF) [Airborne Combination]
yŏp tol-lyŏ ch'a-gi	Side Turning Kick (ITF)
yŏp ttae-ri-gi	Side Strike (ITF)
yŏp ttul-ki	Side Thrust (ITF)
yŏp t'ŏk	Side Jaw
yŏp-guri	Flank or side (ITF)
yŏp-mom	Side Facing (ITF), side of the body
yŏp twit ttae-ri-gi	Side Back Strike (ITF)
yŏp twit ttul-ki	Side Back Thrust (ITF)
yŏ-sŏt	Six [in Native Korean]
yŏ-sŏt-tchae	Sixth [in Native Korean]

yu 유

yu-in mak-ki	Luring Block (ITF) [yu-in is derived from the verb yu-in-ha-da (유인하다), meaning to tempt, to allure, to lure, to decoy, to induce, to entice, or to seduce]
yuk	Six [in Sino-Korean] - originating from the Chinese term for six, 六 (pronounced in Chinese as *liu*)
yuk-dan	Sixth Degree Black Belt (ITF&WTF)
yuk-gŭp	Sixth Grade (ITF&WTF) [Low Green Belt]

Yul-Gok t'ŭl	ITF pattern practiced by 5th Grade [Pseudonym of the great philosopher and scholar Yi I (1536 - 1584), nicknamed the "Confucius of Korea." The pattern diagram is in the shape of the Chinese character 士 pronounced in Chinese as *shi*), meaning scholar, officer, or soldier and therefore represents scholar]
Yun-Mu Kwan	Korean Martial Art school founded by Sup Jun Song in 1945
yu-ri	yu-ri is defined as isolation or separation
yu-ri nŭk-gol	Floating Rib [Sino-Korean]
Yu-Shin t'ŭl	ITF pattern practiced by 3rd Degree [Named after General Kim Yu Shin (595 A.D. - 673 A.D.), a commanding general during the Shilla Dynasty]

Chapter 4
(제 4 장)

Nomenclature by Category

The relationship between words is sometimes more evident when they are grouped together. The terms in Chapter 4 have been arranged into 21 sections of related terms. For example, some of the categories are numbers, commands, rank, strikes, blocks, and kicks. Each category is arranged in a logical sequence for the specific subject, allowing the reader to quickly find terms grouped together instead of paging through Chapters 2 or 3 to find individual entries such as numbers. It should be noted that several terms in this chapter may not be found elsewhere in this book (e.g., a short section on Korean phrases like; How are you?, Thank you very much, etc.). Another unique section (see page 295) deals with the translation rules for complex combinations of technical terms, such as, "flying side pushing kick with a punch.."

To find out how to write any terms in Chapter 4 which do not have Han-gŭl entries, simply look up each term in Chapter 2. In order to find out more information on the meaning of individual terms, look them up in Chapter 3. Hints on Han-gŭl pronunciation can be found in the appendices.

Class

Commands

myŏng-nyŏng-ŏ (명 령 어)

Korean terms listed in this section are those most often used in conducting Korean based martial arts classes and often have military commands as their basis. All terms in this section are listed in alphabetical order according to their English equivalent.

About Face (ITF&WTF)	twi to-ra or twi-ro to-ra
Again	tas-hi
At Ease	swi-ŏt
Attention	ch'a-ryŏt
Begin	shi-jak
Bow [salute]	kyŏng-nye
Break [separate]	kal-lyŏ
Change Direction (ITF)	pang-hyang pa-kku-gi
Commence (ITF)	shi-jak
Continue	gye-sok
Dismissed	hae-san

191

Face the [national] Flag	kuk-gi-e tae-ha-yŏ
Face the Instructor	sa-bŏm-nim kke
Kneel [sit down]	an-jŏ
Line Up	chul-lo-sŏ
Meditate	mung-nyŏm
Ready	chun-bi
Return [to a position]	pa-ro
Salute	kyŏng-nye
Salute the [National] Flag	kuk-gi-e tae-ha-yŏ kyŏng-nye
Sit Down	an-jŏ
Sitting Stance Punch (ITF)	an-nŭn sŏ tchi-rŭ-gi
Start	shi-jak
Stop	kŭ-man or chŏng-ji
Turn Around (ITF&WTF) [about face]	twi-ro to-ra

Taekwon-Do

Moral

Culture

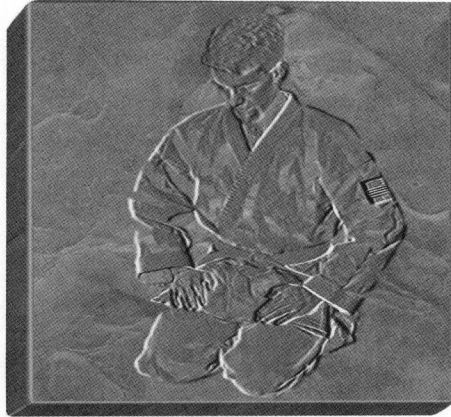

T'ae-kwŏn-Do chŏng-shin su-yang
(태권도 정신 수양)

This section brings together Korean terms which are related to the behavior of a martial artist, both inside and outside the to-jang. It includes the ancient Korean code of the Hwa-rang, the Tenets of Taekwon-Do, the Student Oath, and additional terms related to the philosophy of Taekwon-Do. Most of these concepts are also common in modified forms in other Korean martial arts as they are based on mutual historical values from the Korean culture. The section also includes additional terms associated with the spirit of the martial artist. These terms often stem from Buddhism or Confucianism teachings although many are also common in other religions (i.e., nobility; wisdom; trust worthiness; loyalty to family, friends, school, nation, etc.; humbleness, following the path of the righteous warrior; etc.) All of the terms in this section are listed in a logical sequence by topic.

Student Oath

I Shall Observe the Tenets of Taekwon-Do .
Na-nŭn T'ae-kwŏn-Do chŏng-shi-nŭl chun-su-han-da .
나 는 태권도 정신을   준수한다 ·

I Shall Respect the Instructor and Seniors .
Na-nŭn sabŏm-kwa sŏn-bae-rŭl chon-gyŏng-han-da .
나 는 서범과 선배를 존경한다 ·

I Shall Never Misuse Taekwon-Do .
Na-nŭn T'ae-kwŏn-Do-rŭl chŏl-dae nam-yong-ch'i an-ket-da .
나 는 태권도를 절대 남용치 않겠다 ·

I Shall be a Champion of Freedom and Justice .
Na-nŭn cha-yu-wa chŏng-ŭi-ŭi sa-do-ga twi-ket-da .
나 는 자유와 정의의 사도가 되겠다 ·

I Shall Build a More Peaceful World .
Na-nŭn po-da dŏ p'yŏng-hwa-sŭ-rŏ-un
    il-lyu-sa-hwi-rŭl i-ruk-ha-get-da .
나 는 보다 더 평화스러 운 인류사회를 이룩하겠다 ·

Tenets   chŏng-shin (정 신)

Courtesy	ye-ŭi
Integrity	yŏm-ch'i
Perseverance	in-nae
Self Control	kŭk-gi
Indomitable Spirit	paek-jŏl-bul-gul

Other Terms

Cold Showers and Baths	naeng-su ma-ch'al
Concentration (ITF&WTF)	ki-hap
Etiquette	ye-jŏl
Humanity	in-gan-mi
Humility	kyŏm-son
Hwa-rang Code of Ethics	Hwa-rang Do
Moral Culture	chŏng-shin su-yang
Public Service	sa-hoe pong-sa
Righteousness	chŏng-ŭi
Student / Instructor Relationship (ITF)	sa-je-ji-do
Tenets (ITF)	chŏng-shin
Travel	yŏ-haeng
Trust	shin-yong
Virtue	mi-dŏk

Hwa-rang Code of Ethics
Hwa-rang Do

Be Loyal to the King .
Im-gŭ-me, ch'ung-sŏng ha-go .
임금에 충성 하고 ·

Be Dutiful to Your Parents .
Pu-mo-e, hyo-do ha-go .
부모에 효도 하고 ·

Make a Friend in Trust .
Pŏt-gwa-nŭn, shi-ni-mŭ-ro sa-gwi-go .
벗과는 신임 으로 사귀고·

Never Retreat in Battle .
Chŏn-jaeng-e-sŏn, gyŏl-k'o hu-t'wi-ha-ji mal-myŏ .
전쟁에선 결코 후퇴하지 말며 ·

Kill an Animal, if Only Appropriate .
Sal-saeng-ŭn, ttae-wa chang-so-rŭl t'aek-ha-ra .
살생은 때와 장소를 택하라·

Ranking

System

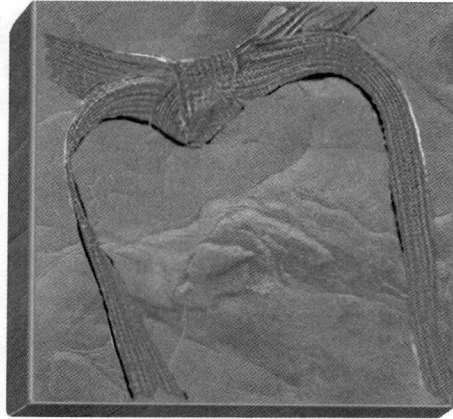

gye-gŭp che-do (계급 제도)

In this section, the Martial Artist can find terms relating to rank, seniority, and belt colors. General terms (both ITF & WTF) and colors are listed first, then belt colors (in rank order), followed by the gŭp ranking order and then the dan ranking order.

General Terms

Assistant Instructor (ITF)	pu-sa-bŏm
Certificate	cha-gyŏk-jŭng
Classification of Instructor (ITF)	sa-bŏm pu-ryu
Degree Certificate (ITF)	tan-jŭng
Grade Certificate	kŭp-jŭng
Instructor - Teacher (ITF&WTF)	sa-bŏm
Master Instructor (ITF)	sa-hyŏn
Junior (WTF)	hu-bae

General Terms - (continued)

Promotion Test	sŭng-kŭp shim-sa
Rank (ITF)	gye-gŭp
Rank, Grade (WTF)	p'um-gye
Grand Master	sa-sŏng (ITF) or kwan-jang (WTF)
Senior (WTF)	sŏn-bae
Student (WTF)	su-ryŏn-saeng
System of Ranking	tan-gŭp che-do
Test for Rank Promotion	shim-sa

Colors   saek (색)

White	hin saek
Yellow	no-ran saek
Green	ch'o-rok saek
Blue	p'u-rŭn saek
Red	ppal-gan saek
Black	kŏ-mŭn saek

Belt Colors (ITF&WTF)   tti saek (띠 색)

White Belt	hin tti
White Belt with a Yellow Stripe	hin tti-e no-ran sŏn
Yellow Belt	no-ran tti
Yellow Belt with a Green Stripe	no-ran tti-e ch'o-rok sŏn
Green Belt	ch'o-rok tti
Green Belt with a Blue Stripe	ch'o-rok tti-e p'u-rŭn sŏn
Blue Belt	p'u-rŭn tti
Blue Belt with a Red Stripe	p'u-rŭn tti-e ppal-gan sŏn
Red Belt	ppal-gan tti
Red Belt with a Black Stripe	ppal-gan tti-e kŏ-mŭn sŏn
Black Belt	kŏ-mŭn tti

Grade (ITF&WTF)
Colored Belt Ranking

kŭp (급)

Tenth Grade (Low White Belt)	ship-gŭp
Ninth Grade (High White Belt)	ku-gŭp
Eighth Grade (Low Yellow Belt)	p'al-gŭp
Seventh Grade (High Yellow Belt)	ch'il-gŭp
Sixth Grade (Low Green Belt)	yuk-gŭp
Fifth Grade (High Green Belt)	o-gŭp
Fourth Grade (Low Blue Belt)	sa-gŭp
Third Grade (High Blue Belt)	sam-gŭp
Second Grade (Low Red Belt)	i-gŭp
First Grade (High Red Belt)	il-gŭp

Degree (ITF&WTF)
Black Belt Ranking

tan

(단)

Beginning Black Belt	ch'ŏt-dan
Beginning Junior Black Belt	ch'ŏt-pum
Degree Certificate	tan-jŭng
First Degree Black Belt	il-dan
First Degree Junior Black Belt (WTF only)	il-pum
Second Degree Black Belt	i-dan
Second Degree Junior Black Belt (WTF only)	i-pum
Third Degree Black Belt	sam-dan
Third Degree Junior Black Belt (WTF only)	sam-pum
Fourth Degree Black Belt	sa-dan
Fifth Degree Black Belt	o-dan
Sixth Degree Black Belt	yuk-dan
Seventh Degree Black Belt	ch'il-dan
Eighth Degree Black Belt	p'al-dan
Ninth Degree Black Belt	ku-dan
Tenth Degree Black Belt	ship-dan

Numbering

sut-ja (숫 자)

Korean numbers are often used in martial arts. For example, a stretching exercise may be held for a certain count and degree ranking and certain patterns are numbered first, second, third etc. In this section we will only present the numbers most often used by martial artists. The reader should refer to the bibliography for more detailed information.

In written text, Koreans not only use Han-gŭl to represent the numbers (일, 이, 삼 , ... ; or 하나, 둘 , 셋 , ...), but they also use Roman numerals (I, II, III, ...), Arabic numbers (1, 2, 3, ...), and Chinese characters (一 , 二 , 三 , ...). However, there are basically two numbering systems; Sino-Korean and native Korean. Both are used for either counting, ordering, and identifying.

Sino-Korean cardinal numbers stem from Chinese, but are pronounced a bit differently in Korean, and are written in either Chinese or Han-gŭl. Native Korean cardinal numbers are purely Korean and are only written in Han-gŭl. Native Korean cardinal numbers are often used when counting aloud. For example, you would say, "ha-na, tul, set, .." while executing a series of kicks. It should be noted that native Korean cardinal numbers only extend to the number 99. After this, Sino-Korean numbers are used.

When numbering items for placement, ordinal numbers are used (first, second, third, etc.). Native Korean ordinal numbers begin with ch'ŏt-tchae, tul-tchae, se-tchae, etc., while Sino-Korean ordinal numbers begin with che-il, che-i, che-sam, etc. in Sino-Korean. There are also several identifies which are used to specify the type of object being counted. In this section we will present only representative numbers (both Sino-Korean and native Korean) which might apply to martial arts. We will not discuss the identifiers needed to specify the types of objects being counted. Much of the information in this section is not found in previous chapters, and as such, Han-gŭl letters have been included to aid the reader. Terms in this section are listed in sequence in cardinal and ordinal numbering tables.

Cardinal Numbers

#	Sino-Korean		Native Korean	
1	il	일	ha-na (han-)	하나 (한)
2	i	이	tul (tu-)	둘 (두)
3	sam	삼	set (se-)	셋 (세)
4	sa	사	net (ne-)	넷 (네)
5	o	오	ta-sŏt	다섯
6	yuk	육	yŏ-sŏt	여섯
7	ch'il	칠	il-gop	일곱
8	p'al	팔	yŏ-dŏl	여덟
9	ku	구	a-hop	아홉
10	ship	십	yŏl	열

Cardinal Numbers -continued

#	Sino-Korean		Native Korean	
11	shi-bil	십 일	yŏl-ha-na	열 하나
12	shi-bi	십 이	yŏl-tul	열 둘
13	ship-sam	십 삼	yŏl-set	열 셋
14	ship-sa	십 사	yŏl-net	열 넷
15	shi-bo	십 오	yŏl-ta-sŏt	열다섯
16	shim-yuk	십 육	yŏl-yŏ-sŏt	열 여섯
17	ship-ch'il	십 칠	yŏl-il-gop	열 일곱
18	ship-p'al	십 팔	yŏl-yŏ-dŏl	열여덟
19	ship-ku	십 구	yŏl-a-hop	열 아홉
20	i-ship	이 십	sŭ-mul	스물
21	i-shi-bil	이십일	sŭ-mul-ha-na	스물 하나
22	i-shi-bi	이 십 이	sŭ-mul-dul	스물 둘
23	i-ship-sam	이 십 삼	sŭ-mul-set	스물 셋
24	i-ship-sa	이 십 사	sŭ-mul-net	스물 넷
30	sam-ship	삼 십	sŏ-rŭn	서른
40	sa-ship	사 십	ma-hŭn	마흔
50	o-ship	오십	swin	쉰
60	yuk-ship	육 십	ye-sun	예순
70	ch'il-ship	칠 십	il-hŭn	일흔
80	p'al-ship	팔 십	yŏ-dŭn	여든
90	ku-ship	구 십	a-hŭn	아흔

Cardinal Numbers -continued

#	Sino-Korean		Native Korean
100	paek	백	native Korean numbers only go up to 99, after that Sino-Korean numbers are used
1,000	ch'ŏn	천	
10,000	man	만	
100,000	ship-man	십만	
1,000,000	paek-man	백만	

Ordinal Numbers

#	Sino-Korean		Native Korean	
1st	che-il-	제 일 -	ch'ŏt-tchae	첫 째
2nd	che-i-	제 이 -	tul-tchae	둘 째
3rd	che-sam-	제 삼 -	se-tchae	세 째
4th	che-sa-	제 사 -	ne-tchae	넷 째
5th	che-o-	제 오 -	ta-sŏt-tchae	다섯 째
6th	che-yuk-	제 육-	yŏ-sŏt-tchae	여섯 째
7th	che-ch'il-	제 칠-	il-gop-tchae	일곱 째
8th	che-p'al-	제 팔-	yŏ-dŏl-tchae	여덟 째
9th	che-ku-	제 구 -	a-hop-tchae	아홉째
10th	che-ship-	제 십-	yŏl-tchae	열 째

Taekwon-Do

Principles and

Theory

$$F=m\int\frac{\Delta V}{\Delta t}$$

$$E=1/2\,mv^2$$

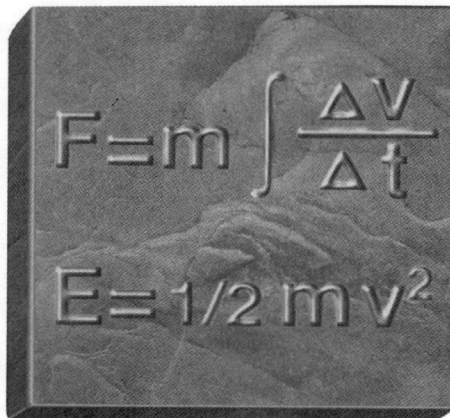

T'ae-kwŏn-Do wŏl-li-wa i-ron
(태권도 원리와 이론)

In this section we have grouped terms which are related to the theory of Taekwon-Do. Many of these terms are common to all martial arts, as they all include concepts such as balance, power, concentration, etc. All of the terms in this section are listed in alphabetical order according to their English equivalent.

Balance	chung-shim
Breath Control (ITF)	ho-hŭp cho-jŏl
Center of Gravity	chung-nyŏk chung-shim
Cold Showers and Baths	naeng-su ma-ch'al
Composition (ITF)	ku-sŏng
Concentration (WTF)	chip-jung
Concentration (ITF&WTF)	ki-hap
Dynamic Stability (ITF)	tong-jŏk an-jŏng

Equilibrium	kyun-hyŏng
Exercise (ITF)	un-dong
Exercises (ITF)	yŏn-sŭp
Flexibility	shin-ch'uk
Force	him
Fundamental Exercises	ki-bon yŏn-sŭp
Horizontal Wave (ITF)	su-p'yŏng p'a-do
Mass	chil-lyang
Movement	tong-jak
Motion	tong-jak
Philosophy	ch'ŏl-hak
Power	him
Public Service	sa-hoe pong-sa
Reaction Force (ITF)	pan-dong-nyŏk
Reflex (ITF)	pa-nŭng
Saw-tooth Wave (ITF)	t'om-nal p'ado
Sine Wave (ITF)	hwal-dŭng p'ado
Speed	sok-do
Speed and Reflex (ITF)	sok-do-wa pa-nŭng
Static Stability (ITF)	chŏng-jŏk an-jŏng
Theory of Power (ITF)	hi-mŭi wŏl-li
Wisdom	chi-hye

Physical

Tools

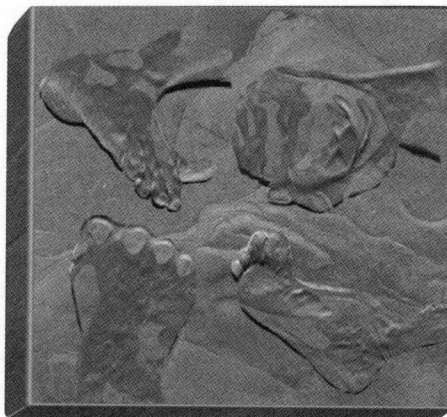

shin-ch'e ki-gu (신체 기구)

This section provides a grouping of many Korean terms used to identify the tools of the body that the martial artist might use for blocking or attacking (e.g., fist, angle fingertip, inner forearm, footsword, knifehand, etc.). There are many words that can be used to describe parts of the body. Individuals may choose as many words as they like to describe a specific part. Individual martial arts organizations, on the other hand, tend to standardize their terms for tools. The reader can further investigate the definitions of specific terms using Chapter 3. All of the terms listed in this section are in alphabetical order according to their English equivalent.

Angle Fingertip (ITF)	ho-mi son-kkŭt
Arc-fist (WTF)	a-gwi-son
Arc-hand (ITF)	pan-dal-son
Attacking Tools (ITF)	kong-gyŏk pu-wi
Back Elbow	twit p'al-gup
Backfist (ITF&WTF)	tŭng chu-mŏk
Back of Forearm [at Wrist]	tŭng p'al-mok

Backhand (ITF)	son-dŭng
Back Heel	twi-ch'uk
Back Sole [heel area] (ITF)	twi-kkum-ch'i
Back Sole	twi-ch'uk
Ball of the Foot	ap-kkum-ch'i
Base of Knifehand (ITF)	son-k'al pa-t'ang
Bear-hand (ITF&WTF)	kom-son
Blocking Tools (ITF)	mak-ki pu-wi
Bow Wrist	son-mok dŭng (ITF) or ku-p'in son-mok (WTF)
Chestnut Fist (WTF)	pam chu-mŏk
Combined All-fingertip (WTF)	mo-dŭm p'yŏn son-kkŭt
Combined Three Flat-fingertip (WTF)	mo-ŭn se p'yŏn son-kkŭt
Combined Two Flat-fingertip (WTF)	mo-ŭn tu p'yŏn son-kkŭt
Covering Fist (WTF)	po chu-mŏk
Double Backhand (ITF)	tu-son-dŭng
Double Finger (ITF)	tu-son-ga-rak
Double Finger Spear (ITF)	ka-wi son-kkŭt
Double Forearm (ITF)	tu-p'al-mok
Double Side Elbow (ITF)	tu yŏp p'al-gup
Edge of the Foot (ITF) [see Foot-blade or Footsword]	pal-lal
Edge of the Hand (ITF) [see hand-blade or Knifehand]	son-nal

Elbow [bottom]	p'al-gup
Elbow [general area]	p'al-kkum-ch'i
Finger Belly [bottom] (ITF)	son-ga-rak pa-dak
Finger Pincers WTF	chip-ge-son
Fingertip	son-kkŭt
Fist (ITF&WTF)	chu-mŏk
Flat Fingertip	ŏ-pŭn son-kkŭt (ITF) or p'yŏn son-kkŭt (WTF)
Flat-fist (WTF)	p'yŏn chu-mŏk
Foot	pal or t'ae [Sino-Korean]
Foot-back	pal-dŭng
Foot Back Sole [Heel] (ITF)	pal twi-kkum-ch'i
Foot-blade (WTF) [see Edge of the Foot or Footsword]	pal-lal
Foot-blade Back (WTF)	pal-lal dŭng
Foot Parts [lower half of body]	ha-ban-shin
Foot Sole [foot bottom]	pal-ba-dak
Front-sole	ap-ch'uk
Footsword [See Edge of the Foot or Foot-blade]	pal-k'al (ITF) or pal-lal (WTF)
Forearm [near the elbow]	p'al- kkum-ch'i or p'al-gup
Forearm [near the wrist]	p'al-mok
Forefinger (ITF)	han son-ga-rak
Forefist (ITF)	ap chu-mŏk
Fore-knuckle Fist (ITF)	in-ji chu-mŏk
Front Elbow (ITF)	ap p'al-gup

Hammer-fist (WTF)	me chu-mŏk
Hand	son
Hand-back (WTF)	son-dŭng
Hand-blade (WTF) [see Edge or the Hand or Knifehand]	son-nal
Hand-blade Back (WTF)	son-nal tŭng
Hand Parts [upper half of body]	sang-ban-shin
Head	mŏri
Heel [foot back sole] (ITF)	pal twi-kkum-ch'i
Heel [foot back sole, foot back heel] (WTF)	pal twi-ch'uk
Heel [back sole]	twi-ch'uk
Heel	twi-kkum-ch'i
Horizontal Forearm	su-p'yŏng p'al-mok
Inner Forearm [at wrist] (ITF&WTF)	an p'al-mok
Instep	pal-dŭng
Knee	mu-rŭp
Knifehand [see Edge of the Hand or Hand-blade]	son-k'al (ITF) or son-nal (WTF)
Knuckle Fist (ITF)	son-ga-rak chu-mŏk
Leg	ta-ri
Long Fist (ITF)	kin chu-mŏk
Middle Finger	chung-ji
Middle Knuckle Fist (ITF)	chung-ji chu-mŏk
Open-fist (ITF)	p'yŏn chu-mŏk

Outer Forearm [at the wrist] (WTF)	pa-kkat p'al-mok
Outside Forearm (ITF)	pa-kkat-p'al-mok
Palm [hand bottom] (ITF)	son-ba-dak
Palm Hand (WTF)	pa-t'ang-son
Palm-upward Fist (WTF)	che-ch'in chu-mŏk
Palm-upward Flat Fingertip (WTF)	che-ch'in p'yŏn son-kkŭt
Pincers Fist (WTF)	chip-ge chu-mŏk
Press Finger (ITF)	chi-ap
Reverse Footsword (ITF)	pal-k'al dŭng
Reverse Knifehand (ITF)	son-k'al dŭng
Scissors Fingertip (WTF)	ka-wi son-kkŭt
Shin	chŏng-gang-i
Side Elbow	yŏp p'al-gup
Side Fist (ITF)	yŏp chu-mŏk
Side Foot (bottom) Sole (ITF)	yŏp pal-ba-dak
Side Instep	yŏp pal-dŭng
Side Knee (ITF&WTF)	yŏp mu-rŭp
Single Fingertip (WTF)	han son-kkŭt
Single Fist (ITF)	oe chu-mŏk
Single Straight Forearm (ITF)	oe sŏn p'al-mok
Single Straight Knifehand (ITF)	oe sŏn son-k'al
Spear Hand (ITF)	p'yŏn son-kkŭt
Straight Elbow (ITF)	sŏn p'al-gup

Straight Fingertip (ITF)	sŏn son-kkŭt
Straight Forearm (ITF)	sŏn p'al-mok
Thumb Knuckle Fist (ITF)	ŏm-ji chu-mŏk
Thumb Ridge (ITF)	ŏm-ji pa-t'ang
Toes	pal-kkŭt
Toe Edge (ITF)	pal-ga-rak-nal
Twin Backfist (ITF)	ssang dŭng chu-mŏk
Twin Backhand (ITF)	ssang son-dŭng
Twin Elbow (ITF)	ssang p'al-gup
Twin Fist (ITF)	ssang chu-mŏk
Twin Knifehand (ITF)	ssang son-k'al
Twin Side Fist (ITF)	ssang yŏp chu-mŏk
Twin Straight Forearm (ITF)	ssang sŏn p'al-mok
Twin Straight Knifehand (ITF)	ssang sŏn son-k'al
Under Fist (ITF)	mit chu-mŏk
Under Forearm [at wrist] (ITF&WTF)	mit p'al-mok
Upper Elbow	wi p'al-gup
Upset Fingertip (ITF)	twi-ji-bŭn son-kkŭt
Upset Flat-fingertip (WTF)	ŏ-pŭn p'yŏn son-kkŭt
Vertical Fist (WTF)	se-un chu-mŏk
Vertical Flat-fingertip (WTF)	se-un p'yŏn son-kkŭt
Wrist	son-mok or p'al-mok
X-Backhand (ITF)	kyo-ch'a son-dŭng
X-Fist (ITF)	kyo-ch'a chu-mŏk
X-Knifehand (ITF)	kyo-ch'a son-k'al

Vital Spots

and

Body Parts

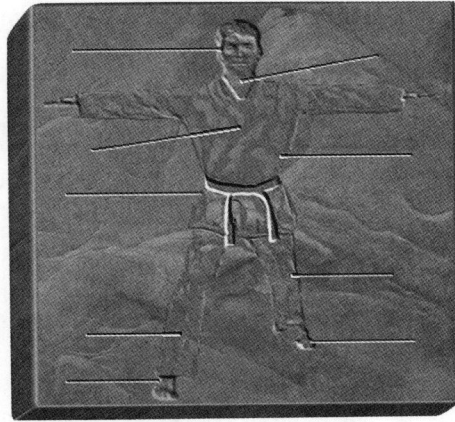

kŭp-so-wa shin-che pu-bun (급소와 신체 부분)

In this section we have grouped Korean terms which describe general body parts or places the martial artist might consider points of attack on an opponent. There are many words that can be used to describe parts of the body. Individuals may choose as many words as they like to describe a specific part. Individual martial arts organizations, on the other hand, tend to standardize their terms for vital spots and targets. The reader can further investigate the definitions of specific terms using Chapter 3. All of the terms in this section are listed in alphabetical order according to their English equivalent.

Abdomen	pok-bu
Achilles Heel	twi-ch'uk yak-jŏm
Achilles Tendon	twi-ch'uk him-jul
Adam's Apple	kyŏl-hu
Angle of the Mandible [upper jaw]	wit t'ŏk
Ankle	pal-mok

Ankle Joint	pal-mok kwan-jŏl
Arm	p'al
Armpit	kyŏ-dŭ-rang-i
Artery	tong-maek
Back	tŭng
Back Leg	twit-da-ri
Back Tibia [Achilles tendon area]	twit kyŏng-gol
Back Wrist Artery	tŭng son-mok tong-maek
Body	mom
Body - Middle Part	mom-t'ong pu-wi
Bone	ppyŏ or -gol [Sino-Korean]
Brachial Plexus	sang-wan shin-gyŏng
Bridge of the Nose	mi-gan
Cervical Bundle	kyŏng-bu
Cervical Vertebrae	kyŏng-gol
Cheek Bone	kwang-dae ppyŏ
Chest	ka-sŭm
Chin	t'ŏk
Clavicle	swae-gol
Coccyx	mi-gol
Ear	kwi
Elbow [bottom]	p'al-gup
Elbow [general area]	p'al-kkum-ch'i
Elbow Joint	p'al-gup kwan-jŏl

Extremities	p'al-gwa-da-ri
Eye	nun
Eyes [region]	an-bu
Eyeball	an-gu
Face	ŏl-gul
Face Area	an-myŏn [Sino-Korean]
Face Parts	ŏl-gul pu-wi
Femur	tae-t'wi-gol
Fibula	pi-gol
Finger Joint	son-ga-rak kwan-jŏl
Floating Rib	yu-ri nŭk-gol
Focus Point (ITF)	ch'o-jŏm
Foot	pal or t'ae [Sino-Korean]
Forehead	i-ma
Fossa of the Knee	o-gŭm
Front Leg (ITF)	ap ta-ri
Groin	sa-t'a-gun-i
Hand	son
Head	mŏ-ri
Heart	shim-jang
Heel [foot back sole] (ITF)	pal twi-kkum-ch'i
Heel [foot back sole, foot back heel] (WTF)	pal twi-ch'uk
Heel [back sole]	twi-ch'uk
Heel	twi-kkum-ch'i

High Abdomen	sang-bok-bu
Hip Joint	ŏng-dŏng-i kwan-jŏl
Humerous	sang-bak-gol
Inner Ankle Joint	an pal-mok kwan-jŏl
Inner Tibia	an kyŏng-gol
Inside Thigh	an-tchok hŏ-bŏk-da-ri
Instep	pal-dŭng
Intercostal Nerve	nŭk-gol shin-gyŏng
Jaw	t'ŏk
Joint	kwan-jŏl
Kidney	k'ong-p'at
Knee Hollow (WTF)	o-gŭm
Knee Joint	mu-rŭp kwan-jŏl
Lead Leg	ap ta-ri
Left Arm	oen p'al
Left Foot	oen pal
Left Hand	oen son
Left Leg	oen ta-ri
Leg	ta-ri
Lips	ip-sul
Liver	kan-jang
Low Part [body]	a-rae pu-bun
Lower Abdomen	ha-bok-bu
Mandible Bone	ha-ak-gol

Mandibula	t'ŏk kwan-jŏl
Mastoid	hu-i-bu
Maxilla Bone	sang-ak-gol
Median Nerve	chung-gan shin-gyŏng
Muscle	kŭn-yuk
Neck	mok
Neck Artery [Carotid]	mok tong-maek
Nerve	shin-gyŏng
Nose	k'o
Occiput	hu-du-bu
Occipital Bone	hu-du-gol
Outside Ankle Joint	pa-kkat pal-mok kwan-jŏl
Outside Tibia [Fibula]	pa-kkat kyŏng-gol
Patella	sŭl-gae-gol
Philtrum	in-jung
Point of the Chin	mit t'ŏk
Pubic Region (ITF)	ch'i-bu
Pubis (WTF)	ch'i-gol
Radial Artery	maek-bak son-mok tong-maek
Radial Nerve	yo-gol shin-gyŏng
Radius	yo-gol
Rear Leg	twit ta-ri
Ribs	nŭk-gol [Sino-Korean]
Right Arm	o-rŭn p'al

Right Foot	o-rŭn pal
Right Hand	o-rŭn son
Right Leg	o-rŭn ta-ri
Sciatic Nerve	chwa-gol shin-gyŏng
Shin	chŏng-gang-i
Shoulder	ŏ-kkae
Shoulder Joint	ŏ-kkae kwan-jŏl
Side Jaw	yŏp t'ŏk
Skull	tu-gae-gol
Small of the Back	kyŏng-ch'u
Solar Plexus	myŏng-ch'i
Spinal Chord [nerve]	ch'ŏk-ch'u shin-gyŏng
Spine	ch'ŏk-ju
Spleen	pi-jang
Sternum	hyung-gol
Temporal Bone	ch'ŭk-du-gol
Temporo-mandibular Joint	kwan-ja-no-ri
Temple	no-ri
Tendon	him-jul
Thenar [thumb knuckle web]	ŏm-ji-gu
Throat	mok-gu-mŏng
Thumb	ŏm-ji son-ga-rak
Thumb Joint	ŏm-ji kwan-jŏl

Tibia (ITF)	kyŏng-gol
Tibial Nerve	kyŏng-gol shin-gyŏng
Toe	pal-ga-rak
Trunk of the Body	mom-t'ong
Ulna	ch'ŏk-gol
Ulnar Nerve	ch'ŏk-gol shin-gyŏng
Umbilicus	pae-kkob
Upper Abdomen	sang-bok-bu
Upper Arm	p'al-juk-ji
Upper Back	kyŏn-gap
Upper Neck	wit mok
Vital Spots (ITF)	kŭp-so
Waist	hŏ-ri
Windpipe	sum-t'ong
Wrist	son-mok or p'al-mok
Wrist Joint	son-mok kwan-jŏl

Locations

and

Directions

wi-chi-wa pang-hyang (위치와 방향)

Terms listed in this section are those used to specify general locations of techniques, directions of movement, and levels at which techniques are performed. There are many words that can be used to describe directions or locations. Individuals may choose as many words as they like to describe these. Individual martial arts organizations, on the other hand, tend to standardize these terms. The reader can further investigate the definitions of specific terms using Chapter 3. All terms in this section are listed in alphabetical order according to their English equivalent.

Back	twi , twit or tŭng
Change Direction (WTF)	pang-hyang pa-kku-gi
Clockwise [turn] (ITF)	o-rŭn-tchok-ŭ-ro to-nŭn
Counter Clockwise [turn] (ITF)	oen-tchok-ŭ-ro to-nŭn
Downward	nae-ryŏ
End or Tip	kkŭt
Face [High Section] (WTF)	ŏl-gul

Flank or Side	yŏp-gu-ri
Front	ap
Full Facing (ITF)	on-mom
Half Facing (ITF)	pan-mom
High (ITF)	no-p'ŭn-dae
High Level (ITF)	sang-dan
High Section (ITF)	no-p'ŭn pu-bun
High Section (WTF)	ŏl-gul
Inner	an-
Inside [area]	an-tchok
Inward	an-ŭ-ro
Left -	oen-
Left Side [direction]	oen-tchok
Low (ITF)	na-jŭn-dae
Low Level	ha-dan
Low Section (ITF)	na-jŭn pu-bun
Low Section (WTF)	a-rae
Middle (ITF)	ka-un-dae
Middle Level	chung-dan [Sino-Korean]
Middle Section (ITF)	ka-un-dae pu-bun
Middle Section (WTF)	mom-t'ong
Obverse (ITF)	pa-ro
Outer	pa-kkat
Outside	pa-kkat

Outward	pak-kŭ-ro
Reverse (ITF)	pan-dae
Right -	orŭn-
Right Side [direction]	orŭn-tchok
Section of the Body (ITF)	mom- t'ong pun or mom pu-bun
Side	yŏp
Side Facing (ITF)	yŏp-mom
Side [flank, lateral] (ITF)	ch'ŭk-myŏn
Tip or End	kkŭt
Toward - "A"	"A" -bang
Toward - "B"	"B" -bang
Toward - "C"	"C" -bang
Toward - "D"	"D" -bang
Trunk [Middle Section] (WTF)	mom-t'ong
Under	mit or a-rae
Upper	wi
Upward	ol-lyŏ or wi-ro

Stances

sŏ-gi (서기)

Terms listed in this section are associated with stances. They are listed in alphabetical order according to their English equivalent. There are many words that can be used to describe stance positioning. Individuals may choose as many words as they like to describe a specific stance. Individual martial arts organizations, on the other hand, tend to standardize their terms for a given stance. The reader can further investigate definitions of specific terms using Chapter 3.

Assisting Stance (WTF)	kyŏt-da-ri sŏ-gi
At Ease Stance (WTF)	p'yŏn-hi sŏ-gi
Attention Stance (ITF&WTF)	ch'a-ryŏt sŏ-gi
Attention Stance (WTF)	twi-ch'uk mo-a sŏ-gi
Back Inflection Stance (WTF)	twit ku-bi
Backward Cross Stance (WTF)	twit kko-a sŏ-gi
Basic Ready Stance (WTF)	ki-bon chun-bi sŏ-gi
Bending Ready Stance (ITF)	ku-bu-ryŏ chun-bi sŏ-gi

227

Bending Stance (ITF)	ku-bu-ryŏ sŏ-gi
Close Attention Stance (WTF)	mo chu-ch'um sŏ-gi
Close Ready Stance (ITF)	mo-a chun-bi sŏ-gi
Close Stance (ITF&WTF)	mo-a sŏ-gi
Covered-Fist Ready Stance (WTF)	po chu-mŏk chun-bi sŏ-gi
Crane Stance (WTF)	hak-da-ri sŏ-gi
Cross Stance (WTF)	kko-a sŏ-gi
Crouched Stance (ITF)	o-gŭ-ryŏ sŏ-gi
Diagonal Stance (ITF)	sa-sŏn sŏ-gi
Fighting Stance (WTF)	kyŏ-rum-se sŏ-gi
Fists on the Waist Ready Stance (WTF)	tu chu-mŏk hŏ-ri chun-bi sŏ-gi
Fixed Stance (ITF)	ko-jŏng sŏ-gi
Forward Cross Stance (WTF)	ap kko-a sŏ-gi
Forward Inflection Stance (WTF)	ap ku-bi
Forward Riding Stance (WTF)	ap chu-ch'um sŏ-gi
Forward Stance (WTF)	ap sŏ-gi
Heaven Hand Stance (ITF)	ha-nŭl-son sŏ-gi
Inflection (WTF)	ku-bi
Inner Open Stance (ITF)	an p'al-ja sŏ-gi
Inverted "T"-Shape Stance (WTF)	o-ja sŏ-gi
Inward Riding Stance (WTF)	an-tchok chu-ch'um sŏ-gi
Inward Stance (WTF)	an-tchok sŏ-gi

Left at Ease Stance (WTF)	oen p'yŏn-hi sŏ-gi
Left-hand Stance (WTF)	oen sŏ-gi
Low Stance (ITF)	nat-ch'wŏ sŏ-gi
L-Ready Stance (ITF)	ni-ŭn-ja chun-bi sŏ-gi
L-Stance (ITF)	ni-ŭn-ja sŏ-gi
Oblique Angle Riding Stance (WTF)	mo chu-ch'um sŏ-gi
Oblique Angle Stance (WTF)	mo sŏ-gi
One-Leg Stance (ITF)	oe-bal sŏ-gi
Open Ready Stance (ITF)	p'al-ja chun-bi sŏ-gi
Open Stance (ITF)	p'al-ja sŏ-gi
Outside Open Stance (ITF)	pa-kkat p'al-ja sŏ-gi
Overlapped Hands Ready Stance (WTF)	kyŏp-son chun-bi sŏ-gi
Parallel Ready Stance (ITF)	na-ran-hi chun-bi sŏ-gi
Parallel Stance (ITF&WTF)	na-ran-hi sŏ-gi
Pushing-hands Ready Stance (WTF)	t'ong mil-gi chun-bi sŏ-gi
Ready Stance (ITF&WTF)	chun-bi sŏ-gi
Rear-foot Stance (ITF)	twit-bal sŏ-gi
Reverse Attention Stance (WTF)	ap-ch'uk mo-a sŏ-gi
Reverse Crane Stance (WTF)	o-gŭm sŏ-gi
Right at Ease Stance (WTF)	o-rŭn-tchok p'yŏn-hi sŏ-gi
Right-hand Stance (WTF)	o-rŭn sŏ-gi
Sitting Ready Stance (ITF)	an-nŭn chun-bi sŏ-gi

Sitting Stance (ITF)	an-nŭn sŏ-gi
Stance (ITF&WTF)	sŏ-gi (ITF&WTF) or ku-bi (WTF)
Tiger Stance (WTF)	pŏm sŏ-gi
Twin Fist on the Waist (WTF)	tu chu-mŏk hŏri
Vertical Stance (ITF)	su-jik sŏ-gi
Walking Ready Stance (ITF)	kŏn-nŭn chun-bi sŏ-gi
Walking Stance (ITF)	kŏn-nŭn sŏ-gi
Warrior Ready Stance (ITF)	mu-sa chun-bi sŏ-gi
X-Ready Stance (ITF)	kyo-ch'a chun-bi sŏ-gi
X-Stance (ITF)	kyo-ch'a sŏ-gi

Blocks

mak-ki (막기)

Terms listed in this section are associated with blocking techniques. All terms in this section are listed in alphabetical order according to their English equivalent. There are many words that can be used to describe a blocking action. Individuals may choose as many words as they like to describe a specific block. Individual martial arts organizations, on the other hand, tend to standardize their terms for blocking. The reader can further investigate the definitions of specific terms using Chapter 3.

Arc-hand Rising Block (ITF)	pan-dal-son ch'u-k'yŏ mak-ki
Assisting Block (WTF)	kŏ-dŭ-rŏ mak-ki
Assisting Face Block (WTF)	kŏ-dŭ-rŏ ŏl-gul mak-ki
Assisting Face Side Block (WTF)	kŏ-dŭ-rŏ ŏl-gul yŏp mak-ki
Assisting Hand-blade Block (WTF)	kŏ-dŭ-rŏ son-nal mak-ki
Assisting Trunk Block (WTF)	kŏ-dŭ-rŏ mom-t'ong mak-ki
Assisting Underneath Block (WTF)	kŏ-dŭ-rŏ a-rae mak-ki

Barrel Pushing (WTF)	t'ong mil-gi
Block - Backward Stepping (ITF)	ma-gŭ-myŏ tŭ-rŏ o-gi
Block - Forward Stepping (ITF)	ma-gŭ-myŏ na-ga-gi
Block or Blocking (ITF&WTF)	mak-ki
Boulder Pushing (WTF)	pa-wi mil-gi
Bow Wrist Block (ITF)	son-mok dŭng mak-ki
Bow Wrist Face Block (ITF)	ku-p'in son-mok ŏl-gul mak-ki
Bow Wrist Trunk Block (ITF)	ku-p'in son-mok mom-t'ong mak-ki
Bull Block (WTF)	hwang-so mak-ki
Checking Block (ITF)	mŏm-ch'wo mak-ki
Circular Block (ITF)	tol-li-myŏ mak-ki
Crane Diamond Block (WTF)	hak-da-ri kŭm-gang mak-ki
Cross Block (WTF)	ŏt-gal-lyŏ mak-ki
Cross Underneath Block (WTF)	ŏt-gal-lyŏ a-rae mak-ki
Diamond Block (WTF)	kŭm-gang mak-ki
Diamond Trunk Block (WTF)	kŭm-gang mom-t'ong mak-ki
Double Arc-hand Block (ITF)	tu-ban-dal-son mak-ki
Double Forearm Block (ITF)	tu-p'al-mok mak-ki
Downward Block (ITF)	nae-ryŏ mak-ki
Downward X-Block (ITF)	nae-ryŏ kyo-ch'a mak-ki
Downward X-Fist Block (ITF)	nae-ryŏ kyo-ch'a chu-mŏk mak-ki
Downward X-Knifehand Block (ITF)	nae-ryŏ kyo-ch'a son-k'al mak-ki

Face Block (WTF)	ŏl-gul mak-ki
Face Cross Block (WTF)	ŏl-gul ŏt-gal-lyŏ mak-ki
Face Foot-blade Rising Block (WTF)	ŏl-gul yŏp ch'a-ol-lyŏ mak-ki
Face Front-sole Rising Block (WTF)	ŏl-gul ap ch'a-ol-lyŏ mak-ki
Face Inner Block (WTF)	ŏl-gul an mak-ki
Face Outer Block (WTF)	ŏl-gul pa-kkat mak-ki
Face Pushing Block (WTF)	ŏl-gul he-ch'yŏ mak-ki
Face Side Block (WTF)	ŏl-gul yŏp mak-ki
Face Twist Block (WTF)	ŏl-gul pi-t'ŭ-rŏ mak-ki
Foot-blade Underneath Counter Block (WTF)	a-rae pa-da mak-ki
Forearm Wedging Block (ITF)	p'al-mok he-ch'yŏ mak-ki
Front Block (ITF)	ap mak-ki
Grasping Block (ITF)	put-ja-ba mak-ki
Guarding Block (ITF)	tae-bi mak-ki
Hand-blade Back Face Block (WTF)	son-nal tŭng ŏl-gul mak-ki
Hand-blade Back Trunk Block (WTF)	son-nal tŭng mom-t'ong mak-ki
Hand-blade Back Trunk Pushing Block (WTF)	son-nal tŭng mom-t'ong he-ch'yŏ mak-ki
Hand-blade Back Underneath Block (WTF)	son-nal tŭng a-rae mak-ki
Hand-blade Back Wide-open Block (WTF)	son-nal tŭng san-t'ŭl mak-ki

Hand-blade Diamond Block (WTF)	son-nal kŭm-gang mak-ki
Hand-blade Single-hand Wide-open Block (WTF)	son-nal oe-san-t'ŭl mak-ki
Hand-blade Trunk Block (WTF)	son-nal mom-t'ong mak-ki
Hand-blade Trunk Pushing Block (WTF)	son-nal mom-t'ong he-ch'yŏ mak-ki
Hand-blade Trunk Side Block (WTF)	son-nal mom-t'ong
Hand-blade Underneath Block (WTF)	son-nal a-rae mak-ki
Hand-blade Underneath Cross Block (WTF)	son-nal a-rae ŏt-gal-lyŏ mak-ki
Hand-blade Underneath Pushing Block (WTF)	son-nal a-rae he-ch'yŏ mak-ki
High Block (ITF)	no-p'ŭn-dae mak-ki
Hooking Block (ITF)	kŏl-ch'ŏ mak-ki
Horizontal Forearm Block	su-p'yŏng p'al-mok mak-ki
Inner-Block	an mak-ki (WTF) or an-tchok mak-ki
Inner-forearm Assisting Trunk Block (WTF)	an p'al-mok kŏ-dŭ-rŏ mom-t'ong mak-ki
Inner-forearm Block (WTF)	an p'al-mok mak-ki
Inner-forearm Face Outer Block (WTF)	an p'al-mok ŏl-gul pa-kkat mak-ki
Inner-forearm Face Twist Block (WTF)	an p'al-mok ŏl-gul pi-t'ŭ-rŏ mak-ki

Inner-forearm Trunk Outer Block (WTF)	an p'al-mok mom-t'ong pa-kkat mak-ki
Inner-forearm Trunk Pushing Block (WTF)	an p'al-mok mom-t'ong he-ch'yŏ mak-ki
Inner-forearm Trunk Twist Block (WTF)	an p'al-mok mom-t'ong pi-t'ŭ-rŏ mak-ki
Inside Block	an mak-ki (ITF) or an-tchok mak-ki
Inward Block (ITF)	an-ŭ-ro mak-ki
Knifehand Block (ITF)	son-k'al mak-ki
Knifehand Wedging Block (ITF)	son-k'al he-ch'yŏ mak-ki
Low Block (ITF)	na-jŭn-dae mak-ki
L-Stance High Block (ITF)	ni-ŭn-ja sŏ no-p'ŭn-dae mak-ki
Luring Block (ITF)	yu-in mak-ki
Middle Block (ITF)	ka-un-dae mak-ki
Mountain Pushing (WTF)	t'ae-san mil-gi
Mountain Shape Block (WTF)	san-t'ŭl mak-ki
Mountain Shape Cross Block (WTF)	san-t'ŭl ŏt-gal-lyŏ mak-ki
Nine-Shape Block (ITF)	ku-ja mak-ki
Outer Block (WTF)	pa-kkat mak-ki
Outer-forearm Block (WTF)	pa-kkat p'al-mok mak-ki
Outer-forearm Face Side Block (WTF)	pa-kkat p'al-mok ŏl-gul yŏp mak-ki
Outer-forearm Trunk Side Block (WTF)	pa-kkat p'al-mok mom-t'ong yŏp mak-ki

Outside Block (ITF)	pa-kkat mak-ki
Outward Block (ITF)	pak-kŭ-ro mak-ki
Palm Assisting Side Block (WTF)	son-ba-dak kŏ-dŭ-rŏ yŏp mak-ki
Palm-hand Face Inner Block (WTF)	pa-t'ang-son ŏl-gul an mak-ki
Palm-hand Trunk Block (WTF)	pa-t'ang-son mom-t'ong mak-ki
Palm-hand Trunk Pressing Block (WTF)	pa-t'ang-son mom-t'ong nul-lŏ mak-ki
Palm-hand Underneath Block (WTF)	pa-t'ang-son a-rae mak-ki
Parallel Block (ITF)	na-ran-hi mak-ki
Part Mountain Shape Block (WTF)	oe-san-t'ŭl mak-ki
Part Mountain Shape Side Block (WTF)	oe-san-t'ŭl yŏp mak-ki
Pole Block or U-Shape Block (ITF)	mong-dung-i mak-ki
Pole Grasping Block (ITF)	mong-dung-i chap-go mak-ki
Pressing Block (ITF&WTF)	nul-lŏ mak-ki
Pressing X-Fist Block (ITF)	nul-lŏ kyo-ch'a chu-mŏk mak-ki
Push Barrel (WTF)	t'ong mil-gi
Push Boulder (WTF)	pa-wi mil-gi
Pushing Block (WTF)	he-ch'yŏ mak-ki
Pushing Block (ITF)	mi-rŏ mak-ki

Pushing Wide-open Block (WTF)	he-ch'yŏ san-t'ŭl mak-ki
Push Mountain (WTF)	tae-san mil-gi
Rising Block (ITF)	ch'u-k'yŏ mak-ki
Rock Pushing (WTF)	pa-wi mil-gi
Scattered Block (WTF)	he-ch'yŏ mak-ki
Scissors Block (WTF)	ka-wi mak-ki
Scooping Block (ITF)	ttŭ-rŏ mak-ki
Shin Counter Block (WTF)	chŏng-gang-i pa-da mak-ki
Side Block (ITF&WTF)	yŏp mak-ki
Side Front Block (ITF)	yŏp ap mak-ki
Single Hand-blade Block (WTF)	han son-nal mak-ki
Single Hand-blade Face Inner Block (WTF)	han son-nal ŏl-gul an mak-ki
Single Hand-blade Face Outer Block (WTF)	han son-nal ŏl-gul pa-kkat mak-ki
Single Hand-blade Face Twist Block (WTF)	han son-nal ŏl-gul pi-t'ŭ-rŏ mak-ki
Single Hand-blade Trunk Block (WTF)	han son-nal mom-t'ong mak-ki
Single Hand-blade Trunk Inner Block (WTF)	han son-nal mom-t'ong an mak-ki
Single Hand-blade Underneath Side Block (WTF)	han son-nal a-rae yŏp mak-ki
Single Hand-blade Underneath Twist Block (WTF)	han son-nal a-rae pi-t'ŭ-rŏ mak-ki
Single-hand Wide-open Side Block (WTF)	oe-san-t'ŭl yŏp mak-ki

237

A Martial Artist's Guide to Korean Terms

Single-hand Wide-open Block and Side Kick (WTF)	oe-san-t'ŭl yŏp ch'a-gi
Single-hand Wide-open Block (WTF)	oe-san-t'ŭl mak-ki
Single Straight Forearm Block (ITF)	oe sŏn p'al-mok mak-ki
Single Straight Knifehand Block (ITF)	oe sŏn son-k'al mak-ki
Spot Block (ITF)	kŭ-ja-ri mak-ki
Straight Forearm Block (ITF)	sŏn p'al-mok mak-ki
Target Block (WTF)	p'yo-jŏk mak-ki
Trunk Block (WTF)	mom-t'ong mak-ki
Trunk Inner Block (WTF)	mom-t'ong an mak-ki
Trunk Outer Block (WTF)	mom-t'ong pa-kkat mak-ki
Trunk Pushing Block (WTF)	mom-t'ong he-ch'yŏ mak-ki
Trunk Side Block (WTF)	mom-t'ong yŏp mak-ki
Trunk Twist Block (WTF)	mom-t'ong pi-t'ŭ-rŏ mak-ki
Twin Forearm Block (ITF)	ssang p'al-mok mak-ki
Twin Knifehand Block (ITF)	ssang son-k'al mak-ki
Twin Palm (hand bottom) Rising Block (ITF)	ssang son-ba-dak ch'u-k'yŏ mak-ki
Twin Straight Forearm Block (ITF)	ssang sŏn p'al-mok mak-ki
Twin Straight Knifehand Block (ITF)	ssang sŏn son-k'al mak-ki
Twist Block (WTF)	pi-t'ŭ-rŏ mak-ki
Underneath Block (WTF)	a-rae mak-ki

Underneath Pushing Block (WTF)	a-rae he-ch'yŏ mak-ki
Underneath Side Block (WTF)	a-rae yŏp mak-ki
Underneath Twist Block (WTF)	a-rae pi-t'ŭ-rŏ mak-ki
Upward Block (ITF)	ol-lyŏ mak-ki
U-Shape Block (ITF)	ti-gŭt-ja mak-ki or mong-dung-i mak-ki
U-Shape Grasp (ITF)	ti-gŭt-ja put-jap-gi
U-Shape Grasping Block (ITF)	mong-dung-i chap-go mak-ki
Waist Block (ITF)	hŏ-ri mak-ki
Wedging Block (ITF)	he-ch'yŏ mak-ki
Wide-open Block (WTF)	san-t'ŭl mak-ki
Wing Spreading (WTF)	nal-gae p'yŏ-gi
Wrist Block (WTF)	p'al-mok mak-ki
W-Shape Block (ITF)	san mak-ki
X-Fist Block (ITF)	kyo-ch'a chu-mŏk mak-ki
X-Fist Rising Block (ITF)	kyo-ch'a chu-mŏk ch'u-k'yŏ mak-ki
X-Knifehand Block (ITF)	kyo-ch'a son-k'al mak-ki
X-Knifehand Rising Block (ITF)	kyo-ch'a son-k'al ch'u-k'yŏ mak-ki

Punches

chi-rŭ-gi / tchi-rŭ-gi (지르기 / 찌르기)

Terms listed in this section are associated with punching techniques. All terms in this section are listed in alphabetical order according to their English equivalent.

There are many words that can be used to describe a punching type action. Individuals may choose as many words as they like to describe this action. Individual martial arts organizations, on the other hand, tend to standardize their terms for striking (i.e., chi-rŭ-gi or tchi-rŭ-gi, etc.). The reader can further investigate the detailed definitions of these and other terms using Chapter 3.

Angle Punch (ITF)	ki-yŏk-ja tchi-rŭ-gi
Back Punch (WTF)	twi chi-rŭ-gi
Backward Sliding Punch (ITF)	mi-kkŭ-rŭm-bal-lo tchi-rŭ-myŏ tŭrŏ-o-gi
Crescent Punch (ITF)	pan-dal tchi-rŭ-gi
Diamond Forward Punch (WTF)	kŭm-gang ap tchi-rŭ-gi
Diamond Side Punch (WTF)	kŭm-gang yŏp tchi-rŭ-gi

241

Dodging Punch (ITF)	p'i-ha-myŏ tchi-rŭ-gi
Double Fist Punch (ITF)	tu-ju-mŏk tchi-rŭ-gi
Downward Punch (ITF)	nae-ryŏ tchi-rŭ-gi
Erected-Fist Punch (WTF)	se-wŏ chi-rŭ-gi
Face Punch (WTF)	ŏl-gul chi-rŭ-gi
Flat-fingertip Palm-upward Punch (WTF)	p'yŏn son-kkŭt che-ch'yŏ chi-rŭ-gi
Flat-fingertip Vertical Punch (WTF)	p'yŏn son-kkŭt se-wŏ chi-rŭ-gi
Flat-fist Reverse Straight Punch (WTF)	p'yŏn chu-mŏk pan-dae chi-rŭ-gi
Flat-fist Reverse Straight Vertical Punch (WTF)	p'yŏn chu-mŏk pan-dae se-wŏ chi-rŭ-gi
Flat-fist Straight Punch (WTF)	p'yŏn chu-mŏk pa-ro chi-rŭ-gi
Flat-fist Straight Vertical Punch (WTF)	p'yŏn chu-mŏk pa-ro se-wŏ chi-rŭ-gi
Flying Consecutive Punch [jumping] (ITF)	ttwi-myŏ yŏn-sok tchi-rŭ-gi
Flying Punch [jumping] (ITF)	ttwi-myŏ tchi-rŭ-gi
Flying Overhead Punch [jumping] (ITF)	ttwi-yŏ nŏ-mŏ tchi-rŭ-gi
Fork-shape Punch (WTF)	ch'et-da-ri chi-rŭ-gi
Forward Sliding Punch (ITF)	mi-kkŭ-rŭm-bal-lo tchi-rŭ-myŏ na-ga-gi
Front Punch (ITF)	ap tchi-rŭ-gi
Front Punching Kick (ITF)	ap tchi-rŭ-myŏ ch'a-gi

Ground Punch (ITF)	nu-wŏ tchi-rŭ-gi
High Punch (ITF)	no-p'ŭn-dae tchi-rŭ-gi
Hooking Punch (ITF)	kŏ-rŏ tchi-rŭ-gi
Horizontal Punch (ITF)	su-p'yŏng tchi-rŭ-gi
Knuckle Fist Punch (ITF)	son-ga-rak chu-mŏk tchi-rŭ-gi
Long Fist Punch (ITF)	kin chu-mŏk tchi-rŭ-gi
Low Punch (ITF)	na-jŭn-dae tchi-rŭ-gi
Mid-air Punch [Jump-rotating] (ITF)	ttwi-yŏ tol-myŏ tchi-rŭ-gi
Middle Punch (ITF)	ka-un-dae tchi-rŭ-gi
Obverse Punch (ITF)	pa-ro tchi-rŭ-gi
Open-fist Punch (ITF)	p'yŏn chu-mŏk tchi-rŭ-gi
Opposite Straight Punch (WTF)	pan-dae chi-rŭ-gi
Palm-upward Punch (WTF)	che-ch'yŏ chi-rŭ-gi
Pulling the Jaw Punch (WTF)	tang-gyŏ t'ŏk chi-rŭ-gi
Punch - Backward Stepping (ITF)	tchi-rŭ-myŏ tŭ-rŏ o-gi
Punch - Forward Stepping (ITF)	tchi-rŭ-myŏ na-ga-gi
Punch or Punching (WTF)	chi-rŭ-gi
Punch or Punching (ITF)	tchi-rŭ-gi
Punching Kick (ITF) [Airborne Combination]	tchi-rŭ-myŏ ch'a-gi
Punching Technique (WTF)	chu-mŏk ki-sul
Reverse Punch (ITF)	pan-dae tchi-rŭ-gi
Side Front Punch (ITF)	yŏp ap tchi-rŭ-gi

Side Punch (ITF)	yŏp tchi-rŭ-gi
Side Punch (WTF)	yŏp chi-rŭ-gi
Side Punching Kick (ITF) [Airborne Combination]	yŏp tchi-rŭ-myŏ ch'a-gi
Side Vertical Punch (ITF)	yŏp se-wŏ tchi-rŭ-gi
Sitting Stance Punch (ITF)	an-nŭn sŏ tchi-rŭ-gi
Skip Punch (ITF)	tŭ-rŏ-ka-myŏ tchi-rŭ-gi
Spiral Punch (WTF)	tol-lyŏ chi-rŭ-gi
Spring-up Punch (WTF)	so-sŭm chi-rŭ-gi
Spot Punch (ITF)	kŭ-ja-ri tchi-rŭ-gi
Straight Punch (WTF)	pa-ro chi-rŭ-gi
Target Punch (WTF)	p'yo-jŏk chi-rŭ-gi
Thumb Knuckle Punch (ITF)	ŏm-ji chu-mŏk tchi-rŭ-gi
Triple Punch (ITF)	sam-jung tchi-rŭ-gi
Trunk Punch (WTF)	mom-t'ong chi-rŭ-gi
Tug and Punch (WTF)	tang-gyŏ chi-rŭ-gi
Tug the Jaw Punch (WTF)	tang-gyŏ t'ŏk chi-rŭ-gi
Turning Punch (ITF)	tol-lyŏ tchi-rŭ-gi
Twin-fist Palm-upward Punch (WTF)	tu chu-mŏk che-ch'yŏ chi-rŭ-gi
Twist Punch (WTF)	tol-lyŏ chi-rŭ-gi
U-letter-Shape Punch (WTF)	U-ja chi-rŭ-gi
Underneath Punch (WTF)	nae-ryŏ chi-rŭ-gi or a-rae chi-rŭ-gi
Upset Punch (ITF)	twi-ji-bŏ tchi-rŭ-gi

Upward Punch (ITF)	ol-lyŏ tchi-rŭ-gi
U-Shape Punch (ITF)	ti-gŭt-ja tchi-rŭ-gi or U-ja tchi-rŭ-gi
U-Shape Punching Kick (ITF)	ti-gŭt-ja tchi-rŭ-myŏ ch'a-gi
U-Shape Trunk Punch (WTF)	mom-t'ong U-ja chi-rŭ-gi
Vertical Punch (ITF)	se-wŏ tchi-rŭ-gi
Vertical Punch (WTF)	se-wŏ chi-rŭ-gi
Walking Stance Obverse Punch (ITF)	kŏn-nŭn sŏ pa-ro tchi-rŭ-gi
Walking Stance Reverse Punch (ITF)	kŏn-nŭn sŏ pan-dae tchi-rŭ-gi
Wing Punch (WTF)	nal-gae chi-rŭ-gi

Strikes

ch'i-gi / ttae-ri-gi （치기 / 때리기）

Terms listed in this section are associated with strikes or hits. There are many words that can be used to describe a striking type action. Individuals may choose any word they like to describe this action. Individual martial arts organizations, on the other hand, tend to standardize their terms for striking (i.e., ch'i-gi, or ttae-ri-gi, etc.). The reader can further investigate the detailed definitions of these and other terms using Chapter 3. All terms in this section are listed in alphabetical order according to their English equivalent.

Assisting Face Outer Hit (WTF)	kŏ-dŭ-rŏ ŏl-gul pa-kkat ch'i-gi
Back Elbow Strike (ITF)	twit p'al-gup ttae-ri-gi
Backfist Assisting Face Front Hit (WTF)	tŭng chu-mŏk kŏ-dŭ-rŏ ŏl-gul ap ch'i-gi
Backfist Face Front Hit (WTF)	tŭng chu-mŏk ŏl-gul ap ch'i-gi
Backfist Face Outer Hit (WTF)	tŭng chu-mŏk ŏl-gul pa-kkat ch'i-gi
Backfist Strike (ITF)	tŭng chu-mŏk ttae-ri-gi
Back Hit (WTF)	twi ch'i-gi

Back Strike (ITF)	twi ttae-ri-gi
Combined All-fingertip Hit (WTF)	mo-dŭm son-kkŭt ch'i-gi
Combined Three-fingertip Hit (WTF)	mo-ŭn se son-kkŭt ch'i-gi
Combined Two-fingertip Hit (WTF)	mo-ŭn tu son-kkŭt ch'i-gi
Crescent Strike (ITF)	pan-dal ttae-ri-gi
Dodging Strike (ITF)	p'i-ha-myŏ ttae-ri-gi
Double Strike (ITF)	i-jung ttae-ri-gi
Downward Strike (ITF)	nae-ryŏ ttae-ri-gi
Downward Strike (WTF)	nae-ryŏ ch'i-gi
Elbow Back Strike (WTF)	p'al-gup twi ch'i-gi
Elbow Downward Strike (ITF)	p'al-gup nae-ryŏ ttae-ri-gi
Elbow Downward Strike (WTF)	p'al-gup nae-ryŏ ch'i-gi
Elbow Front Strike (WTF)	p'al-gup ap ch'i-gi
Elbow Rise-up Strike (WTF)	p'al-gup ol-lyŏ ch'i-gi
Elbow Side Strike (WTF)	p'al-gup yŏp ch'i-gi
Elbow Strike (ITF)	p'al-gup ttae-ri-gi
Elbow Strike (WTF)	p'al-gup ch'i-gi
Elbow Target Strike (WTF)	p'al-gup p'yo-jŏk ch'i-gi
Elbow Turning Strike (WTF)	p'al-gup tol-lyŏ ch'i-gi
Face Front Hit (WTF)	ŏl-gul ap ch'i-gi

Flying Consecutive Strike [jumping] (ITF)	ttwi-myŏ yŏn-sok ttae-ri-gi
Flying Strike [jumping] (ITF)	ttwi-myŏ ttae-ri-gi
Front Downward Strike (ITF)	ap nae-ryŏ ttae-ri-gi
Front Elbow Strike (ITF)	ap p'al-gup ttae-ri-gi
Front Hit (WTF)	ap ch'i-gi
Front Strike (ITF)	ap ttae-ri-gi
Ground Strike (ITF)	nu-wŏ ttae-ri-gi
High Elbow Strike (ITF)	no-p'ŭn-dae p'al-gup ttae-ri-gi
High Strike (ITF)	no-p'ŭn-dae ttae-ri-gi
Hitting (WTF)	ch'i-gi
Horizontal Elbow Strike (ITF)	su-p'yŏng p'al-gup ttae-ri-gi
Horizontal Strike (ITF)	su-p'yŏng ttae-ri-gi
Horizontal Striking Kick (ITF)	su-p'yŏng ttae-ri-myŏ ch'a-gi
Inward Hit (WTF)	an ch'i-gi
Inward Strike (ITF)	an-ŭro ttae-ri-gi
Knee Rising Hit (WTF)	mu-rŭp ol-lyŏ ch'i-gi
Knee Strike (WTF)	mu-rŭp ch'i-gi
Knee Turning Hit (WTF)	mu-rŭp tol-lyŏ ch'i-gi
Knifehand Stike (ITF)	son-k'al ttae-ri-gi
Low Strike (ITF)	na-jŭn-dae ttae-ri-gi
Mid-air [jump-rotating] Strike (ITF)	ttwi-yŏ tol-myŏ ttae-ri-gi
Middle Strike (ITF)	ka-un-dae ttae-ri-gi
Outward Hit (WTF)	pa-kkat ch'i-gi

249

Outward Strike (ITF)	pak-kŭ-ro ttae-ri-gi
Rise-up Strike (WTF)	ol-lyŏ ch'i-gi
Side Back Strike (ITF)	yŏp twit ttae-ri-gi
Side Downward Strike (ITF)	yŏp nae-ryŏ ttae-ri-gi
Side Front Strike (ITF)	yŏp ap ttae-ri-gi
Side Hit (WTF)	yŏp ch'i-gi
Side Strike (ITF)	yŏp ttae-ri-gi
Single Elbow Strike (ITF)	oe p'al-gup ttae-ri-gi
Single Side Elbow Strike (ITF)	oe yŏp p'al-gup ttae-ri-gi
Skip Strike (ITF)	tŭ-rŏ-ka-myŏ ttae-ri-gi
Spot Strike (ITF)	kŭ-ja-ri ttae-ri-gi
Strike - Backward Stepping (ITF)	ttae-ri-myŏ tŭ-rŏ o-gi
Strike - Forward Stepping (ITF)	ttae-ri-myŏ na-ga-gi
Strike or Striking (WTF)	ch'i-gi
Strike or Striking Technique (ITF)	ttae-ri-gi
Swallow-shape Jaw Hit (WTF)	che-bi-p'um t'ŏk ch'i-gi
Swallow-shape Neck Hit/Strike (WTF)	che-bi-p'um mok ch'i-gi
Target Strike (WTF)	p'yo-jŏk ch'i-gi
Triple Strike (ITF)	sam-jung ttae-ri-gi
Trunk Outer Hit (WTF)	mom-t'ong pa-kkat ch'i-gi
Tug and Hit (WTF)	tang-gyŏ ch'i-gi
Tug and Jaw Hit (WTF)	tang-gyŏ t'ŏk ch'i-gi

Twin Knifehand Strike (ITF)	ssang son-k'al ttae-ri-gi
Twin Reverse Knifehand Strike (ITF)	ssang son-k'al dŭng ttae-ri-gi
Upper and Back Elbow Strike (ITF)	wi twit p'al-gup ttae-ri-gi
Upper Elbow Strike (ITF)	wi p'al-gup ttae-ri-gi
Yoke Hit (WTF)	mŏng-e ch'i-gi

Thrusts

tchi-rŭ-gi / ttul-ki (찌르기 / 뚫기)

Terms listed in this section are associated with thrusting techniques. There are many words that can be used to describe a thrusting type action. Individuals may choose any word they like to describe this action. Individual martial arts organizations, on the other hand, tend to standardize their terms for striking (i.e., ch'i-gi, tchi-rŭ-gi, ttul-gi, etc.). The reader can further investigate the detailed definitions of these and other terms using Chapter 3. All terms in this section are listed in alphabetical order according to their English equivalent.

Back Elbow Thrust (ITF)	twit p'al-gup ttul-ki
Combined Three-fingertip Thrust (WTF)	mo-ŭn se son-kkŭt tchi-rŭ-gi
Combined Two-fingertip Thrust (WTF)	mo-ŭn tu son-kkŭt tchi-rŭ-gi
Crane Thrust (WTF)	hak-da-ri tchi-rŭ-gi
Dodging Thrust (ITF)	p'i-ha-myŏ ttul-ki
Double Finger Spear [Thrust] (ITF)	tu-son-ga-rak ttul-ki

Double Side Elbow Thrust (ITF)	tu yŏp p'al-gup ttul-ki
Downward Thrust (ITF)	nae-ryŏ ttul-ki
Flat-fingertip Erect Thrust (WTF)	p'yŏn son-kkŭt se-wŏ tchi-rŭ-gi
Flat-fingertip Flat Thrust (WTF)	p'yŏn son-kkŭt ŏ-p'ŭn tchi-rŭ-gi
Flat-fingertip Front Thrust (WTF)	p'yŏn son-kkŭt ap tchi-rŭ-gi
Flat-fingertip Palm Upward Thrust (WTF)	p'yŏn son-kkŭt che-ch'yŏ tchi-rŭ-gi
Flying Consecutive Thrust [jumping] (ITF)	ttwi-myŏ yŏn-sok ttul-ki
Flying Thrust [jumping] (ITF)	ttwi-myŏ ttul-ki
Front Elbow Thrust (ITF)	ap p'al-gup ttul-ki
Ground Thrust (ITF)	nu-wŏ ttul-ki
High Elbow Thrust (ITF)	no-p'ŭn-dae p'al-gup ttul-ki
High Thrust (ITF)	no-p'ŭn-dae ttul-ki
Horizontal Thrust (ITF)	su-p'yŏng ttul-ki
Low Thrust (ITF)	na-jŭn-dae ttul-ki
Mid-air [jump-rotating] Thrust (ITF)	ttwi-ŏ tol-myŏ ttul-ki
Middle Thrust (ITF)	ka-un-dae ttul-ki
Scissors Fingertip Thrust (WTF)	ka-wi son-kkŭt tchi-rŭ-gi
Side Back Thrust (ITF)	yŏp twit ttul-ki
Side Elbow Thrust (ITF)	yŏp p'al-gup ttul-ki
Side Front Thrust (ITF)	yŏp ap ttul-ki

Side Thrust (ITF)	yŏp ttul-ki
Single Elbow Thrust (ITF)	oe p'al-gup ttul-ki
Single Fingertip Thrust (WTF)	han son-kkŭt tchi-rŭ-gi
Single Finger Spear [Thrust ITF]	han son-ga-rak ttul-ki
Single Side Elbow Thrust (ITF)	oe yŏp p'al-gup ttul-ki
Skip Thrust (ITF)	tŭ-rŏ-ka-myŏ ttul-ki
Spot Thrust (ITF)	kŭ-ja-ri ttul-ki
Straight Elbow Thrust (ITF)	sŏn p'al-gup ttul-ki
Thrust - Backward Stepping (ITF)	ttu-rŭ-myŏ tŭ-rŏ o-gi
Thrust - Forward Stepping (ITF)	ttu-rŭ-myŏ na-ga-gi
Thrusting (WTF)	tchi-rŭ-gi
Thrust or Thrusting (ITF)	ttul-ki
Triple Thrust (ITF)	sam-jung ttul-ki
Twin Elbow Thrust (ITF)	ssang p'al-gup ttul-ki
Twin Side Back Elbow Thrust (ITF)	ssang yŏp twit p'al-gup ttul-ki
Twin Side Elbow Thrust (ITF)	ssang yŏp p'al-gup ttul-ki

Kicks

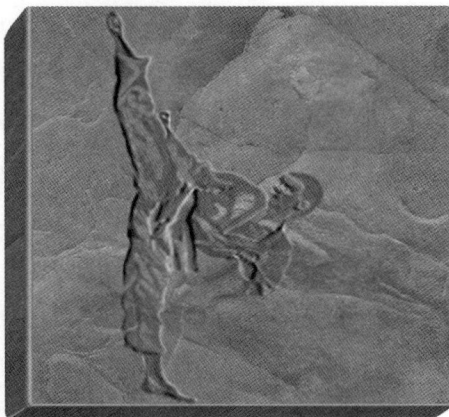

ch'a-gi (차기)

Terms listed in this section are associated with kicking techniques. There are many words that can be used to describe a kicking type action. Individuals may choose as many words as they like to describe this action. Additionally, when describing a term, there are specific words that may be placed in different orders. Individual martial arts organizations, on the other hand, tend to standardize their terms for kicking (i.e., ch'a-gi, ch'i-gi, or ch'a- followed by a descriptor such as mil-gi, e.g., ch'a-mil-gi). The reader can further investigate the detailed definitions of these and other terms using Chapter 3. All terms in this section are listed in alphabetical order according to their English equivalent.

Arc Kick [Half Turning Kick] (WTF)	pan tol-lyŏ ch'a-gi
Back Kick (ITF&WTF)	twit ch'a-gi
Back Piercing Kick (ITF)	twit ch'a-tchi-rŭ-gi
Back Pushing Kick (ITF)	twit ch'a-mil-gi
Back Snap Kick (ITF)	twit ch'a-pu-su-gi

257

Backward Lifting Kick (WTF)	twi ol-lyŏ ch'a-gi
Body Turning Kick (WTF)	mom tol-lyŏ ch'a-gi
Checking Kick (ITF)	ch'a mŏm-ch'u-gi
Combination Kick (ITF)	hon-hap ch'a-gi
Consecutive Kick [continuous] (ITF)	yŏn-sok ch'a-gi
Counter Kick (ITF)	pa-da ch'a-gi
Crescent Kick (ITF)	pan-dal ch'a-gi
Dichotomy Kick (WTF)	pan-dal ch'a-gi
Dodging Kick (ITF)	p'i-ha-myŏ ch'a-gi
Double Front Snap Kick [smashing] (ITF)	i-jung ap ch'a-pu-su-gi
Double Kick (ITF)	i-jung ch'a-gi
Downward Kick (ITF&WTF) [Ax kick]	nae-ryŏ ch'a-gi
Flying Combination Kick [jumping] (ITF)	ttwi-myŏ hon-hap ch'a-gi
Flying Consecutive Kick (WTF)	kong-jung yŏn-sok ch'a-gi
Flying Consecutive Kick [jumping] (ITF)	ttwi-myŏ yŏn-sok ch'a-gi
Flying Double Foot Side Pushing Kick [jumping] (ITF)	ttwi-myŏ tu-bal yŏp ch'a-mil-gi
Flying Front and Twisting Kick [jumping] (ITF)	ttwi-myŏ ap ch'a-go pi-t'ŭ-rŏ ch'a-gi
Flying Kick [jumping] (ITF)	ttwi-myŏ ch'a-gi
Flying Overhead Kick [jumping] (ITF)	ttwi-myŏ nŏ-mŏ ch'a-gi

Flying Scissors-shape Kick [jumping] (ITF)	ttwi-myŏ ka-wi ch'a-gi
Flying Spiral Kick [jumping] (ITF)	ttwi-myŏ ra-sŏn-shik ch'a-gi
Flying Twin-foot Closed Kick (WTF)	kong-jung mo-dŭm-bal ch'a-gi
Flying Twisting Kick [jumping] (ITF)	ttwi-myŏ pi-t'ŭ-rŏ ch'a-gi
Four-direction Kick (ITF)	sa-bang ch'a-gi
Four-direction Kick (WTF)	sa-bang hyang ch'a-gi
Front Checking Kick (ITF)	ap ch'a-mŏm-ch'u-gi
Front Kick (ITF&WTF)	ap ch'a-gi
Front Leg Kick (ITF)	ap ta-ri ch'a-gi
Front Piercing Kick (ITF)	ap ch'a-tchi-rŭ-gi
Front Punching Kick (ITF)	ap tchi-rŭ-myŏ ch'a-gi
Front Pushing Kick (ITF)	ap ch'a-mil-gi
Front Rising Kick (ITF)	ap ch'a-ol-li-gi
Front Rising Kick (WTF)	pal ap ol-lyŏ ch'a-gi
Front Snap Kick (ITF)	ap ch'a-pu-su-gi
Grasp and Kick (ITF)	put-jap-go ch'a-gi
Ground Kick (ITF)	nu-wŏ ch'a-gi
Half Turning Kick [Arc Kick] (WTF)	pan tol-lyŏ ch'a-gi
High Kick (ITF)	no-p'i ch'a-gi
High Twisting Kick (ITF)	no-p'i pi-t'ŭ-rŏ ch'a-gi
Holding Front Kick (WTF)	chap-go ap ch'a-gi

Holding Kick (WTF)	chap-go ch'a-gi
Holding Side Kick (WTF)	chap-go yŏp ch'a-gi
Holding Turning Kick (WTF)	chap-go tol-lyŏ ch'a-gi
Hook Kick (ITF)	kŏ-rŏ ch'a-gi
Hook Kick (WTF)	na-ga ch'a-gi
Hooking Kick (ITF)	kŏl-ch'ŏ ch'a-gi
Horizontal Striking Kick (ITF)	su-p'yŏng ttae-ri-myŏ ch'a-gi
Inner Downward Kick (WTF)	an nae-ryŏ ch'a-gi
Inward Kick (ITF)	an-ŭ-ro ch'a-gi
Inward Vertical Kick (ITF)	an-ŭ-ro se-wŏ ch'a-gi
Joint-feet Kick (WTF)	mo-dŭm-bal ch'a-gi
Jump High Kick (WTF)	ttwi-ŏ ol-lyŏ ch'a-gi
Jump Kick (WTF)	ttwi-ŏ ch'a-gi
Kick or Kicking (ITF&WTF)	ch'a-gi
Kick - Backward Stepping (ITF)	ch'a-myŏ tŭ-rŏ o-gi
Kick - Forward Stepping (ITF)	ch'a-myŏ na-ga-gi
Kick while Grasping (ITF)	put-jap-go ch'a-gi
Knee Rising Kick (WTF)	mu-rŭp ol-lyŏ ch'a-gi
Knee Turning Kick (WTF)	mu-rŭp tol-lyŏ ch'a-gi
Lead Leg Kick (ITF)	ap ta-ri ch'a-gi
Low Kick (ITF)	na-jŭn-dae ch'a-gi
Mid-air [jump-rotating] Kick (ITF)	ttwi-yŏ tol-myŏ ch'a-gi
Middle Kick (ITF)	ka-un-dae ch'a-gi
Mixed Kicks (WTF)	sŏk-kŏ ch'a-gi

Multi-direction Kick (WTF)	ta-bang-hyang ch'a-gi
Outer Downward Kick (WTF)	pa-kkat nae-ryŏ ch'a-gi
Outward Kick (ITF)	pak-kŭ-ro ch'a-gi
Outward Vertical Kick (ITF)	pak-kŭ-ro se-wŏ ch'a-gi
Pick-shape Kick (ITF)	kok-gwaeng-i ch'a-gi
Piercing Kick (ITF)	ch'a tchi-rŭ-gi
Pressing Kick (ITF)	nul-lŏ ch'a-gi
Punching Kick (ITF) [Airborne Combination]	tchi-rŭ-myŏ ch'a-gi
Pushing Kick (ITF)	ch'a mil-gi
Pushing Kick (WTF)	mi-rŏ ch'a-gi
Quadruple Kick (ITF)	sa-jung ch'a-gi
Reflex Kick (ITF)	pan-sa ch'a-gi
Repeated Kick (WTF)	kŏ-dŭp ch'a-gi
Reverse Turning Kick (ITF)	pan-dae tol-lyŏ ch'a-gi
Rising Kick (ITF)	ch'a ol-li-gi
Scissors Front Kick (WTF)	ka-wi ap ch'a-gi
Scissors Kick (WTF)	ka-wi ch'a-gi
Scissors Pushing Side Kick (WTF)	ka-wi mi-rŏ yŏp ch'a-gi
Scissors Side Kick (WTF)	ka-wi yŏp ch'a-gi
Scissors Turning Kick (WTF)	ka-wi tol-lyŏ ch'a-gi
Side Checking Kick (ITF)	yŏp ch'a-mŏm-ch'u-gi
Side Front Kick (ITF)	yŏp ap ch'a-gi
Side Front Pushing Kick (ITF)	yŏp ap ch'a-mil-gi

Side Front Snap Kick (ITF)	yŏp ap ch'a-pu-su-gi
Side Kick (ITF&WTF)	yŏp ch'a-gi
Side Piercing Kick (ITF)	yŏp ch'a-tchi-rŭ-gi
Side Punching Kick (ITF) [Airborne Combination]	yŏp tchi-rŭ-myŏ ch'a-gi
Side Pushing Kick (ITF)	yŏp ch'a-mil-gi
Side Rising Kick (ITF)	yŏp ch'a-ol-li-gi
Side Thrusting Kick (ITF)	yŏp ch'a-ttul-ki
Side Turning Kick (ITF)	yŏp tol-lyŏ ch'a-gi
Single-hand Wide-open Block and Side Kick (WTF)	oe san-t'ŭl yŏp ch'a-gi
Single Line Kicks (WTF)	il-ch'a ch'a-gi
Skip Kick (ITF)	tŭ-rŏ-ka-myŏ ch'a-gi
Snap Kick (ITF)	ch'a pu-su-gi
Spot Kick (ITF)	kŭ-ja-ri ch'a-gi
Stamping Kick (ITF)	ch'a pap-gi
Stamping Front Kick (WTF)	kul-lŏ ap ch'a-gi
Stamping Kick (WTF)	kul-lŏ ch'a-gi
Stamping Side Kick (WTF)	kul-lŏ yŏp ch'a-gi
Stamping Turning Kick (WTF)	kul-lŏ tol-lyŏ ch'a-gi
Straight Kick (ITF)	tchi-gŏ ch'a-gi
Stretch Kick (WTF)	ppŏ-dŏ ch'a-gi
Sweeping Kick (ITF)	ssŭ-rŏ ch'a-gi
Target Kick (WTF)	p'yo-jŏk ch'a-gi
Thrashing Kick (WTF)	hu-ryŏ ch'a-gi

Three-direction Kick (ITF)	sam-bang ch'a-gi
Thrusting Kick (ITF)	ch'a ttul-ki
Triple Kick (ITF)	sam-jung ch'a-gi
Turning Kick (ITF&WTF)	tol-lyŏ ch'a-gi
Twin-foot Kick (ITF)	ssang-bal ch'a-gi
Twist Kick (WTF)	pi-t'ŭ-rŏ ch'a-gi
Twisting Kick (ITF)	pi-t'ŭ-rŏ ch'a-gi
Two-direction Kick (ITF)	i-bang ch'a-gi
Upward Kick (ITF)	ol-lyŏ ch'a-gi
U-Shape Punching Kick (ITF)	ti-gŭt-ja tchi-rŭ-myŏ ch'a-gi
Vertical Kick (ITF)	se-wŏ ch'a-gi

Additional

Relevant

Techniques

ch'u-ga ki-sul (추가 기술)

Terms listed in this section are associated with additional techniques such as jumping, breaking, dodging, faking, holding, grasping, etc. All terms in this section are listed in alphabetical order according to their English equivalent.

Actions	tong-jak
Attack	kong-gyŏk
Attack Techniques	kong-gyŏk-ki (ITF) or kong-gyŏk ki-sul (WTF)
Backward Double Step-turning (ITF)	twi-ro i-bo om-gyŏ ti-di-myŏ tol-gi
Backward Stepping (ITF)	tŭ-rŏ o-gi
Backward Step-turning (ITF)	twi-ro om-gyŏ ti-di-myŏ tol-gi
Body Dropping (ITF)	mom nat-ch'u-gi
Bowing Posture (ITF)	kyŏng-nye cha-se
Breaking	kyŏk-p'a-gi
Checking (ITF)	mŏm-ch'u-gi

265

Chin-up	t'ŏk-gŏ-ri
Clockwise [turn] (ITF)	o-rŭn-tchok-ŭ-ro to-nŭn
Combination Attack (ITF)	hon-hap kong-gyŏk
Connecting Motion (ITF)	i-ŏ-jin tong-jak
Consecutive Attack (ITF)	yŏn-sok kong-gyŏk
Continuous Motion (ITF)	yŏn-sok tong-jak
Counter Attack (ITF)	pan-gyŏk
Counter Clockwise[turn] (ITF)	oen-tchok-ŭ-ro to-nŭn
Covering (ITF)	ka-ri-u-gi
Crane Stance Hinge (WTF)	hak-da-ri tol-tchŏ-gwi
Cross-cut (ITF)	kŭt-gi
Crossing	kko-gi
Defense	pang-ŏ
Defense Against a Bayonet (ITF)	tae ch'ong-gŏm
Defense Against a Club (ITF)	tae kon-bong
Defense Against a Dagger (ITF)	tae tan-do
Defense Against a Pistol (ITF)	tae kwŏn-ch'ong
Defense Against a Pole (ITF)	tae mong-dung-i
Defense Against a Sudden Attack (ITF)	tae pu-ri kong-gyŏk
Defense Against an Armed Opponent (ITF)	tae mu-gi
Defensive Techniques (ITF)	pang-ŏ-gi
Dodging (ITF&WTF)	p'i-ha-gi

Dodging Attack (ITF)	p'i-ha-myŏ kong-gyŏk
Dodging Technique (ITF&WTF)	p'i-ha-myŏ ki-sul
Double Attack (ITF)	i-jung kong-gyŏk
Double Stepping (ITF)	i-bo om-gyŏ ti-di-gi
Double Stepping Turn (ITF)	i-bo om-gyŏ ti-di-myŏ tol-gi
Drawing the Feet Together (ITF)	mo-dŭm-bal
Drawing up (WTF)	kkŭ-rŏ ol-li-gi
Ducking (ITF)	nat-ch'u-gi
Fake (ITF)	so-gim
Fall or Falling (ITF)	ttŏ-rŏ-ji-gi
Flying [jumping] (ITF)	ttwi-gi
Flying Combination Attack [jumping] (ITF)	ttwi-myŏ hon-hap kong-gyŏk
Flying Consecutive Attack [jumping] (ITF)	ttwi-myŏ yŏn-sok kong-gyŏk
Flying Double Attack [jumping] (ITF)	ttwi-myŏ i-jung kong-gyŏk
Flying Triple Attack [jumping] (ITF)	ttwi-myŏ sam-jung kong-gyŏk
Flying Techniques [jumping] (ITF)	ttwi-myŏ ki-sul
Flying to Evade [jumping] (ITF)	ttwi-gi
Foot Lifting (ITF)	pal tŭl-gi
Foot Tackling (ITF)	pal kŏl-gi
Foot Techniques (ITF&WTF)	pal ki-sul

267

Forward Double Step-turning (ITF)	a-p'ŭ-ro i-bo om-gyŏ ti-di-myŏ tol-gi
Forward Stepping (ITF)	na-ga-gi
Forward Step-turning (ITF)	a-p'ŭ-ro om-gyŏ ti-di-myŏ tol-gi
Ground Dodging (ITF)	nu-wŏ p'i-ha-gi
Ground Techniques (ITF)	nu-wŏ ki-sul
Ground Foot Techniques (ITF)	nu-wŏ pal ki-sul
Ground Hand Techniques (ITF)	nu-wŏ son ki-sul
Ground Knee Bending (ITF)	nu-wŏ mu-rŭp ku-bu-ri-gi
Ground Leg Crossing (ITF)	nu-wŏ ta-ri-kko-gi
Hand Techniques (ITF)	son ki-sul
Head-on Attack (ITF)	mat-ba-da kong-gyŏk
Heaven Hand (ITF)	ha-nŭl-son
High Attack (ITF)	no-p'ŭn-dae kong-gyŏk
Holding (ITF)	pat-ch'i-gi
Instantaneous Attack (ITF)	chŭk-shi kong-gyŏk
Inward Cross-cut	an-ŭ-ro kŭt-gi
Large Hinge (WTF)	k'ŭn tol-tchŏ-gwi
Large Hinge Shape (WTF)	k'ŭn tol-tchŏ-gwi hyŏng
Leg Stretching (ITF)	tari-p'yŏ-gi
Lifting	tŭl-gi
Low Attack (ITF)	na-jŭn-dae kong-gyŏk
Jumping to Evade (ITF)	ttwi-gi
Mid-air [jump-rotating] Techniques (ITF)	ttwi-yŏ tol-myŏ ki-sul

Middle Attack (ITF)	ka-un-dae kong-gyŏk
Motion (ITF)	tong-jak
Movement (ITF)	tong-jak
Outward Cross-cut (ITF)	pak-kŭ-ro kŭt-gi
Overlap Backhand (WTF)	p'o-gaen son-dŭng
Push Barrel (WTF)	t'ong mil-gi
Push Boulder (WTF)	pa-wi mil-gi
Pushing (ITF&WTF)	mil-gi
Reverse Turning Techniques	pan-dae tol-lyŏ ki-sul
Rising (ITF)	ol-li-gi
Rolling (ITF)	kul-lŭ-gi
Self Defense (ITF)	ho-shin-sul
Shifting the Body by Moving Both Feet (ITF)	mi-kkŭ-rŏm pal
Shifting Feet Quickly - Stepping (ITF)	cha-jŭn-bal om-gyŏ ti-di-gi
Shifting Feet Quickly [Dodging] (ITF)	cha-jŭn-bal
Shout (ITF&WTF)	ki-hap
Side Cross-cut (ITF)	yŏp kŭt-gi
Single Stepping (ITF)	il-bo om-gyŏ ti-di-gi
Skipping Techniques (ITF)	tŭ-rŏ-ka-myŏ ki-sul
Sliding (ITF)	mi-kkŭl-gi
Sliding the Feet to Cover Long Distances (ITF)	o-myŏ mi-kkŭl-gi

Slow Motion (ITF)	nŭ-rin tong-jak
Small Hinge (WTF)	cha-gŭn tol-tchŏ-gwi
Small Hinge Shape (WTF)	cha-gŭn tol-tchŏ-gwi hyŏng
Smashing	pu-su-gi
Spot Turning (ITF)	kŭ-ja-ri tol-gi
Stamping Motion (ITF)	ku-rŭ-nŭn tong-jak
Stepping (ITF)	om-gyŏ ti-di-gi
Stepping and Shifting Foot Changing (ITF)	om-gyŏ ti-di-myŏ cha-jŭn-bal
Stepping and Shifting (ITF)	om-gyŏ ti-di-gi
Stepping and Shifting Turn (ITF)	om-gyŏ ti-di-myŏ tol-gi
Stretching (ITF)	p'yŏ-gi
Technique (ITF&WTF)	ki-sul
Technique	tong-jak
Throw or Throwing (ITF)	tŏn-ji-gi
Triple Attack (ITF)	sam-jung kong-gyŏk
Triple Stepping (ITF)	sam-bo om-gyŏ ti-di-gi
Turning (ITF&WTF)	tol-gi
Underneath Pull-out (WTF)	mi-t'ŭ-ro ppae-gi
Upward Pull-out (WTF)	wi-ro ppae-gi
U-Shape Grasp (ITF)	mong-dung-i chap-gi
U-Shape Grasp (ITF)	ti-gŭt-ja put-jap-gi
Vital Point Attacking (ITF)	kŭp-so tchi-rŭ-gi
Yell (ITF&WTF)	ki-hap
Yoke Pull-out (WTF)	mŏng-e ppae-gi

Patterns

p'um-se / t'ŭl

(품세 / 틀)

This section contains general terms relating to patterns practiced by both the ITF and the WTF, and a brief description of pattern meanings taken from official organizational references (additional information can be obtained from many of the references in the bibliography). Some of the information in this section is not found in previous chapters, and as such, Han-gŭl letters have often been included to aid the reader. Pattern entries in this section are listed in order of both organizational structure, and by the rank at which the pattern is practiced.

Miscellaneous Patterns Terms

Ch'ang-Hŏn 창 헌	Patterns system (ITF) named for the penname of General Choi Hong Hi who developed this set of patterns for Taekwon-Do
T'ae-gŭk 태극	Patterns system (WTF)- also means The Great Absolute; Large, Big; Eternity - in Chinese philosophy, it is the source of the Yin and the Yang
P'al-gwae 팔괘	Patterns system (WTF) - also means the 8-Diagrams - from the eight divination symbols in Chinese Book of Changes (i-ching)

t'ŭl 틀	"ITF" term for patterns
hyŏng 형	Old "ITF" term for patterns
p'um-se 품세	"WTF" term for patterns

ITF Colored Belt Patterns

Sa-ju tchi-rŭ-gi 사 주 찌르기	Four-direction Punch (ITF exercise practiced by 10th Grade)
Sa-ju mak-ki 사 주 막기	Four-direction Block (ITF exercise practiced by 10th Grade)
Sa-ju ttul-ki 사 주 뚫기	Four-direction Thrust (ITF exercise practiced by 2nd Grade)
Ch'ŏn-Ji t'ŭl 천 지 틀	ITF pattern practiced by 9th Grade [Chon-Ji means literally "the Heaven the Earth." Interpreted as the creation of the world or the beginning of human history]
Dan-Gun t'ŭl 단 군 틀	ITF pattern practiced by 8th Grade [Named after the holy Dan-Gun, the legendary founder of Korea in the year of 2,333 B.C.]
Do-San t'ŭl 도 산 틀	ITF pattern practiced by 7th Grade [Pseudonym of the patriot Ahn Chang Ho (1876-1938), who devoted his entire life to furthering the education of Korea and its independence movement]
Wŏn-Hyo t'ŭl 원 효 틀	ITF pattern practiced by 6th Grade [Named after noted monk, Wŏn Hyo (617 A.D. - 686 A.D.) who introduced Buddhism to the Shilla Dynasty in the year 686 A.D.]

Yul-Gok t'ŭl 율곡 틀	ITF pattern practiced by 5th Grade [Pseudonym of the great philosopher and scholar Yi I (1536 - 1584), nicknamed the "Confucius of Korea." The pattern diagram is in the shape of the Chinese character 士 (pronounced in Chinese as *shi*), meaning scholar, officer, or soldier and therefore represents scholar]
Jung-Gŭn t'ŭl 중근 틀	ITF pattern practiced by 4th Grade [Named after the patriot Ahn Jung Gŭn (1879-1910), who assassinated Ito, Hiro Bumi, the first Japanese Governor-General of Korea]
T'oi-Gye t'ŭl 퇴계 틀	ITF pattern practiced by 3rd Grade [Pen name of the noted scholar Yi Hwang (1501-1570), an authority on neo-confucianism." The pattern diagram is in the shape of the Chinese character 士 (pronounced in Chinese as *shi*), meaning scholar, officer, or soldier and therefore represents scholar]
Hwa-rang t'ŭl 화랑 틀	ITF pattern practiced by 2nd Grade [Named after the Hwa-rang youth group which eventually became the actual driving force for the unification of the three kingdoms of Korea during the 1st Century A.D.]
Ch'ung-Mu t'ŭl 충무 틀	ITF pattern practiced by 1st Grade [Represents the posthumous title, meaning Loyalty and Valor, given to the great Admiral Yi Sun Shin (1545-1598) of the Yi Dynasty, who invented the first armored battleship (Kobukson) in 1592]

ITF Black Belt Patterns

Kwang-Gae t'ŭl
광개 틀

ITF pattern practiced by 1st Degree [Named after the famous Korean King Kwang Gae Tae Wang (375-418), who regained all the previously lost territories including the greater part of Manchuria. The pattern diagram is in the shape of the Chinese character 土 (pronounced in Chinese as *tu*), meaning earth, ground, or soil and therefore represents the recovery of the lost territory]

Gye-Baek t'ŭl
계백 틀

ITF pattern practiced by 1st Degree [Named after Gye Baek, a great general in the Baek-je Dynasty (660 A.D.)]

P'o-Ŭn t'ŭl
포은 틀

ITF pattern practiced by 1st Degree [Pseudonym of the loyal subject and famous poet Chong Mong Chu (1337-1392), whose poem, "I Would Not Serve a Second Master Though I Might be Crucified a Hundred Times," is well known in Korea]

Ko-Dang t'ŭl
고당 틀

Retired ITF pattern practiced by 2nd Degree [Pseudonym of the patriot Cho Man Shik, who dedicated his life to the Korean Independence Movement and to the education of his people]

Ŭi-Am t'ŭl
의암 틀

ITF pattern practiced by 2nd Degree [Pseudonym of Son Byong Hi, leader of the Korean Independence Movement on March 1, 1919]

Ch'ung-Jang t'ŭl
충장 틀

ITF pattern practiced by 2nd Degree [Pseudonym given to General Kim Duk Ryang who lived during the Yi Dynasty in the 14th century]

274

Ju-ch'e t'ŭl
주체 틀

ITF pattern practiced by 2nd Degree
[Represents the philosophical idea that
was rooted in Baek-du Mountain, that
man is the master of everything and
decides everything. The pattern diagram
is in the shape of the Chinese character
山 (pronounced in Chinese as *shan*),
meaning hill, mountain, or range and
therefore represents Baek-du Mountain]

Ch'oi-Yŏng t'ŭl
최영 틀

ITF pattern practiced by 3rd Degree
[Named after General Choi Yŏng,
Premier and Commander-in-Chief of the
Armed forces during the 14th century
Koryo Dynasty. Choi Yong was greatly
respected for his loyalty, patriotism and
humility]

Sam-Il t'ŭl
삼일 틀

ITF pattern practiced by 3rd Degree
[Denotes the historical date of the
Independence Movement of Korea
which began throughout the country on
March 1, 1919 (thus, the terms "sam"
representing (3) March; and "il"
representing the first day (1)]

Yu-Shin t'ŭl
유신 틀

ITF pattern practiced by 3rd Degree
[Named after General Kim Yu Shin
(595 A.D. - 673 A.D.), a commanding
general during the Shilla Dynasty]

Mun-Mu t'ŭl
문무 틀

ITF pattern practiced by 4th Degree
[Named for the 30 th king of the Shilla
Dynasty, Mun Mu (661 A.D. - 680 A.D.).
According to his will, his body was placed
in the sea where his soul could forever
defend his land against the Japanese]

Yŏn-Gae t'ŭl
연 개 틀

ITF pattern practiced by 4th Degree
[Named after a famous general during
the Koguryo Dynasty, Yŏn Gae So
Moon, who forced the Chinese Tang
Dynasty to quit it's invasion of Korea in
649 A.D.]

Ŭl-Ji t'ŭl
을 지 틀

ITF pattern practiced by 4th Degree
[Named after General Ŭl Ji Mun Dok who
successfully defended Korea against a
Tang's invasion force of nearly a million
soldiers led by Yang Je in 612 A.D.]

Se-jong t'ŭl
세 종 틀

ITF pattern practiced by 5th Degree
[Named after the greatest Korean king,
Se-jong (1397-1450), who invented,
Han-gŭl, the Korean alphabet in 1443.
The pattern diagram is in the shape of the
Chinese character 王 (pronounced in
Chinese as *wang*), meaning king or ruler
and therefore represents king]

Sŏ-San t'ŭl
서 산 틀

ITF pattern practiced by 5th Degree
[Pseudonym of the great monk Choi
Hyong Ung (1520-1604), who lived
during the Yi Dynasty, and organized a
corps of monk soldiers to repulse the
Japanese pirates in 1592]

T'ong-Il t'ŭl
통 일 틀

ITF pattern practiced by 6th Degree
[Denotes the resolution of the unification
of Korea which has been divided since
1945]

WTF Colored Belt Patterns

P'al-gwae il-jang p'um-se 팔괘 일장 품세	WTF P'al-gwae pattern practiced by 9th Grade - representing "Heaven", the sun, the light (the source of the creation of all things in the universe), and depicting one of the eight divination symbols in the Chinese Book of Changes (i-ching)
P'al-gwae i-jang p'um-se 팔괘 이장 품세	WTF P'al-gwae pattern practiced by 8th Grade - representing "Joyfulness" (strength of mind, inner firmness and outer gentleness), and depicting one of the eight divination symbols in the Chinese Book of Changes (i-ching)
P'al-gwae sam-jang p'um-se 팔괘 삼장 품세	WTF P'al-gwae pattern practiced by 7th Grade - representing "Fire" and sun (brightness, representing light and heat), and depicting one of the eight divination symbols in the Chinese Book of Changes (i-ching)
P'al-gwae sa-jang p'um-se 팔괘 사장 품세	WTF P'al-gwae pattern practiced by 6th Grade - representing "Thunder and Lightning" (great power and dignity), and depicting one of the eight divination symbols in the Chinese Book of Changes (i-ching)
P'al-gwae o-jang p'um-se 팔괘 오장 품세	WTF P'al-gwae pattern practiced by 5th Grade - representing "Wind" (mighty force, strength, flexibility, and calmness), and depicting one of the eight divination symbols in the Chinese Book of Changes (i-ching)

P'al-gwae yuk-jang
    p'um-se
팔괘 육장 품세

WTF P'al-gwae pattern practiced by 4th Grade
- representing "Water" (incessant flow,
formless flexibility, and softness), and
depicting one of the eight divination
symbols in the Chinese Book of Changes
(i-ching)

P'al-gwae ch'il-jang
    p'um-se
팔괘 칠장 품세

WTF P'al-gwae pattern practiced by 3rd Grade
- representing "Mountain" (the immovable,
stable, firmness, solemn majesty, and
tranquillity), and depicting one of the eight
divination symbols in the Chinese Book of
Changes (i-ching)

P'al-gwae p'al-jang
    p'um-se
팔괘 팔장 품세

WTF P'al-gwae pattern practiced
by 2nd Grade -representing "Earth"
(the source of life, the root, and also the
beginning and the end), and depicting one
of the eight divination symbols in the
Chinese Book of Changes (i-ching)

T'ae-gŭk il-jang
    p'um-se
태극 일장 품세

WTF T'ae-gŭk pattern practiced by 9th Grade
- representing "Heaven", the sun, the light
(the creation of all things in the universe),
and depicting one of the eight divination
symbols in the Chinese Book of
Changes (i-ching)

T'ae-gŭk i-jang
    p'um-se
태극 이장 품세

WTF T'ae-gŭk pattern practiced by 8th Grade
- representing "Joyfulness" (strength of
mind, inner firmness and outer gentleness),
and depicting one of the eight divination
symbols in the Chinese Book of
Changes (i-ching)

T'ae-gŭk sam-jang p'um-se 태극 삼장 품세	WTF T'ae-gŭk pattern practiced by 7th Grade - representing "Fire" and sun (brightness, representing light and heat), and depicting one of the eight divination symbols in the Chinese Book of Changes (i-ching)
T'ae-gŭk sa-jang p'um-se 태극 사장 품세	WTF T'ae-gŭk pattern practiced by 6th Grade - representing "Thunder and Lightning" (great power and dignity), and depicting one of the eight divination symbols in the Chinese Book of Changes (i-ching)
T'ae-gŭk o-jang p'um-se 태극 오장 품세	WTF T'ae-gŭk pattern practiced by 5th Grade - representing "Wind" (mighty force, strength, flexibility, and calmness), and depicting one of the eight divination symbols in the Chinese Book of Changes (i-ching)
T'ae-gŭk yuk-jang p'um-se 태극 육장 품세	WTF T'ae-gŭk pattern practiced by 4th Grade - representing "Water" (incessant flow, formless flexibility, and softness), and depicting one of the eight divination symbols in the Chinese Book of Changes (i-ching)
T'ae-gŭk ch'il-jang p'um-se 태극 칠장 품세	WTF T'ae-gŭk pattern practiced by 3rd Grade - representing "Mountain" (the immovable, stable, firmness, solemn majesty, and tranquillity), and depicting one of the eight divination symbols in the Chinese Book of Changes (i-ching)
T'ae-gŭk p'al-jang p'um-se 태극 팔장 품세	WTF T'ae-gŭk pattern practiced by 2nd Grade - representing "Earth" (the source of life, the root, and also the beginning and the end), and depicting one of the eight divination symbols in the Chinese Book of Changes (i-ching)

| Kor-yŏ p'um-se
고려 품세 | WTF pattern practiced by 1st Grade
[Representing the Koryŏ Dynasty of
ancient Korea] |

WTF Black Belt Patterns

Kŭm-Gang p'um-se 금강 품세	WTF pattern practiced by 1st Degree [Meaning "Diamond"]
T'ae-Baek p'um-se 태백 품세	WTF pattern practiced by 2nd Degree [Meaning Big, Bright, Saint Mountain - Representing the area around Baek-du Mountain]
P'yŏng-Wŏn p'um-se 평원 품세	WTF pattern practiced by 3rd Degree [Representing a vast "Plain" or Moorland]
Ship-Jin p'um-se 십진 품세	WTF pattern practiced by 4th Degree [Representing long living things such as mountain, sun, water, stones, clouds, and the "Decimal" system]
Chi-T'ae p'um-se 지태 품세	WTF pattern practiced by 5th Degree [Representing coming out of the "Earth"]
Ch'ŏn-Kwŏn p'um-se 천권 품세	WTF pattern practiced by 6th Degree [Representing the "Sky"]
Han-Su p'um-se 한수 품세	WTF pattern practiced by 7th Degree [Representing the adaptability and flexibility of "Water"]
Il-Yŏ p'um-se 일여 품세	WTF pattern practiced by 8th Degree [Representing the "Oneness" of mind (spirit) and body (material)]

Sparring

mat-sŏ-gi / tae-ryŏn (맞서기 / 대련)

Terms listed in this section are associated with tournament activities, sparring, or step-sparring. There are many words that can be used to describe sparring activities. Individuals may choose any word they like to describe a type of sparring.   Individual martial arts organizations, on the other hand, tend to standardize their terms for sparring activities (i.e., kyŏ-ru-gi, mat-sŏ-gi, tae-ryŏn, etc.).   The reader can further investigate the detailed definitions of these and other terms using Chapter 3. All terms in this section are listed in alphabetical order according to their English equivalent.

Blue Contestant (WTF)	ch'ŏng sŏn-su
Blue Contestant Mark (WTF)	ch'ŏng k'o-nŏ
Bout	shi-hap or kyŏ-ru-gi
Break [separate fighters]	kal-lyŏ
Commence	shi-jak
Contestant (WTF)	sŏn-su
Continue	gye-sok

Deduction (WTF) [minus-1]	kam-jŏm [ha-na]
Disqualification (WTF)	shil-kyŏk
Foot Sparring (ITF)	pal mat-sŏ-gi
Free Sparring (WTF)	cha-yu tae-ryŏn
Free Sparring (ITF)	cha-yu mat-sŏ-gi
Injury	pu-sang
Judge	pu-shim
Match (ITF&WTF)	shi-hap or kyŏ-ru-gi
Model Sparring (ITF)	mo-bŏm mat-sŏ-gi
One-step Sparring	il-bo mat-sŏ-gi (ITF) or han-bŏn kyŏ-ru-gi (WTF)
One-way Three-step Sparring (ITF)	han-tchok sam-bo mat-sŏ-gi
Pre-arranged Free Sparring (ITF)	yak-sok cha-yu mat-sŏ-gi
Pre-arranged Model Sparring (ITF)	yak-sok mo-bŏm mat-sŏ-gi
Pre-arranged One-step Sparring (ITF)	yak-sok il-bo mat-sŏ-gi
Pre-arranged Sparring (ITF)	yak-sok mat-sŏ-gi
Pre-arranged Sparring (WTF)	ma-ch'u-ŏ kyŏ-ru-gi
Pre-arranged Sparring (WTF)	yak-sok tae-ryŏn
Pre-arranged Three-step Sparring (ITF)	yak-sok sam-bo mat-sŏ-gi
Pre-arranged Two-step Sparring (ITF)	yak-sok i-bo mat-sŏ-gi

Protective Sparring Equipment	ho-gu
Recorder	ki-rok
Red Contestant (WTF)	hong sŏn-su
Red Contestant Mark (WTF)	hong k'o-nŏ
Referee	chu-shim
Round (WTF)	hwi-jŏn
Rules	kyu-jŏng
Semi-free Sparring (ITF)	pan-ja-yu mat-sŏ-gi
Sparring	shi-hap (WTF) or mat-sŏ-gi or tae-ryŏn (ITF)
Start	shi-jak
Stop	kŭ-man or chŏng-ji
Sub-Referee	pu-shim
System of Sparring (ITF)	mat-sŏ-gi che-do
Three-step Sparring (ITF)	sam-bo mat-sŏ-gi
Timer	gye-shi
Two-step Sparring (ITF)	i-bo mat-sŏ-gi
Two-way Three-step Sparring (ITF)	yang-tchok sam-bo mat-sŏ-gi
Warning (WTF) [minus-1]	kyŏng-go [ha-na]
Weight (WTF)	ch'e-gŭp

Martial Arts

Systems

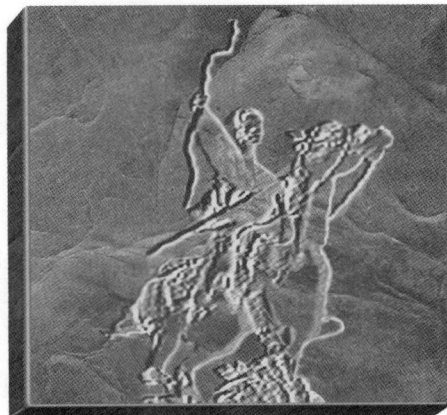

mu-sul che-do (무술 제도)

Terms listed in this section are associated with Martial Arts systems, organizations, or styles. This section does not list all martial arts. It is not meant to be a comprehensive list of all martial art systems, but a list of those that have some relevance to Taekwon-Do. Most of the information in this section is not found in previous chapters, and as such, Han-gŭl letters have been included to aid the reader. All terms in this section are listed in alphabetical order according to their Han-gŭl Romanization.

Ch'ang-Hŏn 창 헌	Patterns System (ITF) created by in 1945 General Choi Hong Hi for Taekwon-Do - also the General's penname
Ch'ang-Mu Kwan 창 무 관	Korean Martial Art school founded by In Yun P'yung in 1946
Chi-Do Kwan 지 도 관	Korean Martial Art school founded by Yun Gae P'yung in 1946
Ch'ung-Mu Kwan 충 무 관	Korean Martial Art school founded by Lee Won Kuk in 1945

Ch'ŏng-Do Kwan
청 도 관

Korean Martial Art school [Civilian] founded by General Choi Hong Hi in 1954 with the help of Nam Tae Hi

Hap-Ki-Do
합 기 도

Korean Martial Art school founded by Choi Yong Shul in 1940

Hwa-Rang-Do
화랑 도

Korean Martial Art school restarted by Joo Bang Lee and Joo Sang Lee in 1960

Ji-Do Kwan
지 도 관

Korean Martial Art school founded by Yun Gae Byang in 1953

Ka-ra-t'e
가라테

Karate, the generic term for the Japanese empty handed Martial Art

Kuk-je T'ae-kwŏn-Do Yŏn-maeng
국제 태권도 연맹

International Taekwon-Do Federation [formed on March 22, 1966]

Kuk-ki-wŏn
국기원

World Headquarters of the World Taekwon-Do Federation

Kwŏn-Bŏp
권법

Chinese Martial Art [Boxing]

Mu-Dŭk Kwan
무 득 관

Korean Martial Art school founded by Hwang Ki in 1945

O-Do Kwan
오 도 관

Korean Martial Art school [Military] founded by General Choi Hong Hi in 1954 with the help of Nam Tae Hi

Sang-Mu Kwan
상 무 관

Korean Martial Art school founded by Ro P'yung Chik in 1953

Se-gye T'ae-kwŏn-Do
  Yŏn-maeng
세계 태권도 연맹

World Taekwon-Do Federation
[formed on May 28, 1973]

Su-Bak-Gi
수 박 기

Ancient Korean Martial Art
[935 A.D. - 1392 A.D.]

Tang-Su-Do
  Mu-Dŭk Kwan
당수도 무득 관

Korean Martial Art school founded
  by Hwang Ki from Mu-Duk
  Kwan founded in 1945

T'ae-kwŏn-Do
태권 도

Korean Martial Art named in 1955
  by General Choi Hong Hi, the
  Father of Taekwon-Do

T'ae-Kyŏn
태 견

Ancient Korean Martial Art
  dating back to 37 B.C.

Yun-Mu Kwan
윤 무 관

Korean Martial Art school founded
  by Sup Chun Song in 1945

Additional

Taekwon-Do

Terms

ch'u-ga T'ae-kwŏn-Do yong-ŏ
(추가 태권도 용어)

This section contains individual terms which are of interest to the martial artist, but may not have logically fit in any of the previous sections in this chapter so that you can easily find individual terms. All terms in this section are listed in alphabetical order according to their English equivalent.

Air Shield (ITF)	kong-gi pang-p'ae
Art	-Do [Sino-Korean]
Assistant Instructor (ITF)	pu-sa-bŏm
Assistant Instructor Sir (ITF)	pu-sa-bŏm-nim
Attack	kong-gyŏk
Balance	chung-shim
Basic - Basic Foundation	ki-bon
Bayonet	ch'ong-gŏm
Belt	tti

Block or Blocking (ITF&WTF)	mak-ki
Blocking Apparatus (ITF)	mak-ki tae
Bout	shi-hap or kyŏ-ru-gi
Breaking	kyŏk-p'a-gi
Breathing	ho-hŭp
Calisthenics (ITF)	to-su-dal-lyŏn
Certain Victory	p'il-sŭng
Certificate	cha-gyŏk-jŭng
Cho-sŏn Dynasty	Cho-sŏn shi-dae (1392 - 1910)
Choi Hong Hi, General [Father of Taekwon-Do]	Choi Hong Hi, Chang-gun
Classification of Instructor (ITF)	sa-bŏm pu-ryu
Classification of Umpire (ITF)	shim-p'an pu-ryu
Club [weapon]	kon-bong
Cold Showers and Baths	naeng-su ma-ch'al
Combination (ITF)	hon-hap
Competition (ITF)	kyŏng-gi
Concentration (ITF)	chip-jung
Concentration (ITF&WTF)	ki-hap
Connecting Motion (ITF)	i-ŏ-jin tong-jak
Continuous (ITF)	yŏn-sok
Continuous Motion (ITF)	yŏn-sok tong-jak
Correct	o-rŭm
Dagger	tan-do

Defense (ITF)	pang-ŏ
Degree Certificate (ITF)	tan-jŭng
Demonstration (ITF)	shi-bŏm
Dynasty	shi-dae
Exercise	un-dong
Exercises (ITF)	yŏn-sŭp
Equipment (ITF)	su-ryŏn chang-bi
Fast Motion (ITF)	ppa-rŭn tong-jak
Federation	yŏn-maeng
Fist	kwŏn [Sino-Korean]
Flag [National]	kuk-gi
Flexibility	shin-ch'uk
Focus Shield (ITF)	ch'o-jŏm pang-p'ae
Foot	pal, -bal, or t'ae [Sino-Korean]
Forging (ITF)	tal-lyŏn
Forging Bag (ITF)	tal-lyŏn ppaek
Forging Post (ITF)	tal-lyŏn chu
Foundation	ki-bon
Fundamental Exercises	ki-bon yŏn-sŭp
Grab [Grasp] (ITF)	chap-gi
Grade Certificate	kŭp-jŭng
Grading Test (ITF)	shim-sa
Guard or Guarding (ITF)	tae-bi
Headquarters for the WTF	Kuk-ki-won
Heaven Hand (ITF)	ha-nŭl-son

History	yŏk-sa
Hwa-rang Code of Ethics	Hwa-rang Do
Incorrect	t'ŭl-lim
Injury	pu-sang
International	kuk-je
International Taekwon-Do Federation (ITF)	Kuk-je T'ae-kwŏn-Do Yŏn-maeng
Knife	k'al
Korean Ancient Kingdoms	Ko-gu-ryŏ, Paek-je, and Shil-la
Headquarters of the World Taekwon-Do Federation	Kuk-ki-wŏn
Life Energy	ki [Sino-Korean]
Koguryo Dynasty	Ko-gu-ryŏ shi-dae (37 B.C. - 668A.D.)
Koryo Dynasty	Ko-ryŏ shi-dae (918 A.D. - 1392)
Lifting	tŭl-gi
Line	sŏn
Martial Art	mu-sul
Match	shi-hap or kyŏ-ru-gi
Mirror	kŏ-ul
Mountain	san
Mountain Climbing	tŭng-san
Movement, motion (WTF)	tong-jak
Paekje Dynasty	Paek-je shi-dae (18 B.C. - 663 A.D.)
Pistol	kwŏn-ch'ong
Pole (staff)	mong-dung-i

Practice Pants (ITF)	pa-ji
Practice Shirt (ITF)	chŏ-go-ri
Practice Suit [Uniform] (ITF&WTF)	to-bok
Protective Sparring Equipment	ho-gu
Pushups	mom-tong pa-ch'im
Rank	gye-gŭp (ITF) or p'um-gye (WTF)
Recorder	ki-rok
Referee	chu-shim
Rules	kyu-jŏng
School	kwan
Senior (WTF)	sŏn-bae
Shilla Dynasty	Shil-la shi-dae (57 B.C. - 935 A.D.)
Shout	ki-hap
Sir	-nim [when added as a suffix]
Slow Motion (ITF)	nŭ-rin tong-jak
Sponge Pad (ITF)	sŭ-p'on-ji pe-gae
Staff (pole)	mong-dung-i
Straight	sŏn
Straw Pad (ITF)	chip pe-gae
Stretching	p'yŏ-gi
Strong	kang-han
Student (ITF)	che-ja
Student (WTF)	su-ryŏn-saeng

Taekwon-Do	T'ae-kwŏn-Do [Korean Martial Art - the individual words originated from the Chinese set of characters 跆 拳 道 (Foot-Fist-Way) pronounced in Chinese as *tai-quan-dao*]
Technique	tong-jak
Technique (ITF&WTF)	ki-sul
Timer	gye-shi
Trainee	su-ryŏn-saeng
Training	su-ryŏn or tal-lyŏn
Training Aids (ITF)	tal-lyŏn-gu
Training Equipment (ITF)	su-ryŏn chang-bi
Training Hall (ITF)	to-jang
Training Schedule (ITF)	su-ryŏn gye-hoek-p'yo
Turtle Ship	kŏ-buk-sŏn
Umpire (ITF)	shim-p'an
Umpire Classification (ITF)	shim-p'an pu-ryu
Way	-Do [Sino-Korean]
Weak	ya-kan
World-wide	se-gye-jŏk
World Taekwon-Do Federation (WTF)	Se-gye T'ae-kwŏn-Do Yŏn-maeng
Yell (ITF&WTF)	ki-hap
Yi Dynasty	I-jo shi-dae (1392 - 1910)

Combinations

of Technical

Terms

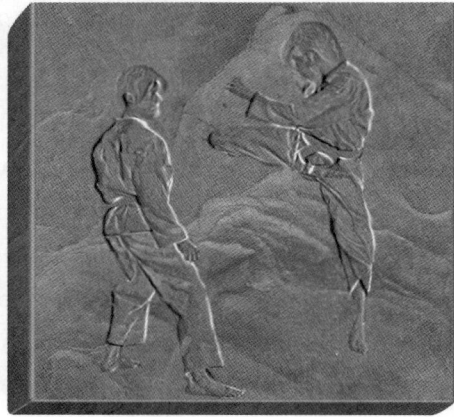

hon-hap yong-ŏ (혼합 용어)

As in all languages, Korean grammar provides many variations and endings for words used in complex phrases. The martial arts student is often faced with a list of detailed technical terms presented in the form of a string of nouns. These are not always presented in sentence form, but in the form of short commands. This command form is representative of many of the terms listed in this book. They are mostly in the form of either individual words, partial noun strings, or partial sentences. This section provides the reader with a small list of examples of strings of technical terms to illustrate how some of these terms might appear in different forms.

As stated in the introduction, it is not our intent to instruct the reader in Korean grammatical rules, however, we have provided a Han-gŭl representation of each phrase to aid the reader in understanding some of the word changes.

There are three syllables often used to connect words in Taekwon-Do terminology have the meaning "with" or "and." They are:

> **-wa** (와), as in

>> Kick with Punch   ch'a-gi-**wa** tchi-rŭ-gi
>>
>> 차기와 찌르기

> **-kwa** (과), as in

>> Hand and Foot   Son-**kwa** pal
>>
>> 손과 발

>> or;

> **-go** (고), as in

>> Grasp and Kick   put-jap-**go** ch'a-gi
>>
>> 붙잡고 차기

These are attached to the end of the first in these two-word strings.

Strings of Technical Terms

Flying Combination Kick with Punch [jumping]	ttwi-myŏ hon-hap ch'a-gi-wa tchi-rŭ-gi 뛰며 혼합 차기와 찌르기
Flying Combination Side Strike [jumping] (ITF)	ttwi-myŏ hon-hap yŏp ttae-ri-gi 뛰며 혼합 옆 때리기
Flying Consecutive Kick [jumping]	ttwi-myŏ yŏn-sok ch'a-gi 뛰며 연속 차기
Flying Double Horizontal Side Thrust [jumping] (ITF)	ttwi-myŏ i-jung su-p'yŏng yŏp ttul-ki 뛰며 이중 수평 옆 뚫기

Flying Double Vertical Front Thrust [jumping] (ITF)	ttwi-myŏ i-jung su-jik ap ttul-ki 뛰며 이 중 수직 앞 뚫기
Flying Four-direction Kick [jumping]	ttwi-myŏ sa-bang ch'a-gi 뛰며 사방 차기
Flying Front and Twisting Kick	ttwi-myŏ ap ch'a-go 　pi-t'ŭ-rŏ ch'a-gi 뛰며 앞 차고 비틀어 차기
Flying Reverse Hook Kick and Double Side Kick [jumping]	ttwi-myŏ pan-dae kŏ-rŏ 　ch'a-go i-jung yŏp ch'a-gi 뛰며 반대 걸어 차고 이 중 옆 차기
Flying Triple Side Front Kick [jumping]	ttwi-myŏ sam-jung yŏp ap ch'a-gi 뛰며 삼 중 옆 앞 차기
Flying Two-direction Kick [jumping]	ttwi-myŏ i-bang ch'a-gi 뛰며 이 방 차기
Front Leg Quadruple Kick	ap ta-ri sa-jung ch'a-gi 앞 다리 사중 차기
Front Leg Sweeping Kick	ap ta-ri ssŭ-rŏ ch'a-gi 앞 다리 쓸어 차기
Mid-air [jump-rotating] Double Kick	ttwi-ŏ tol-myŏ i-jung ch'a-gi 뛰어 돌며 이 중 차기
Skip Pick-shape Kick	tŭ-rŏ-ka-myŏ kok-gwaeng-i ch'a-gi 들어 가 며 곡 괭이 차기
Skip Side Front Pushing Kick	tŭ-rŏ-ka-myŏ yŏp ap ch'a-mil-gi 들어 가 며 옆 앞 차 밀 기
Walking Stance Obverse Punch	kŏn-nŭn sŏ pa-ro tchi-rŭ-gi 걷는 서 바로 찌르기
Walking Stance Reverse Punch	kŏn-nŭn sŏ pan-dae tchi-rŭ-gi 걷는 서 반대 찌르기

Conversational

Phrases

This section provides the reader with a small list of conversational phrases which might be encountered while interacting with other martial artists inside, and outside of the to-jang. (Note: We have only included phrases that are **polite-honorific**, as those are the phrases that should be used in a martial arts class.) As stated in the introduction, it is not our intent to provide the reader with an understanding of the Korean language or grammar, however, we have provided Han-gŭl letters in this section to aid the reader in the pronunciation of these phrases. All terms in this section are listed in alphabetical order according to their English equivalent.

Good morning.	An-nyŏng ha-shim-ni-kka ?
Good evening.	안녕 하십니까 ?
Good afternoon.	
How are you?	

    (formal greeting used any time of day)

    or

Good morning.	An-nyŏng ha-se-yo ?
Good evening.	안녕 하세요 ?
Good afternoon.	
How are you?	

    (informal form of greeting used any time of day)

Fine, and how are you?
(formal)

Ye an-nyŏng ha-shim-ni-kka ?
예 ,안녕 하십니까 ?

or

Fine, and how are you?
(informal)

Ye an-nyŏng ha-se-yo ?
예 ,안녕 하세요 ?

Good bye. (formal)
[to person (s) who are leaving]

An-nyŏng-hi ka-ship-shi-o .
안녕 히 가십시오 .

or

Good bye. (informal)
[to person (s) who are leaving]

An-nyŏng-hi ka-se-yo .
안녕히 가세요 .

Good bye. (formal)
[to person (s) who are staying]

An-nyŏng-hi gye-ship-shi-o .
안녕히 계십시오 .

or

Good bye. (informal)
[to person (s) who are staying]

An-nyŏng-hi gye-se-yo .
안녕히 계세요 .

Good night. (formal)

An-nyŏng-hi chu-mu-ship-shi-o
안녕히 주무십시오 .

or

Good night. (informal)

An-nyŏng-hi chu-mu-se-yo .
안녕히 주무세요 .

Thank you. (formal)
[Native Korean]

Ko-map sŭm-ni-da .
고맙 습니다 .

or

Thank you. (formal)
[kam-sa is Sino-Korean]

Kam-sa ham-ni-da .
감사 합니다 .

Thank you very much. (formal)
   [Native Korean]

  or

Thank you very much. (formal)
   [kam-sa is Sino-Korean]

Tae-dan-hi ko-map sŭm-ni-da .
대단히 고맙 습니다 ·

Tae-dan-hi kam-sa ham-ni-da .
대단히 감사 합니다 ·

Pardon me.
Excuse me.

Shil-lye ham-ni-da .
실례 합니다 ·

I am sorry.

Mi-an ham-ni-da .
미안 합니다 ·

That's all right.
You're welcome.
Not at all.

Ch'ŏn ma-ne-yo .
천 만에요 ·

Yes

ye or ne
예   or 네

No

a-ni-o
아니오

Sir, father, honorable master,
   mister, esquire

- nim
- 님

[a suffix attached to a title expressing respect, e.g., sa-bŏm-**nim**]

Appendix A
The Structure of Han-gŭl

Han-gŭl is a phonetic alphabet which was invented by King Se-jong in 1443. It originally consisted of twenty-eight letters containing seventeen consonants and eleven vowels (see Chapter 1, "Korea's King Se-jong and the Development of Han-gŭl"). Over the years, the original twenty-eight letters have been consolidated to fourteen consonants and ten basic vowels.

Individual syllables in Han-gŭl are written with consonants and vowels arranged in groups. These syllables consist of either; a consonant+vowel (e.g., 주 , 지), a consonant+vowel+consonant (e.g., 톡, 선 , 끝), or infrequently, as a consonant+vowel+consonant-cluster (e.g., 긁 , 많). The basic placement and pronunciation of individual Han-gŭl consonants and vowels are more fully illustrated in the McCune-Reischauer Romanization Table in Appendix D.

The syllables formed with Han-gŭl letters always start with a consonant. Primarily, syllables begin with one of the fourteen basic consonants [ki-yŏk (ㄱ), ni-ŭn (ㄴ), ti-gŭt (ㄷ), ri-ŭl (ㄹ), mi-ŭm (ㅁ), pi-ŭp (ㅂ), shi-ot (ㅅ), i-ŭng (ㅇ), chi-ŭt (ㅈ), ch'i-ŭt (ㅊ), ki-ŭk (ㅋ), t'i-ŭt (ㅌ), p'i-ŭp (ㅍ), and hi-ŭt (ㅎ)]. When a syllable begins with a vowel sound, that vowel is proceeded by the initial consonant i-ŭng (ㅇ), which has a silent sound when it is in the initial position [see table in Appendix C]. A syllable can also start with one of the five "twin" consonants [ssang ki-yŏk (ㄲ), ssang ti-gŭt (ㄸ), ssang pi-ŭp (ㅃ), ssang shi-ot (ㅆ), or ssang chi-ŭt (ㅉ)]. These "twin" consonants are not like a "double" version of their single consonant counterparts, as their written form might lead one to speculate. They actually sound like a very tense form of their single consonant counterpart. When two different consonants appear together at the end of a syllable they are described as a consonant-cluster (e.g., 앉).

Examples and pronunciation of both "twin" consonants and consonant-clusters are discussed further in Appendix C.

The initial consonant is placed in one of two positions. If the vowel is a vertical vowel (i.e., ㅏ, ㅐ, ㅓ, ㅔ, or ㅣ, etc.), then the consonant is placed to the left of the vowel (i.e., 가 , 내 , 머 , 데 , 리 , etc.). If it is a horizontal vowel, (i.e., ㅗ , ㅜ, ㅡ , ㅠ , etc.), the consonant is placed above the vowel (i.e., 고 , 누 , 므 , 듀 , etc.). Compound vowels, which include combinations of the basic vertical and horizontal vowels (i.e., 세 , 계 , 원 , 뛰 , 흰, etc.), follow these same rules.

The best way to write the Korean language is in vernacular Han-gŭl, essentially because it is a phonetic representation of that language. As in many languages, letters form syllables which make words that flow together in a conversation. As the language is spoken, the mixture of consonants and vowels combine to modify the sound of each syllable in a word. The pronunciation of an individual syllable may change, depending upon its combination with other syllables in a word. This pronunciation change is created by the linkage between syllables. When two syllables are adjacent to each other in a word, the sound of the first syllable links with the sound of the second. This creates variations in the pronunciation of words, as opposed to the pronunciation of each of the individual letters or syllables in the word.

Some of the letters in a word may change their pronunciation, as some consonants fall silent or become soft, and others become aspirated or tense (see discussions in Appendix C). Whether the sound of a letter remains the same, or becomes silent, soft, aspirated or tense depends upon its placement in a word and its linkage with surrounding letters. The placement of consonants can be either: as the "initial" consonant of the first syllable of a word; in the "medial" position (the first consonant in the next, or following syllables) of a word; or as the "final" consonant in a syllable or word. The terms initial, medial, and final are therefore used to represent the position of a consonant in a word, and are discussed and illustrated in Appendix C. The following paragraphs contain additional information which the authors have included to allow the reader to better understand the Romanization of Han-gŭl.

Some individual consonants that change their pronunciation with their placement in syllables and words are; ki-yŏk (ㄱ), ti-gŭt (ㄷ), ri-ŭl (ㄹ), pi-ŭp (ㅂ), shi-ot (ㅅ), chi-ŭt (ㅈ), and hi-ŭt (ㅎ). As an example, the letter ki-yŏk is pronounced similar to an English **k** when in the initial position in a word, but similar to an English **g**, when in the medial position of a word. At the end, or final position of a syllable, the ki-yŏk is pronounced similar to an un-aspirated English **k** where the tongue stays put and air is not released. The pronunciation of the Korean letters ni-ŭn (ㄴ) and mi-ŭm (ㅁ) does not change much. However, because they are nasal consonants, they tend to modify consonants they are linked with to produce other sounds in the linkages like **n**, **m**, and **ng** [e.g., 묵 녑 sounds like **mung-nyŏm** as if it were written in Han-gŭl as 뭉 녑]. A better understanding of the effect that syllable linkages have on the pronunciation of words is illustrated both in Appendix C, and in the many Romanized Han-gŭl entries throughout Chapter 2.

When consonant clusters are followed by a syllable that begins with a vowel sound [having an i-ŭng (ㅇ) as the initial consonant], the sound of one of the consonants is pronounced as the final consonant of that syllable; and the other is pronounced as the initial consonant of the next syllable (e.g., 앉 어 sounds like **an-jŏ** as if it were written in Han-gŭl as 안 저). When the consonant-cluster is followed by a syllable that begins with a consonant, one of the consonants in the cluster becomes silent, and the initial consonant in the next syllable generally becomes tense (e.g., 뚫 기 sounds like **ttul-ki** instead of "ttulh-gi"). Consonant rules are discussed in greater detail in the books College Korean and Functional Korean, in the Bibliography, and to some extent in Appendix C.

When Han-gŭl is arranged in syllable groups to form words that are then used to make up sentences, it is sometimes written as a continuous string of syllables with no definitive spacing. To allow Romanized Han-gŭl to be more easily pronounced and to appear more recognizable, most transliteration systems provide spaces, capitals, special letters/symbols, and hyphens within words. There are many ways to represent words and syllable connections in a Romanized form (e.g., T'aeKwŏnDo, Taekwondo, Tae Kwon Do, T'ae-kwŏn-do, or mixtures such as Taekwŏn-do and T'aekwŏn-Do). In this book we have chosen to place spaces between individual Korean words, and hyphens between individual syllables within a Romanized word, to allow the reader the most information concerning the meaning, pronunciation, and Han-gŭl spelling for each term (e.g., T'ae-kwŏn-Do). Hyphens enhance the readers understanding of Korean by breaking out individual syllables which frequently occur, such as "pal" or "son" (as seen in Chapter 2). English entries in this book [not those in Romanized Korean form] have been retained in their usual accepted English forms (e.g., Taekwon-Do). We hope this format will allow more insight into the formation of the words and terms in this book, and help the reader to recognize the variety of options that can be used by others in spelling Korean terms in English.

It should be noted that there is no distinction in Han-gŭl between capital or lower-case letters. Therefore, it is appropriate to represent all Romanized Korean words in lower-case letters. There are notable exceptions to this rule such as; proper names, countries, titles, pattern names, martial art systems, and the beginning of sentences.

Appendix B
A Guide to
Han-gŭl Vowels

Han-gŭl has twenty-one vowels, consisting of ten basic vowels, of which six are simple vowels, and four are palletized forms of these simple vowels. There are also eleven vowels that are compound versions of the ten basic vowels.

Included in the six simple vowels are four that correspond well with English letters [**a** (ㅏ), **o** (ㅗ), **u** (ㅜ), and **i** (ㅣ)]. The Korean vowel **i** (ㅣ) is sometimes pronounced like the English sound **yi** when it is used in the beginning of proper nouns. The other two simple vowels have a unique pronunciation not represented in the English vowel set (i.e., ㅓ and ㅡ). The modified McCune-Reischauer Romanization system uses **ŏ** (ㅓ) and **ŭ** (ㅡ) to represent these sounds.

Pronunciation rules for individual, palatalized and compound vowels are illustrated in the table at the end of this appendix. The sound for a palletized vowel is formed by pushing on the palate with the back of the tongue at the beginning of the vowel sound, resulting in a tense **y** sound being added to the basic simple vowel [e.g., **ya** (ㅑ), **yŏ** (ㅕ), **yo** (ㅛ), and **yu** (ㅠ)].

Compound vowels are created by combining two or three of the ten basic vowels. The resulting pronunciation is a combination of the sounds of these basic vowels [i.e., **ae** (ㅐ), **yae** (ㅒ), **e** (ㅔ), **ye** (ㅖ), **oe** (ㅚ), **ŭi** (ㅢ), etc.].

Compound vowels that have an initial sound like the English letter **w,** occur when the Korean letters **o** (ㅗ) and **u** (ㅜ) combine with other basic vowels [e.g., **wa** (ㅘ), **wae** (ㅙ), **wŏ** (ㅝ), **we** (ㅞ), **wi** (ㅟ)]. These compound vowels, and their Romanization, represent contractions of their basic vowel components [e.g., **o** (ㅗ) + **a** (ㅏ) = **wa** (ㅘ) ; **u** (ㅜ) + **ŏ** (ㅓ) = **wŏ** (ㅝ)]. These Korean letters are also illustrated in the table at the end of this appendix and in the books College Korean and Functional Korean, in the Bibliography.

The Korean language and the English language have several letters that do not transliterate from one language to the other. The letters in each language have their own pronunciation. Therefore, it is very important to note these differences, so that the English speaking reader can obtain the best possible understanding of vowel pronunciation throughout this book.

The vowels listed in the following table have been presented in Korean alphabetical order.

Vowel	Roman-ization	Sound	English word with Sound		
ㅏ	a	ah	f**a**ther	or	f**a**r
ㅐ	ae	ae	c**a**ke	or	b**a**yonet
ㅑ	ya	ya	**ya**rd	or	**ya**cht
ㅒ	yae	yae	**ya**m	or	**Ya**nkee
ㅓ	ŏ	auh	c**au**ght	or	**Au**gust
ㅔ	e	eh	p**e**t	or	fl**e**sh
ㅕ	yŏ	yah	**ya**wn	or	be**yo**nd
ㅖ	ye	ye	**ye**s	or	**ye**llow
ㅗ	o	oh	n**o**te	or	t**o**e
ㅘ	wa	wa	**wa**ter	or	**wa**ll
ㅙ	wae	way	q**ua**ke	or	**wa**ke
ㅚ	oe	weh	**wi**nter	or	**wi**ndow
ㅛ	yo	yo	**yo**ke	or	**yo**ga
ㅜ	u	oo	m**oo**n	or	Z**u**lu
ㅝ	wŏ	wuh	**wo**n	or	**wo**nder
ㅞ	we	we	**we**t	or	**we**lt
ㅟ	wi	wee	s**wee**p	or	**we**ak
ㅠ	yu	you	**Yu**kon	or	**u**se
ㅡ	ŭ	uh	h**u**nt	or	c**u**t
ㅢ	ŭi	uh-ee	sound of "**u**gl**y**" without *gl*, or "m**u**dd**y**" without *m* or *dd*.		
ㅣ	i	ee	f**ee**t	or	p**ee**ve
	(Yi)	yee	or beginning proper nouns		
			yield	or	**ye**ast

Appendix C
A Guide to
Han-gŭl Consonants

Consonants have different pronunciations depending on their position in a word. Two variations of a given consonant often heard in spoken Korean as either aspirated and unaspirated. Whether the consonant is aspirated or not depends both on the characteristics of the letter itself, and on its linkage with other syllables. The pronunciation of a consonant may change if it is located in the initial, medial, or final position of a syllable or word. Thus, the terms **initial**, **medial**, and **final** refer to the placement of the consonant within syllables and words, as discussed in Appendix A. Korean syllables always begin with a consonant, but depending on the individual word, it may or may not have a final consonant.

Aspirated consonants have an explosion of air released at the end, and unaspirated consonants do not. Final unaspirated consonants result from the formation of the mouth at the end of Korean words, allowing no release of air. We denote aspirated consonants with an apostrophe [e.g., **p'** (ㅍ) as in **p'**il-sŭng], so the reader will know the correct pronunciation of a given letter, and will be able to tell the difference between variations of similar letters like pi-ŭp (ㅂ) and p'i-ŭp (ㅍ).

The Korean language and the English language have several letters that do not transliterate from one language to the other. The letters in each language have their own pronunciation. Because of differences in pronunciation, it is difficult to find an English letter that easily represents some sounds in Korean. It is important to note the differences, so that the English speaking reader can obtain the best possible understanding of individual pronunciations for a particular letter or word. These sounds can be approximated if one tries to pronounce a word so that it can not be determined which of

311

the two is being spoken (i.e., saying the word **kill** in such a way that the listener can not determine if it is **kill** or **gill**). This approximates the sound of the Han-gŭl letter ki-yŏk (ㄱ) which has a pronunciation somewhere between the English letters **k** and **g** (e.g., blending the initial sounds of **k**ill and **g**ill), and is created with a different area of the mouth than either the English **k** or **g**. The pronunciation can have more emphasis on either the **k**, or the **g,** depending on its placement in a syllable or word and how it is affected by other consonants in a linkage. The Korean letters ti-gŭt (ㄷ), ri-ŭl (ㄹ), pi-ŭp (ㅂ), shi-ot (ㅅ), and chi-ŭt (ㅈ) also contain sounds that are slightly different than those of English letters. The Korean letter ti-gŭt (ㄷ) has a pronunciation somewhere between the English letters **t**, and **d** (e.g., blending the initial sounds of the words **tip** and **dip**). The ri-ŭl (ㄹ) has a pronunciation somewhere between the English letters **r**, and **l** (e.g., blending the initial sounds of the words **right** and **light**). The pi-ŭp (ㅂ) has a pronunciation somewhere between the English letters **p**, and **b** (e.g., blending the initial sounds of the words **pill** and **bill**). The shi-ot (ㅅ) has a pronunciation somewhere between the English letters **s**, and **sh** (e.g., blending the initial sounds of the words **she** and **see**). The chi-ŭt (ㅈ) has a pronunciation somewhere between the English letters **ch**, and **j** (e.g., blending the initial sounds of the words **cheap** and **jeep**).

The five "twin" consonants [ssang ki-yŏk (ㄲ), ssang ti-gŭt (ㄸ), ssang pi-ŭp (ㅃ), ssang shi-ot (ㅆ), and ssang chi-ŭt (ㅉ)] sound like a very tense version of their single consonant counterparts followed by a very slight aspiration. There are no really good examples in English of the sounds of these "twin" consonants, however, they can be approximated. When pronouncing the examples in the table at the end of this section, exaggerate the tense-ness on the consonants in the English words and follow with only a slight aspiration.

To give the reader a better understanding of changes in consonant pronunciation for consonant-vowel or consonant-consonant linkages between syllables, it may be helpful to illustrate some of the guidelines for their pronunciation:

• When a syllable ending in a consonant is followed in the same word by a syllable beginning with a vowel sound, the final consonant of the first syllable is pronounced as the beginning consonant of the second syllable [e.g., 높은 대 is pronounced **no-p'ŭn-dae** as if it were written in Han-gŭl as 노픈 대 ; or 속임 is pronounced **so-gim** as if it were written 소김].

• When a ni-ŭn (ㄴ) and a ri-ŭl (ㄹ) form the link between syllables, they both sound like a ri-ŭl (ㄹ) [e.g., 신 라 is pronounced **Shil-la** as if it were written in Han-gŭl as 실 라]. Additionally, the letter ri-ŭl (ㄹ) sounds like a ni-ŭn (ㄴ) if it follows any consonant other than a ni-ŭn (ㄴ) [e.g.,; 발 날 sounds like **pal-lal** as if it were written in Han-gŭl as 발랄].

• When the first syllable of two linked syllables ends with a hi-ŭt (ㅎ), that hi-ŭt is often silent, and the other consonant involved in this type of linkage is often modified to a more aspirated or tense form [e.g., 놓 자 is pronounced **no-ch'a** as if it were written in Han-gŭl as 노차 ; 노랗 고 is pronounced **no-ra-k'o** as if it were written in Han-gŭl as 노라코].

• When the second syllable of two linked syllables begins with a hi-ŭt (ㅎ), the hi-ŭt is often silent, and the other consonant involved in this type of linkage is often pronounced as the beginning consonant of the second syllable in a more aspirated or tense form [e.g., 굽 힌 is pronounced **ku-p'in** as if it were written in Han-gŭl as 구핀].

• Consonant clusters at the end of one syllable are usually pronounced like one of the consonants, with the other being silent [e.g., 앉 is pronounced **an** as if it were written in

313

Han-gŭl as 안 , and 뚫 is pronounced **ttul** as if it were written in Han-gŭl as 뚤]. However, when followed by a syllable beginning with the consonant iŭng (a vowel sound), the first consonant in the consonant cluster is pronounced as the final consonant of that syllable and the second consonant is pronounced as the beginning consonant of the second syllable [e.g., 앉 아 요 is pronounced **an-ja-yo** as if it were written in Han-gŭl as 안 자 요]. When a consonant cluster is followed by a syllable beginning in a consonant other than i-ŭng, the three consonants are often modified, since three consonants are never pronounced together in Korean speech. The modification of these consonants varies depending on the combination of consonants involved [e.g., 뚫 기 is pronounced **ttul-ki** as if it were written in Han-gŭl as 뚤 끼 ; or 닭다 is pronounced **tam-tta** as if it were written in Han-gŭl as 감 따].

- When the second syllable of two linked syllables begins with a ni-ŭn (ㄴ) or a mi-ŭm (ㅁ), most final consonants involved in these types of linkages are modified to a more nasal form such as **n**, **m**, or **ng** [e.g., 묵 념 is pronounced **mung-nyŏm** as if it were written in Han-gŭl as 뭉념; 걷 는 is pronounced **kŏn-nŭn** as if it were written in Han-gŭl as 건 는 ; or 톱날 is pronounced **t'om-nal** as if it were written in Han-gŭl as 톰날].

For a more in depth understanding of Romanization/pronunciation guidelines, or to learn more about the Romanization rules used in this book, please refer to the books College Korean and Functional Korean, in the Bibliography. Throughout this book, we have Romanized terms according to the McCune-Reischauer Romanization Table in Appendix D, and the pronunciation rules in the book College Korean and Functional Korean.

The consonants listed in the following table have been presented in Korean alphabetical order.

Con-sonant	Romanization			English word with Sound		
	initial	medial	final	initial	medial	final
ㄱ	k	g	k⌐	**k**ing	be**g**in	kic**k**⌐
ㄲ	kk	kk	k⌐	s̸**k**ill*	s**k**y	pic**k**⌐
ㄴ	n	n	n	**n**eck	pa**n**el	pai**n**
ㄷ	t	d	t⌐	**t**ie	un**d**one	hi**t**⌐
ㄸ	tt	tt	- -	s̸**t**ill*	uns**t**ick	- -
ㄹ	r	r	l	**r**ed	pa**r**allel	ki**ll**
ㅁ	m	m	m	**m**editate	de**m**and	ja**m**
ㅂ	p	p	p⌐	**p**ail	re**b**ate	shar**p**⌐
ㅃ	pp	pp	- -	s̸**p**ill*	s**p**ike	- -
ㅅ	s	s	t⌐	**s**at **sh**in	wind**s**ock battle**sh**ip	cu**t**⌐
ㅆ	ss	ss	t⌐	**sc**ience	un**sc**enic	hi**t**⌐
ㅇ	silent	silent	ng	φ	φ	so**ng**
ㅈ	ch	j	t⌐	**ch**op	in**j**ury	upse**t**⌐
ㅉ	tch	tch	- -	**t**ruck	ca**tch**er	- -
ㅊ	ch'	ch'	t⌐	**ch**eck	pun**ch**ing	foo**t**⌐
ㅋ	k'	k'	k⌐	**k**arma	trac**k**ing	atta**ck**⌐
ㅌ	t'	t'	t⌐	**t**ickle	thrus**t**ing	cu**t**⌐
ㅍ	p'	p'	p⌐	**p**unch	ins**p**ire	sla**p**⌐
ㅎ	h	h	t⌐	**h**it	back**h**and	fla**t**⌐

The footnote	⌐	denotes a unaspirated consonant in this table.
The symbol	'	denotes an aspirated consonant, both in this table and throughout this book.
The footnote	- -	denotes that there are no examples of this Korean consonant as a final position in a syllable.
The footnote	*	pronounce the example as if you were trying to say the word that starts with "s", but without making the "s" sound.

Appendix D
McCune-Reischauer
Romanization Table

The two-page table in this appendix is provided as a quick and easy Han-gŭl transliteration and pronunciation reference for the martial artist. It uses a matrix (Korean consonants listed top to bottom and Korean vowels listed left to right) to illustrate the relationship between the two alphabets, Han-gŭl and English, and is a modified version of the McCune-Reischauer Romanization system.

In 1939, Korea was still under Japanese rule. At that time, there was a Hepburn system for Romanizing Japanese and a Wade-Giles system for Romanizing Chinese, but no system for Romanizing Korean. This was seen as a communication barrier between the occidental and Korean scholars. Two scholars, G. M. McCune and Edwin O. Reischauer, published their transliteration system in 1939 in the "Transactions of the Korea Branch of the Royal Asiatic Society" volume 29, pages 1-55. This system is still widely used today in many dictionaries, Korean language books, and reference material. Reischauer (1910-1990) later became the U.S. Ambassador to Japan from 1961 to 1966. He also co-authored several other publications including "East Asia, The Great Tradition: A History of East Asian Civilization," published in 1966.

Since 1939, there have been several refinements and modifications to the McCune-Reischauer Romanization System. We have also chosen to use a few of these modifications to create a logical and consistent system to base our transliteration on. Although some of the entries in the McCune-Reischauer Romanization table do not necessarily represent actual syllables found in Korean words, all of the entries represent sounds formed with the different combinations of Korean consonants and vowels to reinforce the logical combinations of letters for the reader. Please refer to Appendices B and C and the books College Korean and Functional Korean, in the Bibliography, for further details on Romanizing Han-gŭl.

McCune-Reischauer Romanization Table

C \ V	ㅏ a	ㅐ ae	ㅑ ya	ㅒ yae	ㅓ ŏ	ㅔ e	ㅕ yŏ	ㅖ ye	ㅗ o	ㅘ wa	ㅙ wae
ㄱ k	가 k(g)a	개 k(g)ae	갸 gya	걔 gyae	거 k(g)ŏ	게 k(g)e	겨 gyŏ	계 gye	고 k(g)o	과 k(g)wa	괘 k(g)wae
ㄲ kk	까 kka	깨 kkae	꺄 kkya	꺠 kkyae	꺼 kkŏ	께 kke	껴 kkyŏ	꼐 kkye	꼬 kko	꽈 kkwa	꽤 kkwae
ㄴ n	나 na	내 nae	냐 nya	냬 nyae	너 nŏ	네 ne	녀 nyŏ	녜 nye	노 no	놔 nwa	놰 nwae
ㄷ t	다 t(d)a	대 t(d)ae	댜 t(d)ya	댸 t(d)yae	더 t(d)ŏ	데 t(d)e	뎌 t(d)yŏ	뎨 t(d)ye	도 t(d)o	돠 t(d)wa	돼 t(d)wae
ㄸ tt	따 tta	때 ttae	땨 ttya	떄 ttyae	떠 ttŏ	떼 tte	뗘 ttyŏ	뗴 ttye	또 tto	똬 ttwa	뙈 ttwae
ㄹ r	라 r(l)a	래 r(l)ae	랴 r(l)ya	럐 r(l)yae	러 r(l)ŏ	레 r(l)e	려 r(l)yŏ	례 r(l)ye	로 r(l)o	롸 r(l)wa	뢔 r(l)wae
ㅁ m	마 ma	매 mae	먀 mya	먜 myae	머 mŏ	메 me	며 myŏ	몌 mye	모 mo	뫄 mwa	뫠 mwae
ㅂ p	바 p(b)a	배 p(b)ae	뱌 p(b)ya	뱨 p(b)yae	버 p(b)ŏ	베 p(b)e	벼 p(b)yŏ	볘 p(b)ye	보 p(b)o	봐 p(b)wa	봬 p(b)wae
ㅃ pp	빠 ppa	빼 ppae	뺘 ppya	뺴 ppyae	뻐 ppŏ	뻬 ppe	뼈 ppyŏ	뼤 ppye	뽀 ppo	뽜 ppwa	뽸 ppwae
ㅅ s	사 sa	새 sae	샤 sya	섀 syae	서 sŏ	세 se	셔 syŏ	셰 sye	소 so	솨 swa	쇄 swae
ㅆ ss	싸 ssa	쌔 ssae	쌰 ssya	썌 ssyae	써 ssŏ	쎄 sse	쎠 ssyŏ	쎼 ssye	쏘 sso	쏴 sswa	쐐 sswae
ㅇ silent	아 a	애 ae	야 ya	얘 yae	어 ŏ	에 e	여 yŏ	예 ye	오 o	와 wa	왜 wae
ㅈ ch	자 ch(j)a	재 ch(j)ae	쟈 ch(j)ya	쟤 ch(j)yae	저 ch(j)ŏ	제 ch(j)e	져 ch(j)yŏ	졔 ch(j)ye	조 ch(j)o	좌 ch(j)wa	좨 ch(j)wae
ㅉ tch	짜 tcha	째 tchae	쨔 tchya	쨰 tchyae	쩌 tchŏ	쩨 tche	쪄 tchyŏ	쪠 tchye	쪼 tcho	쫘 tchwa	쫴 tchwae
ㅊ ch'	차 ch'a	채 ch'ae	챠 ch'ya	챼 ch'yae	처 ch'ŏ	체 ch'e	쳐 ch'yŏ	쳬 ch'ye	초 ch'o	촤 ch'wa	쵀 ch'wae
ㅋ k'	카 k'a	캐 k'ae	캬 k'ya	컈 k'yae	커 k'ŏ	케 k'e	켜 k'yŏ	켸 k'ye	코 k'o	콰 k'wa	쾌 k'wae
ㅌ t'	타 t'a	태 t'ae	탸 t'ya	턔 t'yae	터 t'ŏ	테 t'e	텨 t'yŏ	톄 t'ye	토 t'o	톼 t'wa	퇘 t'wae
ㅍ p'	파 p'a	패 p'ae	퍄 p'ya	퍠 p'yae	퍼 p'ŏ	페 p'e	펴 p'yŏ	폐 p'ye	포 p'o	퐈 p'wa	퐤 p'wae
ㅎ h	하 ha	해 hae	햐 hya	햬 hyae	허 hŏ	헤 he	혀 hyŏ	혜 hye	호 ho	화 hwa	홰 hwae

McCune-Reischauer Romanization Table

V / C	ㅚ oe	ㅛ yo	ㅜ u	ㅝ wŏ	ㅞ we	ㅟ wi	ㅠ yu	ㅡ ŭ	ㅢ ŭi	ㅣ i	final* sounds
ㄱ k	괴 k(g)oe	교 gyo	구 k(g)u	궈 k(g)wŏ	궤 k(g)we	귀 k(g)wi	규 gyu	그 k(g)ŭ	긔 k(g)ŭi	기 k(g)i	ㄱ k
ㄲ kk	꾀 kkoe	꾜 kkyo	꾸 kku	꿔 kkwŏ	꿰 kkwe	뀌 kkwi	뀨 kkyu	끄 kkŭ	끠 kkŭi	끼 kki	ㄲ k
ㄴ n	뇌 noe	뇨 nyo	누 nu	눠 nwŏ	눼 nwe	뉘 nwi	뉴 nyu	느 nŭ	늬 nŭi	니 ni	ㄴ n
ㄷ t	되 t(d)oe	됴 t(d)yo	두 t(d)u	둬 t(d)wŏ	뒈 t(d)we	뒤 t(d)wi	듀 t(d)yu	드 t(d)ŭ	듸 t(d)ŭi	디 t(d)i	ㄷ t
ㄸ tt	뙤 ttoe	뚀 ttyo	뚜 ttu	뚸 ttwŏ	뛔 ttwe	뛰 ttwi	뜌 ttyu	뜨 ttŭ	띄 ttŭi	띠 tti	ㄸ tt
ㄹ r	뢰 r(l)oe	료 r(l)yo	루 r(l)u	뤄 r(l)wŏ	뤠 r(l)we	뤼 r(l)wi	류 r(l)yu	르 r(l)ŭ	릐 r(l)ŭi	리 r(l)i	ㄹ l
ㅁ m	뫼 moe	묘 myo	무 mu	뭐 mwŏ	뭬 mwe	뮈 mwi	뮤 myu	므 mŭ	믜 mŭi	미 mi	ㅁ m
ㅂ p	뵈 p(b)oe	뵤 p(b)yo	부 p(b)u	붜 p(b)wŏ	붸 p(b)we	뷔 p(b)wi	뷰 p(b)yu	브 p(b)ŭ	븨 p(b)ŭi	비 p(b)i	ㅂ p
ㅃ pp	쀠 ppoe	뾰 ppyo	뿌 ppu	뿨 ppwŏ	쀄 ppwe	쀠 ppwi	쀼 ppyu	쁘 ppŭ	쁴 ppŭi	삐 ppi	ㅃ p
ㅅ s	쇠 soe	쇼 syo	수 su	숴 swŏ	쉐 swe	쉬 swi	슈 syu	스 sŭ	싀 sŭi	시 shi	ㅅ t
ㅆ ss	쐬 ssoe	쑈 ssyo	쑤 ssu	쒀 sswŏ	쒜 sswe	쒸 sswi	쓔 ssyu	쓰 ssŭ	씌 ssŭi	씨 ssi	ㅆ t
ㅇ silent	외 oe	요 yo	우 u	워 wŏ	웨 we	위 wi	유 yu	으 ŭ	의 ŭi	이 i	ㅇ ng
ㅈ ch	죄 ch(j)oe	죠 ch(j)yo	주 ch(j)u	줘 ch(j)wŏ	줴 ch(j)we	쥐 ch(j)wi	쥬 ch(j)yu	즈 ch(j)ŭ	즤 ch(j)ŭi	지 ch(j)i	ㅈ t
ㅉ tch	쬐 tchoe	쬬 tchyo	쭈 tchu	쭤 tchwŏ	쮀 tchwe	쮜 tchwi	쮸 tchyu	쯔 tchŭ	쯰 tchŭi	찌 tchi	ㅉ t
ㅊ ch'	최 ch'oe	쵸 ch'yo	추 ch'u	춰 ch'wŏ	췌 ch'we	취 ch'wi	츄 ch'yu	츠 ch'ŭ	츼 ch'ŭi	치 ch'i	ㅊ t
ㅋ k'	쾨 k'oe	쿄 k'yo	쿠 k'u	쿼 k'wŏ	쾌 k'we	퀴 k'wi	큐 k'yu	크 k'ŭ	킈 k'ŭi	키 k'i	ㅋ k
ㅌ t'	퇴 t'oe	툐 t'yo	투 t'u	퉈 t'wŏ	퉤 t'we	튀 t'wi	튜 t'yu	트 t'ŭ	틔 t'ŭi	티 t'i	ㅌ t
ㅍ p'	푀 p'oe	표 p'yo	푸 p'u	풔 p'wŏ	풰 p'we	퓌 p'wi	퓨 p'yu	프 p'ŭ	픠 p'ŭi	피 p'i	ㅍ p
ㅎ h	회 hoe	효 hyo	후 hu	훠 hwŏ	훼 hwe	휘 hwi	휴 hyu	흐 hŭ	희 hŭi	히 hi	ㅎ t

* Final sounds are those that a consonant has in the **final** position in a syllable or word

Bibliography

A Guide to Korean Characters, 2nd Edition, Bruce K. Grant, Hollym International Corp., Seoul, Korea, 1989 (ISBN 093878-13-2).

Chon-Ji of Tae Kwon Do Hyung, Jhoon Rhee, Ohara Publications Inc., Santa Clara, California, 1994 (ISBN 0-89750-000-8).

College Korean, Michael C. Rodgers, et.al., University of California Press, Ltd., London, England, 1992 (ISBN 0-520-06994-3).

Die 12 TAEKWONDO HYONG's, Michael Unruh, Verlag Weinmann, Berlin, 1993 (ISBN 3-87892-049-0).

Dong-A's Prime Korean-English Dictionary, Dong-A Publishing & Printing Co., Ltd., Korea, 1981 (ISBN 890000541-3).

Encyclopedia of Taekwon-Do, Gen. Choi Hong Hi, International Taekwon-Do Federation, Ontario, Canada, 1987.

Functional Korean, Namgui Chang and Yong-chol Kim, Hollym International Corp., Seoul, Korea, 1994 (ISBN 0-930878-65-5).

Korean Culture and Language, Byung Kon Cho, 1988.

Korean for Travellers, Berlitz Guides, Si-Sa-Yong-O-Sa, Inc., Seoul, Korea, 1986 (ISBN 0-02-964250-7).

Korean in a Hurry, Samuel E. Martin, Charles E. Tuttle Company, Inc., Tokyo, Japan, 1982 (ISBN 0-8048-0349-8).

Legacy Edition Taekwon-Do Multimedia Encyclopedia, Gen. Choi Hong Hi, COM-DO, Inc., 1997.

Minjung's English-Korean & Korean-English Dictionary, 5th Edition, Registration # 2-61 (July 23, 1979), Kim Min Hwang Publishing Co., Seoul, Korea, 1995 (ISBN 89-387-0408-4).

Minjungseorim's New Little English Dictionary:
English-Korean, Korean-English, 4th Edition, Registration
2-715 (July 23, 1979), Kim Min Hwang Publishing Co.,
Seoul, Korea, 1982.

Moderner Kampfsport 1 - Taekwon-Do, Wilfred Peters, Brasse
& Nolte, Dortmund, 1992   (ISBN 3-923868-02-2).

Official WTF Taekwondo, David Mitchell, Stanley Paul & Co.
Ltd., London, England, 1990 (ISBN 0-09-163441-5).

Pictorial Sino-Korean Characters, Rev. Jacob Chang-Ui Kim,
Hollym International Corp., Seoul, Korea, 1987
(ISBN 093878-58-9).

Taegeuk: the new Forms of Tae Kwon Do, Pu Gill Gwon,
Ohara Publications Inc., Santa Clara, California, 1984
(ISBN 0-89750-097-0).

Taekwon-Do Beginners' Training Manual, Paul McPhail, Paul
M. Publishing, Manurewa, New Zealand, 1995
(ISBN 0-473-03068-3).

Taekwondo - Koreanischer Kampfsport, Konstantin Gil, Falken-
Verlag GmbH, Zembsch' Werkstatt, Munchen, 1992
(ISBN 38068-0347-1).

Tae Kwon Do - Korean Martial Art, CD ROM, - G9605-
CR278, Jeasam Techmedia, 1996.

Tae Kwon Do - Techniques & Training, Kyong Myong Lee,
Sterling Publishing Co., New York, 1996
(ISBN 0-8069-5955-X).

The Complete Tae Kwon Do Hyung - Vol. 2, Hee Il Cho,
Hee Il Cho Publishing, West Los Angeles, California, 1989
(ISBN 1-88-2015-002).

The History of Teakwon-Do Patterns: The Chang-Hon Pattern
Set, Chon-Ji through Choong-Moo, Richard L. Mitchell,
Lilley Gulch TKD Publishing, Littleton, Colorado, 1993
(ISBN 0-9622129-9-7).